FIFTEENTH CENTURY
TRANSLATION
AS AN INFLUENCE ON
ENGLISH PROSE

PRINCETON STUDIES IN ENGLISH

Edited by G. H. GEROULD

18

FIFTEENTH CENTURY TRANSLATION AS AN INFLUENCE ON ENGLISH PROSE

BY

SAMUEL K. WORKMAN

OCTAGON BOOKS

A DIVISION OF FARRAR, STRAUS AND GIROUX

New York   1972

First published in 1940 by Princeton University Press

Reprinted 1972

by special arrangement with Princeton University Press

OCTAGON BOOKS

A DIVISION OF FARRAR, STRAUS & GIROUX, INC.

19 Union Square West

New York, N. Y. 10003

*This book has been reproduced from an original in the
Brown University Library*

Library of Congress Cataloging in Publication Data

Workman, Samuel Klinger, 1907-

Fifteenth century translation as an influence on English prose.

A revision of the author's thesis, Princeton, 1935.

Reprint of the 1940 ed., which was issued as no. 18 of Princeton studies in English.

Bibliography: p.

1. English prose literature—Early modern (to 1700)—History and criticism.   2. English literature—Translations from foreign literature—History and criticism.   3. English language—Style.
I. Title.   II. Series: Princeton University. Princeton studies in English, no. 18.

PR297.W6   1972   828'.08   71-159239

ISBN 0-374-98763-7

Manufactured by Braun-Brumfield, Inc.
Ann Arbor, Michigan

Printed in the United States of America

PRINCETON STUDIES IN ENGLISH

EDITED BY G. H. GEROULD

18

FIFTEENTH CENTURY TRANSLATION AS AN INFLUENCE ON ENGLISH PROSE

BY

SAMUEL K. WORKMAN

PRINCETON · 1940

PRINCETON UNIVERSITY PRESS

Planographic Reproduction of
Author's Manuscript by
EDWARDS BROTHERS, INC.
ANN ARBOR, MICHIGAN
1940

PREFATORY NOTE

Begun as a study in loan-words, my examination of early English translations presently involved me less in vocabulary than in syntax and in rhetoric. The study became one in the history of prose. In June, 1935, with essentially the same conclusions presented here, it was accepted by the department of English at Princeton University as a doctoral dissertation. Since then the materials have been considerably rearranged and two chapters (II and VII) have been added.

Encouragement to follow the new turn of my interest during this study, and a great deal of sound advice, enthusiasm, and patience from the beginning to the present moment, have put me under an obligation to Professor Gordon Hall Gerould which I am most happy once more to acknowledge. Beside giving many detailed suggestions Professor Hoyt N. Hudson was of more help than I think he realized by allowing me to visit his seminar and air my views; and for a similar kind of help I am thankful also to Mr. Edward H. Weatherly, former secretary of the Modern Language Club at Northwestern University. Finally, I am under no small debt to the Pierpont Morgan Library, New York, for kind permission to use books otherwise inaccessible, to the staff of the Princeton University Library, and especially to Mr. Malcolm Young, Reference Librarian at Princeton, who has cheerfully suffered a thousand and one inconveniences from me.

S. K. W.

TABLE OF CONTENTS

Chapter One

PROSE TRANSLATION AS A CHANNEL OF INFLUENCE

The term 'age of transition' can be merely a polite
way of saying that the fifteenth century in England lacks
much literary interest. In the better sense it emphasizes
the importance of the period for literary history. True,
not a single genius appeared then, scarcely one or two good
books. The most conspicuous writers of their own time, Lydgate and Caxton, as well as Malory, the most famous now,
were all conservative souls; the most original, Peacock and
Fortescue, were soon left obscure; while the few progressive
scholars, men like Tiptoft and Free, were occupied abroad.
There was no prevailing consciousness of innovation. In
prose, there was not even a formed technique, much less a
philosophy of composition. Yet in the writing of chronicles
-- to cite only one genre from many which changed as much --
there occurred a great shift, and a rapid one, to native
prose as medium, and also a slow growth in sophistication
of style.[1]
Eventually this change in historical prose may have
had a good part in preparing Thomas More for his Life of
Richard III.[2] But in itself it is unsensational, obscure,
and it has been learned only by an accumulation of many details. The studies in the prose of this period of transition have not discovered brilliant books; but they have shown
the importance of understanding the typical literary experi-
ences -- in reading as well as in writing -- of the average
fifteenth century Englishman. Their value has best been
pointed out, and the best use of them made, by Mr. R. W.
Chambers, in his essay 'On the Continuity of English Prose
from Alfred to More.'[3]

---

1. C. L. Kingsford, English Historical Literature in the
Fifteenth Century, Oxford, 1913, pp. 135-9; 169-71. F. J.
Starke, Populare englische Chroniken des 15 Jahrhunderts:
. . . ihre literarische form. Berlin, 1935, pp. 47-89; 106-
136; 152-164.
2. F. J. Starke, op. cit., pp. 85-89; 163-64.
3. Elsie Vaughan Hitchcock, ed. Harpsfield's Life of More
(EETS os 186). London, 1932, Introduction, pp. xiv-clxxix;
esp. p. c.

These studies have, however, been principally di-
rected into the history of ideas or of genres, and have not
investigated in equal detail the tangible facts of prose composition. When Mr. G. R. Owst, having unearthed dozens of
sermons in English prose, comes to treat them as literature,
he gives no discussion at all of their style.[4] Even Mr.
Chambers, though directly concerned with ways of writing, has
dealt more with the spirit of early prose than with its form.
The continuity which he describes is one of religious devo-
tion, of English realism and English sense of humor. Throughout his essay he has been reluctant to use analytical terms
for the description of prose as a form. He cites the word-
order of Rolle;[5] the devices of alliteration, balance, and
repetition in Rolle, More, and Berners;[6] the sentence-structure of Lupset;[7] and the diction or 'augmenting' of the average fifteenth century writer;[8] but these, in the chapters
linking Rolle and More, are the only terms pertaining to means.
His other terms are of quality, usually the quality of naturalness. Hilton and More are compared for their 'passionate seri-
ousness';[9] early religious prose is 'simple and dignified'
or 'noble in its simple lucidity';[10] Nicholas Love's is
'beautiful yet easy and natural';[11] and, in a quoted comparison,[12] Hilton's is 'natural, lucid and easy,' More's
'direct and intimate.' These terms are not misplaced; and
they rightly insist on the relationship between a writer's
character and the form of his prose. But they are too abstract to tell the whole story. 'Naturalness' will do for
both the primitive and the consummate: Skinner Lovelich and
Chaucer, Joinville and Pascal.[13]

---

    4. Preaching in Medieval England, Cambridge, 1926; Litera-
ture and Pulpit in Medieval England, Cambridge, 1933. In his
chapter on 'Sermon-making' (Preaching, pp. 309-354) Mr. Owst
briefly describes methods of division and order, but he is
chiefly interested in the kinds of matter used for amplifica-
cation.
    5. Op. cit., p. ci.
    6. Ibid., pp. cxxiv; cli, cliv.
    7. Ibid., p. cxlviii.
    8. Ibid., pp. cxv, passim.
    9. Ibid., p. cli.
   10. Ibid., p. cxv.
   11. Ibid., p. cxviii.
   12. Ibid., p. cxxx.
   13. There is, too, the difficulty of distinguishing historical
criticism from personal. For instance, Mr. Chambers thinks
that Caxton's translated prose is 'far better than his own',
(p. cxviii) but M. Legouis that 'the best of his prose occurs
in his explanatory prefaces.' (History of English Literature,
New York 1938, p. 198.)

To go to the other extreme and try to explain a man's writing only in terms of technique would be equally limited. What has led any man to write prose in one way or another -- where he learned all the traits of his style and why he came to adopt them -- is in all conscience a tremendously complex thing to ascertain. Euphuism, for instance, gave modern scholars a puzzle for years, not only over its sources but over its very definition.[14] Yet in prose Euphuism is concretion itself; compared to it a normally stylized prose seems amorphous. To account for early Tudor prose requires a multitude of considerations, but surely technical ones are among them. Though the first English 'Art of rhetoric' appeared after 1520, a great deal of rhetoric had been practised in English -- naturally or artificially, crudely or gracefully -- for perhaps two hundred years before. Now if his rhetoric is not to be completely crude, a writer must have some degree of control over the mere mechanics. To gain any effect through parallelism, balance, or the suspended period, for instance, he must know how to manipulate constructions: he must be aware of the syntactical possibilities of his language, and he must understand the syntactical requirements -- and restrictions -- of the rhetorical device he is trying to use. Indeed, in discussing early prose it is interesting to inquire not only where the writer learned his technical resourcefulness but how he came to realize the advantages, even the very existence of the different kinds of rhetorical and grammatical structure. Many fourteenth and fifteenth century writers would seem from their prose to have been unaware of any thought-relationship which cannot be expressed by and.

The formation of adequate habits of composition in prose is something we might be quite willing to take for granted. Yet in early prose it is necessarily at the bottom of any discussion of a writer's taste. For instance, in describing a late fourteenth century English passage which was based upon Hugh of St. Victor, Mr. Chambers praises 'the liveliness and terseness of the English compared with the more rhetorical Latin.'[15] But whether or not we agree with the modern judgement, it can seriously be doubted that the English writer in question had deliberately reshaped his prose because of his own differing taste. His changes from the Latin were

---

14. Morris W. Croll, 'The Sources of the Euphuistic Rhetoric,' introduction to Croll's and Harry Clemons' edition of Euphues, New York, 1916, p. xv-lxiv. William Ringler, 'The Immediate Source of Euphuism,' PMLA, LIII (1938), 678-686.

15. Op. cit., pp. cv-cvi. References to the Latin are there given.

all toward simplification, and it is perfectly possible that
he merely lacked the technical ability to reconstruct the
somewhat elaborate Latin rhetoric into English.[16] During
the early period of English prose, choice must usually have
waited upon means. And throughout the transition, influences
upon technique are as likely to have been important as influences upon taste or upon thought or spirit.

In respect to their more mechanical nature, at least,
such influences are likely also to be more tangible. Yet in
the manner of their operation they are for many reasons elu-
sive. It is hardly probable that a fifteenth century writer,
any more than a modern one, ever developed his style through
trial and error alone. He must consciously or unconsciously
have learned from some predecessor, English or foreign. If
working consciously, he may have imitated what he admired, and
improved upon what he thought limited; there is some reason
to believe that Reginald Peacock, working from Latin models,
developed his English style in this way. But much of the
influence was unconscious: the result either of a man's reading and listening to well-formed English prose, or else of
his translating foreign prose, in writing or only to himself,

---

16. The English is closest to the Latin in the following
two sentences:

For som men aren so kumbred in nice corious countenaunces in
bodily beryng þat, whan þei schal ouȝt here, þei wriþen here
hedes on side queyntely and up wiþ þe chin, þei gape wiþ
þeire mou es as þei schuld here wiþ hem and not wiþ here
eres . . .

Sunt enim quidam qui nisi buccis patentibus auscultare
nesciunt, et quasi per os sensus ad cor influere debeat,
palatum ad verba loquentis aperiunt . . .

Semeli cher were full fayr wiþ sobre and demure beryng of body
and mirþe in maner.

Temperanda est enim facies et mortificanda in gestu suo, ita
ut nec proterve exasperetur, nec molliter dissolvatur, sed
semper habeat et rigidam dulcedinem et dulcem rigorem.

(English as quoted by Chambers, loc. cit., from MS. Harley
674. Latin from Migne, P.L., CLXXVI, col. 941-2.) The
English does imitate the alliteration of the Latin. But note
the informal if not halting construction of the first sentence.

until rhetorical patterns, large or small, had been clearly
or vaguely impressed on his mind. And it must have been in
the same way that he developed whatever critical discrimination he possessed in regard to the clarity and general ef-
fectiveness of the various technical usages of prose.

Conditioning of this sort, partly because it is elementary to any process of learning, is certain to be a very
difficult thing to trace; especially so in a period where
the writers themselves seem very seldom to have discussed
questions of style. Influences can have appeared from all
directions. Precisely which ones were strongest must be
judged not only from the quantity and the nature of each
but also from the manner of its operation. That influence
can be called most certain which is known to have been im-
parted in the most direct, tangible way.

It is here that the many prose translations of the
fifteenth century may prove to have their principal interest.
With a few exceptions, their context now seems of little literary value, and their literary life in their own time was
often short. But any translation characteristically admits
of a very detailed comparison with its source, not only for
its matter but for its composition. The likenesses and differences may be clearly measured, even isolated, as it were,
so that the form of a prose translation is likely to be easier to account for than that of original writing, no matter
how closely the latter has been made to imitate some model.
In other words, if the prose has been composed by translation, that fact may provide a very tangible explanation for
many or most of its technical characteristics; and so far as
those characteristics have given the translation its qualities of style, the same fact will explain the style as well.

Though this can be true of translations which are
fairly free, it would naturally be most important in those
which are close. In fact, any explanation of the style of
translated prose is likely to be incomplete or misleading
if it leaves out of account the source. Mr. Chambers' remarks on Lady Margaret Beaufort's _Imitation of Christ_ appear to be an example. He says of Lady Margaret, in one
sentence, that she was 'a close student of the works of
Hilton', and of her translation, in the next, that it was
'a best seller during the first half of the sixteenth century';[17] and the implication seems to be that Lady Margaret learned to put prose into such a successful form because she had studied the form of Hilton's prose. Chapter
I of her translation begins:

---

17. R. W. Chambers, _op. cit._; p. cxlii.

> O My lorde Iesu cryst, eternall trouthe, these
> wordes befor-sayd be thy wordes. Albeit they haue
> not ben sayd in one self tyme, nor wrytten on one
> selfe place yet for that they be thy words I ought
> 5 feythfully & agreably to vnderstande them, they be
> thy wordes and thou hast proferred them. And
> they be now myn, for thou hast sayd them for my
> helthe. I will gladlye receyue them of thy mouthe,
> to thende they may be the better sowen & planted in
> 10 my herte. Thy wordes of so great pyte, full of
> loue, swetnes, & dileccion, greatly excyteth me;
> but, lorde, my propre synnes fereth & draweth backe
> my conscience nat pure to receyue so great a mys-
> tery. The swetnes of thy wordes incyteth and pro-
> 15 uoketh me, but the multytude of my sinnes chargeth
> & sore greueth me.[18]

Now this, like Hilton's, may be called good prose, and apparently it was carefully composed. But the influence of Hilton
upon it is another matter. It may be that her reading of
Hilton led Lady Margaret to be more deeply interested in devotional literature and thus to undertake her translation;
though the influence of her chaplain, William Atkynson, who
translated the first three books of the Imitation, would seem
to have been the more immediate. Her admiration for the
'naturalness' of Hilton's prose may have led her not to try
to 'augment' her English version, as Atkynson unfortunately
did his; though her humility beside a master of the copious
style like Atkynson is an equally ready explanation.

    Between Lady Margaret's prose and Hilton's many
traits more specific than naturalness would, I think, be
hard to find in common. But even when found, they would
have to be attributed to a remote common influence -- Latin
rhetoric. For the only direct influence upon the form of
Lady Margaret's prose in her English Imitation was the
French Imitation from which she translated it. Book IV of
the French text begins, in the edition of 1493:

> O Monseigneur iesucrist, verite eternelle, les
> parolles deuantdictes sont tes parolles, combien
> quilz nayent pas etre dictes en ung mesme temps:

---

18. P. 259, ll. 23-35 of the edition by J. K. Ingram (EETS
e s lxiii) London, 1893. For all following quotations from
translations and sources, the references will be confined to
the page and line of the editions cited in Appendix A.

     ne escriptes en ung mesme lieu. Doncques pur ce
   5 que ce sont tes parolles ie les dois feablement
     & agreablement toutes entendre. Ce sont tes pa-
     rolles: & tu les as proferees & elles sont miennes
     car tu les as dictes pour mon salut. Ie les re-
     cois voulentiers de ta bouche, affin que mieulx
  10 soient semees & plantees en mon cueur. Tes pa-
     rolles de so grande pitie, pleines damour de di-
     lection et de doulceur me excitent. Mais mes pro-
     pres pechez me espouuent: & me retire ma consci-
     ence non pure de receuoir si grans mysteres. La
  15 doulceur de tes parolles me incite & prouocque:
     mais la multitudes de mes pechez me charge a grie-
     fue.[19]

Lady Margaret has made only seven very slight alterations in
any detail whatsoever.[20] Some of these may have been due
to her sense of rhythm. Some of them are probably not real
alterations, but only discrepancies between her texts and
ours, either French or English, demonstrably a frequent
source of apparent alterations in early translations. Aside
from these, every detail of the English, ideas, syntax, diction -- even the doublets -- is to be directly accounted for
by its presence in the French source. With recognition of
the differences, often slight, between French and English
syntax, this correspondence might have been the result of
uncritical transference of each phrase or construction, almost of each word, as it came along:

     O Monseigneur iesucrist, verite eternelle
     O My lorde Iesu cryst, eternall trouthe

     les parolles devantdictes sont tes parolles
     these words before-sayd be thy wordes

     combien quilz nayent pas etre dictes
     Albeit they have not ben sayd

---

   19. Feuillet xcii, r.
   20. The punctuation of the first period; the insertion of
'nowe' (English, line 7, French, line 7), of 'greatly' (English, line 11, French, line 12), and of 'lorde' (English,
line 12, French, line 12); the shift in the order of the
adjective 'swetnes' (English, Line 11, French, line 12);
the change to the future tense in 'will . . . receyue' (English, line 8, French, line 8); and the change of construction of the last four words.

en ung mesme temps
in one self time

ne escriptes en ung mesme lieu
nor wrytten in one self place

Doncques pur ce que ce sont tes parolles . . . etc.
Yet for that they be thy words . . . etc.

The process, critical or uncritical -- and there is no need
to consider Lady Margaret uncritical -- may, with due allowances, be conveniently described as stencil translation. It
was, in fact, stencil translation, with greater allowances
for greater syntactical differences, that was used when the
French version was made from the Latin:

O Monseigneur iesucrist, verite eternelle, les parolles
    devantdictes sont tes parolles
Haec sunt verba tua Christi Veritas aeterna

Combien quilz nayent pas etre dictes en ung mesme temps
quamvis non uno tempore prolata

ne escriptes en ung mesme lieu.
nec uno in loco ccnscripta.

Doncques pur ce que ce sont tes parolles
Quia ergo tua sunt et vera [21]

ie les dois feablement & agreablement toutes entendre.
gratanter mihi et fideliter cuncta sunt accipienda

Ce sont tes parolles: & tu les a proferee
Tua sunt   et tu ea protulisti

& elles sont miennes car tu les a dictes pou mon salut.
    Etc.
et mea quoque sunt: quia pro salute mea ea edidisti

Libenter suscipio ea ex ore tuo: ut artius inferantur
cordio meo. Excitant me verba tantae pietatis: plena
dulcedinis et dilectionis. Sed terrent me delicta
propria: et ad capienda tanta mysteria me reverberat
impura conscientia: Provocat me dulcedo verborum

---

21. The omission from the French of any idea for 'vera' may
be an example of an apparent alteration due actually to a discrepancy of text. The Frenchman may have read 'verba'.

tuorum: sed onerat multitudo vitiorum meorum.[22]

Not all the stylistic traits of the Latin have been
transferred to the French; but all the traits of the French
are to be accounted for by their presence in Latin. The
French, of course, does not have the same cadence as the Latin,
though there is a pretty fair equivalent for it. The most conspicuous difference is the absence from the French of the
Latin rhymes. But apparently other sound-and word-schemes have
been used as equivalents. It is quite likely that 'dictes
en ung mesme temps: ne escriptes en ung mesme lieu' (line 3)
is a deliberate use of isocolon and parison; and it is just
possible that 'excitent . . . incite' (lines 12-15) was intended for homeoteleuton. Certainly ornament of sound has
been abundantly provided by alliteration.[23]
It is in the broader structure that the correspondence
is close. The division of the paragraph into sentences and of
the sentences into members; the construction of every member;
and the thought-connection between members: all have been determined by the Latin. Sometimes the Latin constructions and
word-order have had to be re-cast in order to Gallicize them:
'ilz nayent pas etre dictes' for 'non . . . prolata,' 'ie les
dois . . . entendre' for 'mihi . . . sunt accipienda.' But
this does not at all effect the correspondence of these members in their syntactical relationships; and, French for Latin,
scarcely at all in the nature of their form. The first clause
of the passage is somewhat changed in nature, perhaps for the
sake of rhythm. The only other alterations of any sort are
occasional solitary additions: 'semees et plantees' (for 'inferantur'), 'damour,' and 'incite'; but these are too incon-
siderable to affect either the form or the tone of the prose.
So far, at least, as syntactical structure determines style,
the style of the French version is the same as that of the
Latin.
The term 'stencil translation,' emphasizing the mechanical nature of the process, is not intended to belittle either
Lady Margaret's or the Frenchman's achievement. Modern verdict calls a translation good if it reproduces the form and
the spirit of the original, and by such verdict both of these
translations of the Imitatio would be called at least toler-

---

22. Lib. IV, Cap. I, v. 1-16.
23. It is most conspicuous in the latter half of the passage:
'plantees (line 10) . . . parolles . . . pitie, pleines . . .
propres pechez . . . espouuent . . . pure . . . parolles . . .
prouocque'; with other groups intermingled: 'dilection . . .
doulceur,' 'retire . . . receuoir.'

able. The important thing is that in translation the style
is not altogether the man; the personality of the translator
is greatly subordinated. There is nothing surprising in this
as modern theory. But it is well worth demonstrating in a
period when translators abounded but theory was scarcely
formed.

Caxton, the most prolific of them all, translated
among some twenty-five other things, Alain Chartier's Curial,
a French version of an anonymous Latin epistle.[24] The Latin
is a piece of typical medieval dictamen in the well-known
style to be derived ultimately from Gorgias:[25]

> Sic sunt curie opera, ut in pusillanimes spritum, in
> virtuoses livorem, in arrogantis mortis periculum pro-
> vocant. At inter palatinos si infimus es, aliorum
> potestati emulaberis prostratus, si mediocris minus
> tibi sufficies, ad maiora contendes, si ad excelsa et
> usque tremenda archana cortinamque dubiam pertingis,
> tunc miserior cum felicior, tunc prope precipitum es
> cum ad culmen usque ascendisti.[26]

Note especially the extended periodic structure with
ellipsis and parallelism. To meet the needs of his less flex-
ible French syntax, Chartier modified somewhat the kinds of
construction, but his periods and the syntactical patterns of
them were in all basic respects directly transferred from the
Latin.

> Telz sont les ouvraiges de court, que les simples y
> sont mesprisez, les vertueux enviez et les arrogans
> orgueilleux en perilz mortelz. Et se tu y es ravallé
> au dessoubz des autres palatins, tu seras envieux de
> leur pouvoir. Se tu y es en moyen estat, dont tu
> n'ayes suffisance, to estriveras de plus hault monter,
> et se tu peux parvenir jusques aux haulx secrez qui
> sont fort a redoubter et a craindre, a la courtine
> doubteuse des plus haulx princes, adoncques seras tu
> plus meschant de tant que ty cuideras estre plus
> eureux, et de tant seras tu en plus grant peril de
> tresbucher, comme tu seras monté en plus hault lieu.[27]

---

24. Probably by Ambrosius de Miliis. F. Heuckenkamp, Le
Curial d'Alain Chartier, Halle, 1899, p. xxxiv.
25 C. S. Baldwin, Medieval Rhetoric and Poetic, New York,
1928. Chap. VIII, 'Dictamen', pp. 206-227.
26. P. 8, 11.4-10.
27. P. 9, 11.5-15.

Caxton had the advantage of working from a syntax far more
similar to his own; and with one possible exception, every
important detail of his English prose is simply the dupli-
cate of the French.

> Such be the werkes of the courte, that they that be
> symple be mesprysed, the vertuous enuyed, And the
> prowde arrogaunts in mortel peryllis. And yf thou
> be sette doun and put aback vnder the other cour-
> tyours, Thou shalt be enuyous of theyr power; yf
> thou be in mene estate, of whyche thou has not suf-
> fysaunce, thou shalt stryue for to mounte and ryse
> hyer. And yf thou mayst come vnto the hye secrets
> whyche ben strongly for to doubte and drede, in the
> doubtous courteynes of the most hye prynces, Thenne
> shalt thou be most meschaunt. Of so moche as thou
> wenest to be most ewrous and happy, so moche more
> shalt thou be in grete perill to falle, lyke to hym
> that is mounted in to the most hye place.[28]

Caxton's English prose was thus made almost as highly
mannered as that of the Latin epistle its ultimate source.
There are even schemes of word and sound here, though these
may not be deliberate but only accidents of translation.[29]
The rhythms, too may be accident; but climactic rhythm is
certainly outstanding in the second period, with its precisely proportioned increase in the length of the main _cola_.
Most to be stressed, however, are the syntactical devices. There is ellipsis, in the first sentence, to give
brevity to the opening series of three; and clausal parallelism (_anaphora_) in the second sentence, to bind three longer
members into a period effect. In the latter two members of
this sentence, there is the insertion of first one and then
two subordinate parts, to help proportion the climax. But,
while these subordinations are of varied construction, there
is never any relapse into sub-dependence. In short, control
over the mechanical resources of prose appears firm through-

---

28. P. 5, ll. 3-17.
29. 'mesprysed . . . envied,' (_homeoteleuton_); 'to doubt
. . . doubtous,' 'ryse hyer . . . unto the hye . . . the most
hye princes . . . the most hye place.' (_polyptoton_ and alliteration); 'mesprysed . . . mortel,' 'envious . . . estate,'
'surrysaunce . . . stryue . . . secrets,' 'mene . . . mounte,'
'doubt . . . drede . . . doubtous' (alliteration). As for the
possible accidents of translation, note, for instance, that
'place,' though alliterating with 'prince,' is only the standard, almost inevitable translation of 'lieu.'

out. And, if we mistook the Curial for Caxton's original
composition, it would appear that he had employed those resources to indulge a taste for the style of the medieval
Latin epistolographers.

As in the case of Lady Margaret's, it may not seem
fair to explain this piece of English prose simply with the
term 'stencil translation'; though in the case of Caxton I
am more inclined to accept its worst implications. But at
least the style in his English Curial is not the only style
in Caxton's books. He shows an amazing range.

Only three years before his Curial, for instance, he
had written -- as translator -- the following piece of explanation, quite ungarnished, simple to a fault:

> Syth that ye haue vnderstond what it is of the daye
> and of the nyght, wille ye thenne after see the fait
> of the mone, and how she receyeyth lyght of the sonne.
> She receyueth lyght in such maner that she is contyn-
> uelly half full in what someuer place she be. And
> whan we see her round, thenne we calle her full. But
> how moche the ferther she is fro the sonne, so moche
> the more we see of her apparayl; and whan she is right
> vnder the sonne, thenne she apperithe not to vs; ffor
> thenne she is bytwene therthe and the sonne, & thenne
> she shyneth toward the sonne, and toward vs she is all
> derke. And thefore we see her not.[30]

If, once more, we mistook Caxton's translations for his own
original, the contrast between this prose and that in his
Curial would be almost shocking. In the Mirrour he appears
to have no awareness of the resources of his language.
Variety is lacking not only in the length of the sentences
and clauses, but in the kinds of construction and connective
used to relate together the ideas. If such prose were attributed to Caxton's own taste, it would be surprising to find
that in 1481 his taste was so primitive. But, of course, the
Mirrour is a translation; and as precisely as in Caxton's
Curial, this manner of writing, if it can be said to have any,
is the manner of its French original, which dates from the
thirteenth century:

> Puis que jour et nuit extendez, or veez apres de la
> lune comment ele recoit lumiere du souleill. Ele en
> recoit lumiere en tele maniere que ele est touz jourz
> la moitie plainne en quelque lieu que ele soit. Et
> quant nous la veons reonde, adonques si l'apelons

---

30. Mirrour of the World, p. 136.

plainne. Mais quant plus est loing do soleill, tant
i voit l'en plus d'apareill. Et quant ele est tout
droit desouz, lors ne nous apert ele pas. Car ele est
adonques entre la terre et le soleill, si que ele est
clere par dela, et par deca devers hous est oscure, et
pour ce ne la veons nous pas. [31]

But if, continuing to assume Caxton's books as his
original work, we whould try to fix a notion of his taste in
English prose, we could only decide that it was for experi-
mentation. Still a third kind of style appears in most of
his medieval romances and prose epics, a type of literature
he much admired.

By the latter half of the fourteenth century, the
French prose romance writers had developed a narrative style
far more complex than the plain, basically par atactic writing found a hundred years earlier in both narrative and exposition. In this prose, which can hardly be called concise,
the sentences tend to be long and the variety of constructions and connectives fairly wide. These general traits it
has in common with the French prose of the _Curial_. But here
there is little conscious arrangement of the parts, in fact
little discrimination between one construction and another,
so that it is sometimes hard to tell whether a connective was
meant to have a relative or a demonstrative force. For all
its looseness, this prose remains sufficiently controlled and
logical; it can set forth lucidly the easy sequence of the
deeds of the heroes. It is usually an ambling style. But on
occasion, for instance when Charlemagne makes a speech, that
same variety, length, and involvement of its constructions
have been used to give it some dignity, or perhaps pomposity.

Thus when Caxton, as usual adhering closely to his
source, translated, for instance, _The Four Sons of Aymon_, his
English prose fell into a style alrogether different from that
either of his _Mirrour_ or his _Curial_. If we took it for his
own, he would appear to have developed a prose far more pli-
able, more easy, in fact more sophisticated than that of his
Mirrour. But he would seem no longer to know or care how to
control it, how to form his variety of constructions into
stylized devices, as he had done five years before in his
Curial. To show how precisely this third style is to be
explained by the nature of his source, it may be well to arrange the opening two hundred-odd words of his _Aymon_ side by
side with the French:

---

31. _L'Image du Monde_, p. 165-7.

Veritablement nous
trouuons es faitz du
bon roy Charlemaigne
que une fois a une
feste de pentecoste
le dit Charlemaigne
tint une moult grant
et solennelle court à
paris apres ce quil
fut reuenu des parties
de lombardie, ou il
avoit en une moult
grande et merueilleuse
journee a lencontre
des sarrasins et mes-
creans dont le chief
de ditz sarrasins est-
oit nomme guitelin le
sesne le quel ledit
roy Charlemaigne

auoit disconfit et
vaincu. `A la quelle
journee et disconfyt-
ure morut grand nobl-
esse de roys: duez:
contes: princes: bar-
ons et chevaliers . . . .
[a list of them follows]
Lors en icelle feste
et assemblee se dressa
empiez le dit roy
Charlemaigne entre ses
princes et barons dis-
ant en ceste maniere.
Barons mes freres et
amys vous scaues com-
ment jay tant grandes
terres par vostre
ayde et secours. Tant
de sarrasins et mes-
creans mys à mort et
en ma subiection com-
ment nagueres aues veu
du mescreant guitelins
le quel Jay vaincu et
desconfit et remis à
la foy chrestinenne,
Nonobstant que moult
y aye perdu grande

Truelye we finde in the
gestes & faites of the
good king Charlemagne
that vpon a time at a
feast of Penthecoste, the
sayde kyng Charlemagne
kept a ryght great and
solempne court at Parys,
after that he was come
againe fro the partyes of
Lombardy, where he had
had a ryght great and
mervaylous batayle agenst
the Sarasyns and suche
folke as were out of the
beleve, wherof the cheef
of the sayde Sarasins was
named Guithelym the sesne.
The which the said kynge
Charlemagne by hys prow-
esse and valyauntnes had
dyscomfyted & overcomen.
At the which battaylle
and dyscomfyture dyed
great noblenesses of king-
es, princes, Dukes, Erles,
barons, knyghtes, and
squyers . . . .

Than at this assemble and
feast stood the sayd
kynge Charlemagne on his
feete, amonge his prynces
and barons, sayinge in
this wyse, 'barons, my
bretherne and freendes, ye
knowe howe I have conquest-
ed and gotten so many
greate londes by youre
helpe and succours, So many
of the Sarasins and mysbel-
evers brought to death, &
in my subieccion; how but
late agoe ye have seene by
ye paynym Guetelyn, whiche
I have dyscomfyted & overcomen and reduced to the
christen faith. Not with-
standynge we have loste
there ryght great cheurelry

cheualerie et noblesse.   and noblenesse, and for
Et ce par faute de   faute of many of our vas-
plusieurs de nos vais-   sayles and subjectes, that
saulx et subietz que à   to vs dayneth not to come,
nous ne daignerent
venir jacoit ce que   howe be it that we had
mande les eussions, com-   sent for theym, as the
ment le duc richart [etc]   Duke Rycharde [etc.] . . .
. . . qui sont tous trois   that been all three breth-
freres germains Dont a   erne Germayne, Whereof vn-
tout vous me complains   to I complayne me and tell
et tous dy que ce ne   you, that yf it were not
fust messire salemon   syr Salamon, that worthy-
qui vaillament nous   ly came to succoure us
vint secourir à tout
trente mille combat-   with xxx. thousande fyght-
tants[et.] (nous étions   ynge menne [etc.], we were
perdus et déconfits --   alle dyscomfyted and lost,
comme vous le savez   as ye all knowe well. [32]
tous).

If these three books of Caxton's, the _Curial_, the _Mirrour_ and the _Aymon_ are anonymous, and the derivative nature of them unknown, we should certainly assume them to have three different Englishmen as authors. Even as it is, no one of these three styles can be called Caxton's own. What has led this one man to write in such different ways is clearly his habit of close translation.

An equally clear illustration of this subordination of the writer's personality appears from the other direction when a number of Englishmen, working independently, have closely translated the work of one foreign author. The English styles then take on a very close resemblance. [33] In three different 'Revelations' of St. Birgitta, for instance, each the work of a different translator, there has been used

---

32. English from Chapt. I, p. 16-17. French from facsimile of print at Lyons, 1480, in ed. of Jean d'Albingnac, p. xxiv; the last few words are from the modernized text.
33. That is, providing the translator has not kept so close as to Latinize his English syntax. Richard Misyn, for instance, in translating two of Rolle's religious treatises, attempted an outrageous Latinization. His _Mendyng of Lyf_ would, therefore, never be confused with the _Mendyng_ in the Worcester Cathedral MS., which is a close translation, too, but in the best sense, seldom deviating from English syntax. I have analysed the varying degrees of closeness below in Chap. V. The two versions of Rolle are discussed on pp. 96-99.

the same unusual variation on a standard rhetorical pattern.
The plainest of the three is to be found in a Lambeth manu-
script of about 1450.[34]   The Virgin is talking to St.
Birgitta:

> But now shall y schewe the more playnly how I, from
> the begynnyng, whan I herd and undirstonde that godde
> was I was al way besye and ferefull of myne helthe and
> of keping of my selfe And whan y herd mor playnly that
> the same god was my maker and juge of all my dedis, I
> louyd him inwardlye and was fferd contynually and
> thought leest y shuld offend him in worde or dede.
> fferthermore whan y herd that he hadde yeuen a lawe
> vn to the peaple and his commaundementis and wroughte
> with hem so grete meraceylis I purposid sikerly in my
> hert to love right nought but hym, and all worldly
> goddis were right bitter to me.   After this also, whan
> y herd that the same god shulde make redempcion of man-
> kynde and be borne of a virgyn, I was affecte with so
> muche charite and love vnto him that y thought right
> nought but on god; I wold right not love but hym.[35]

The iteration, used to develop a kind of paragraph,
appears both in the opening and in the complementary member
of each successive sentence.   But the more unusual element in
the structure is variety of length: there is a relatively
brief opening sentence, then follows a successive lengthening,
until at the last clause of the last sentence there comes an
incisive shortening.

In the two other 'Revelations,' both in the Garrett
manuscript but about twenty years apart in date[36], we find
the same basic pattern of parallelism that was used by the
Lambeth translator, and the same unusual kind of variation
in length.   In both of these the pattern has been further
varied by the periodic introduction of short explanatory
statements.   The earlier one represents Christ speaking to
the Saint:

> I am maker of heuen and erth and see and of all thynges
> that bene in hem.   I am on wyth the fader and the holy
> goste, nott as goddys of stones or of golde, as some
> tymę was seyde, ne mony goddys, as then was wande; bott

---

34. W. P. Cumming, in EETS os clxxviii, 1929, p. xix.   The
transcript is my own, from a photostatic copy which Mr. Cumming deposited in the Princeton University Library.
   35. Folio 76, r.
   36. W. P. Cumming, op. cit., p. xii, ff.

on God, fader and sone & holy goste, iij in persones
and on in substance, maker of all thynges and made of
none, vnchangeble and almyghty lestyng with-out begynnyng & wyth-out ende. I am he that was borne of the
vyrgyne, notte leuying the godhed bott knytting itt to
the manhode, Þat I shuld be in on person Þe verry sonne
of God and the sonne of the virgyne. I am he that honge
one the crosse and dyede and was beryed, Þe godhed aby-
dynge vn-hurte. For Þough the manhode and body whych
I, sonne, alone toke wer dede, yett ine Þe godhede in
whych I was oo God wyth Þe fader and Þe holy goste I
lyuede all way. I em also Þe same Þat roose frome deth
and styede in-to heuyn that nowe spekys wyth Þe wyth my
spiryte.[37]

In the third, it is again the Virgin who speaks:

For there is no modre that loueth my sone aboue all
thynges and askith the same to hir children, but Þat
I am anone redy to helpe hir to Þe effect of hir askyng.
There is also no widowe Þat stably prayeth aftir the
helpe of God to stonde in widowhod to Þe worship of God
un-to hir deth, but that anone I am redy to fulfille hir
wille with hir. For I was as a widowe, in Þat I hadde
a sone in erthe that had no bodily fadre. There is also
no virgyn that desireth to kepe hir maydenhode to God
vn-to hir deth, but Þat I am redy to defende hir and to
comfort hir. For I myself am verrayly a virgyn.[38]

    Between the first of these three passages and the lat-
ter two, there is some difference in the conciseness of the
constructions. In the two from the Garrett manuscript the effect of precise control is especially strong because of the
presence of word-and sound-schemes other than the anaphora
used in all three.[39] But even in the Lambeth there is shown

---

37. P. 1.
38. P. 99.
39. Polyptoton: in the second passage, 'goddes . . . God,'
'maker . . . made'; and in the third, 'asking . . . asketh,'
'widowe . . . Widowhod . . . widowe.' Alliteration: in the
second passage, 'goste . . . goddes . . . golde . . . God . . .
goste,' 'stones . . . seyd . . . sone . . . substaunce,' 'same
. . . steyde . . . spekys . . . spiryte' (though in this last
case the same sound-play does not occur in the same place in
the Latin); and in the third passage, 'stably . . . stonde,'
'widowe . . . widowhod . . . worship . . . wille . . . widowe,'
'desireth . . . defende,' 'verayly . . . virgyn.' The homeoteleuton in the Lambeth ('herd mor playnly . . . louyd him in-
wardlye and was fferd contynually') has no correspondence with
the Latin, nor have the few examples of alliteration.

a firm sense of the syntactical possibilities of words (compare 'I purposid . . . to love right nought but hym' with 'helpe hir to e effect of hir askyng').

A few lines of parallel text will show how closely these passages of English prose were drawn from the respective Latin 'Revelationes.' The Lambeth text:

But now shall y schewe the more playnly
Nunc autem plenius monstrabo

how I, from the begynnyng
quod ego, a principio

whan I herd and undirstode
cum audirem et intelligerem

that godde was
deum esse

I was al way besye and ferefull
semper sollicita & timorata fui

of myne helthe and of keping of my selfe.   Etc.
de salute & observantia mea.

Cum autem audissem plenius ipsum Deum esse Creatorem meum & Iudicem de omnibus actibus meis, intime dilexi eum & omni hora timui & cogitavi ne eum verbo vel facto offenderem. Deinde cum audissem eum dedisse legem populo & praecepta sua, & fecisse cum eis tanta mirabilia, proposui firmiter in animo meo nihil nisi ipsum diligere, & amara mihi erant mundana vehementer Post haec audito etiam quod ille idem Deus redempturus esset mundum, & nasciturus de Virgine, tanta circa eum charitate affecta fui quod nihil nisi Deum cogitabam, nihil volebam nisi ipsum.[40]

The Garrett text of 1450:

I am maker of heuen and erth and see,
Ego sum Creator caeli, & terrae, maris,

and of all thynges that bene in hem.
& omnium quae in eis sunt.

---

40 Lib. I, cap. x, Vol. I, p. 21-3.

I am on wyth the fader and the holy goste,
Ego sum unus cum Patre, & Spiritu sancto,

nott as goddys of stones or of golde,
non sicut dij lapiei, vel aurei,

as some tyme was seyde,
ut olim dicebatur,

ne mony goddys
nec plures,

as then was wande;
vt tunc putabatur,

bott on God, . . . etc.
sed unus Deus

Pater & Filius, & Spiritus sanctus, trinus in personis,
vnus in substantia. Omnia creans, & a nullo creatus,
immutabilis, & omnipotens, manens sine principio, &
sine fine. Ego sum, qui de Virgine natus sum non amitt-
ens Deitatem, sed eam associans humanitati, vt in vna
persona essem verus Filius Dei, & Filius Virginis. Ego
sum qui in cruce pependi, & mortuus fui, & sepultus,
Deitate illaesa permanente. Quia licit ex humanitate,
& carne, quam ego solus filius assumpsi mortuus fui,
tamen in Deitate, qua cum Patre, & Spiritu sancto vnus
eram Deus, vivebam. Ego idem ipse sum, qui surrexi a
mortuis, & ascendi in caelum, qui, & nunc cum spiritu
meo loquor tecum.[41]

The Garrett of 1470:

For there is no modre
Non enim est mater,

that loueth my son aboue all thynges
quae filium meum diligit super omnia,

and askith the same to hir children,
& illud idem petit filijs suis,

but at I am anone redy to helpe hir
quin non statim parata sum iuuare eam,

---

41. Lib. I, cap. ii, Vol. I, p. 5-6.

to þe effect of hir askyng. Etc.
ad effectum petitionis eius.

Nec etiam est aliqua vidua, quae stabiliter rogat auxilium a Deo standi in viduitate ad honorem Dei vsque ad
mortem, quin non statim parata sum perpicere voluntatem
eius cum ea, quia ego fui quasi vidua, eo quod habui
filium in terris, qui non habuit carnalem patrem. Non
est etiam aliqua virgo, quae virginitatem suam desider-
at seruare Deo vsque ad mortem, quin non paratam sum eam
defendere, & confortare, quia ego sum vere ipsa Virgo.[42]

All three translators have worked in a similar way.
They did not try to 'augment'; and they rephrased only enough
to Anglicize the language. The inevitable consequence was
that the structural characteristics of their English prose,
down to considerable detail, were derived from the foreign
original. Since the style of the Latin was homogeneous, so
was the style of these three Englishmen. It has very little
of their own making; and it is quite possible that when they
wrote their own original English prose, the style of each was
very different.
        In the case of a few fifteenth century translators,
some of their original writing has survived. The comparisons
thus offered made it perfectly clear that as a translator a
man might adopt a different form of prose from that which he
chose to write for himself. This is only to be expected,
though it is important in estimating the influence of translation. Sometimes, however, the man's original writing is
structurally, at least, of the same general kind as some of
his translation. And then there very often appears a marked
difference of degree: the same man will show less ability in
the same form of prose when he is composing his own than when
he is translating.
        An early example of such difference is in the work of
Edward of York. His Master of the Game, of about 1405, is
largely a translation of Le Livre de la Chasse by Gaston de
Foix. Edward himself wrote an opening page of prologue, pro-
ceeding then to translate the prologue of Le Livre; and he
interspersed many short passages of his own throughout the
body of the book and added several original chapters at the
end.[43] Edward's own expository chapters, like those he
translated from Gaston de Foix, were intended as a guide for
confirmed hunters. He was neither making converts nor enter-

---

42. Lib. IV, cap. liii, Vol. I, p. 389.
43. All original passages are printed in italics by the
editor.

taining ladies; to state his directions clearly was probably
his only aim. Yet his original prose is neither plain nor
lucid. The difficulty is not in the variety of constructions
at his command; though there are very few participial phrases
-- the average is one to about five hundred words -- he employs
every kind of relative and adverbial clause. His trouble is
rather that he has used constructions in a haphazard manner.
In a series of subordinate clauses or phrases, his favorite
expository device, he will build up so many members or inter-
ject so much between them, that it quickly becomes impossible
to remember from what principal construction the whole depends.
Edward's first original chapter will illustrate:

> And if it be an hert Þat Þe lymer fyndeÞ of and Þat it
> be new, hym ou t to sewe wiÞ as litel noyse as he may,
> controugle, to undo al his moyng til he fynde his fumes,
> Þe which hym ouȝt to put in Þe grete ende of his horn
> and stoppe it wiÞ gras for fallyng out, and litel re-
> ward his hounde and Þa[t] done come aȝeyn Þer as he gan
> to sewe, and sew forÞ Þe right til he come to Þe entr-
> yng of Þe quarter Þat he troweÞ Þe hert be inne, and
> aye wiÞ litil noyse, and umbicast Þe quarters if it be
> in a grete couert as I said bifore. And also if it be
> in a litil couert to do of scantilon and of alle Þing
> right as I have said before, and if he be voided to an-
> eÞer quarter of wode and Þer be ony oÞer couert nye,
> ay to sewe forÞ and umbicast quartere bi quartere, and
> wode by wode, til he be redely harboured, and whan he
> is harboured of scantilon and of alle oÞer Þinggis do
> as biforne is saide, and Þat [done] than drawe hem fast
> to Þe metyng Þat men callen assemble.[44]

Nine successive sentence-members are referred to the first
'ouȝt,' without any word but and to keep the construction before the reader's mind. On a second 'hym ouȝt,' introduced
in sub-dependence, he has hung an inner series of three members. This manner of sentence building characterizes all of
Edward's original prose. It is rare for him to fit together
a facile sentence, while passages similar to the one just
quoted occur on every page.

In the translated chapters of the Master of Game
there are also long series of matter-of-fact directions. But
here they appear in the form of continuous prose, not simply
in a sort of list; and much of the difference is in the careful repetition of the guiding construction. In the following

44. Chap. XXVI, p. 84.

typical passage -- from the last of the translated chapters
-- the one word 'shuld' makes it seem easy:

> The assemble þat men clepyn gaderyng shuld be makyd
> in is manere. The nyght bifore þat ye lord or the
> mayster of þe game wil go to wode, he <u>must</u> make come
> bifore hym all þe hunters, her helpes, the gromes,
> and þe pages, and <u>shuld</u> assigne to eueryche one of hem
> her questes in a certayn place, and soner þe oon frø
> þe other, and þe oon <u>shuld</u> not come vpon þe quest of
> þat oper, ne do hym non noyaunce ne lett. And eueri-
> chon <u>shuld</u> quest in her best wise in þe maner þat I
> haue said, and shuld assigne hem þe place where þe
> gaderyng shuld be makyd <u>at</u> mooste eese of hem alle
> <u>and</u> <u>at</u> nyghest of her queste . . . and also þei þt
> partyn from home, and alle þe officers þat parten from
> home, <u>shuld</u> bryng ider þat þat hem neden ouerychon in
> his office wel and plenteously, and <u>shuld</u> lay þe
> towailes and boordclothes al about vpon þe grene gras,
> and sette diuers metis vpon a grete plater after þe
> lordis pouere, and some <u>shuld</u> ete sittyng and some
> standynge, some lenyng vpon her elbowes.[45]

The relative clarity of this is more, however, than a matter
of auxiliary verbs. It is partly the result of such a detail as the repetition in 'at moost eese of . . . and at
nyghest of.' And it is likewise due to the absence of com-
plications -- for instance, any length of sub-dependence or
any anacoluthon. Both the mechanics and the simplicity of
the passage come straight from Gaston's French:

> Le quelle assemblée se fet en cieu manière: lay nuyt
> devant que le seigneur de la chasse ou le meistre
> veneur voudra aler en boys, il <u>doit</u> faire venir de-
> vant luy les veneurs, les aydes, les valetz, et les
> pages, et leur <u>doit</u> à chescun assigner leurs questes
> en certain lieu et séparé l'une de l'autre; et l'un
> ne <u>doit</u> point venir sur la queste de l'autre ne faire
> annuy. Et chascun <u>doit</u> quester en la manière que j'ay
> dit du mieulz qu'il peut; et leur <u>doit</u> assigner le
> lieu où l'assemblée sera au plus aisé de tous, at au
> plus près de leurs questes . . . Et aussi ceulz qui
> partent de l'ostel; et tous les officiers del'ostel
> <u>doivent</u> là porter chescun ce que li faut selon son
> office et bien plantureusement et <u>doivent</u> estendre

-----

45. Chap. XXXIII, p. 95.

touailles et napes par tout sur l'erbe vert et metre
viandes diverse et grant foyson dessus selon le
povoir du seinheur de la chasse. Et l'un <u>doit</u> men-
gier assis et l'autre sur piés, l'autre acoute.[46]

The prose in Edward's own prologue also compares very
unfavorably with that which he translated. Even in his single
page he let himself get terribly mixed up in his variety of
ideas:

And for þis cause, for þe matere þat þis book trete
of bene in euery sesoun most durable, and to my thenk-
yng to euery gentils hert oftenest most disportful of
alle games þat is to say huntyng for þough it be so
that hawkyng with gentil houndis haukes for þe heroun
and the Reuere be noble and commundable ðit lasteþ it
seelden at the most not passyng half þe yere, And
though men founden from Maij to Lammas game ynow to
hawke at þere myght no wight fynde no haukes to hauke
with but as of huntyng þere nys no sesoun of al þe
yere þat game ne may in euery good contre ryght wel
be founde and eke houndes redy to enchace it. And
sith þis book shal be alle of huntyng which is so
noble a game and heke lastyng þough alle þe yere to
dyuerse beestis aftir at þe sesoun axeth in gladyng
of man, me þenketh I may wel calle it Maystere of
Game.[47]

With its long, loose sentences and variety of subordinations, this is roughly the same kind of prose observed
above in Caxton's <u>Aymon</u>. But Edward was not able to handle
it. Having started to explain something, he let so many di-
gressive thoughts interrupt him, or let their constructions
get so confused, that he seems never to have finished it.
Only once here has he been able to keep a sequence of thought
properly marked out with constructions ('for though . . . and
though'). Instead, the ideas, often repetitious, simply follow along as best they may. Gaston de Foix wrote in a loose
enough style, sometimes falling into sub-dependence, but he
seldom failed to mark the pattern and progress of his thought.
When Edward continues the prologue by translation, his prose
gains startlingly in firmness:

Now shall I preve how hunters lyuen in þis world most
ioyfully of eny oþer men. For whan þe hunters ryseth
in þe mornyng he sawe a swete and fayre morow, and þe
clere wedir and bryght and here þe songe of the small

---

46. Chap. 38, p. 151
47. Chap. 1, p. 3.

> fowles, þe which syngen swetely with grete melodye and
> ful of loue, everich in his language in the best wyse
> þat he may, after þat he bereth of his owyn kynde.
> And whan þe sonne is arise he shall see þe fressh dewe
> vppon þe smale twygges and grasse, and þe sunne which
> by his vertu shal make hem sheyne; and þat is grete
> lykeng and joye to the hunters hert.[48]

This, like the translated passage of directions, has at least
the virtue of never growing confused. Edward could not catch
Gaston's pleasant rhythm, but the structure of the passage is
taken directly from the French:

> Ore te prouveray comme veneurs vivent en cest monde
> plus joyeusement que autre gent; quar, quant le ven-
> eur se liĕve au matin, il voit la très douce et belle
> matinée et le temps cler et serain et le chant de ces
> oiseletz qui chantent doulcement, mélodieusement et
> amouresuement chascun en son language, du mieulx qu'il
> peuvent selon ce que nature leur aprent. Et quant le
> soleill sera levé il verra cette doulce rosée sur les
> raincelles et herbetes et le soleil par sa vertu les
> fera reluysir. C'est grant plaisance et joye au cuer
> du veneur.[49]

The mixture of a personal and a commendatory tone in
these early prologues tends to make them a kind of prose peculiar to themselves. But in another frequent trait they are
not so peculiar: the tendency to pattern exposition upon cause
and effect. The <u>Life</u> <u>of</u> <u>St</u>. <u>Katherine</u> <u>of</u> <u>Siena</u> contains many
passages which are somewhat hortatory and considerably exposi-
tory after the same pattern. The prose is, then, very similar
in kind to that of the original English prologue to the <u>Life</u>,
enough easily to justify another comparison in degree. It is
the only example available from the middle of the century.
Unfortunately the translator decided to 'leve of' the prologue of the Latin author.

His own prologue, at least when first read, makes him
appear rather naïve about composition. He started out as if
to soar, but his pace grew smaller and smaller, and soon he
was merely plodding back and forth. Later he tried the same
flight again; but there was nothing for it, he was earth-bound.

> Here, doughter, and see fructuous example of vertuous
> liuinge to edyfycacion of thy sowle and to comforte

---

48. pp. 6-7.
49. pp. 5-6.

and encrese of thy gostly labour in all werkes of pyte:
ffor as I truste by the gracious yeftes of oure lorde
5 Ihesu thy wyll is sette to plese hym and to do hym ser-
uyce in all holy excercise by the vertue of obedyence
vnder counseyll and techinge of thy gostely gouernours,
And for as moche as I fele by longe experyens the inward affeccions inclynyng with pyte to comforte of all
10 that haue nede, bothe lyuyng and ded, therefore to
strengthe and comforte of thy wil and of all other of
thi gostely susteren, whiche our lord hath graciously
chowse to serue hym nyght and day in prayer and medica-
cion and to laboure bodely in tyme of nede to socour
15 and helpe of the seke and the poure, here I purpos by
our lordis mercy only in his worshvppe wyth truste of
his grace and leue, by helpe of your prayers to translate in englysshe tongue the legende and the blessed
lyf of an holy mayde and virgyn, whiche was and is
20 callyd Katheryn of sene.
    This legende compyled a worshypfull clerke, fryer
Reymond, of the ordre of saynt dominik, doctor of deu-
ynyte and confessour of this holy virgyn. But in this
translacion, I leue of the two prologues whiche in the
25 begynnyng the same clerke made in latyn -- the whiche
passeth your vnderstondyng, and touche alle maters
only that longeth only to your lernyng; by-cause that
moche maner of her vertuous lyuyng shall be rehersyd
in especial in chapytres of this boke whiche in gener-
30 all wordes he toucheth shortely in his prologue; I
leue of also poyntes of diuynyte whiche passeth your
vnderstondyng, and touche only maters þat longeth to
your lernyng. -- Now than, as I sayde in the begynning,
here, doughter, and see what thou herest or redest of
35 this holy mayde and vyrgyn. And that thou geue full
credence to that I shal wryte; the veryte may be preu-
yd wythout ony feynyng bi scryptures of her confessours
and verefyeng of creatures whiche late lyued in erthe.
Also the vytnes I purpose to put in at the ende of eche
40 chapytre, as that worshypfull clerke dide whiche compyl-
ed this boke in latyn.[50]

    The piece of bathos toward the end is hard to overlook,
and of course the exposition has many crudenesses. But this
cleric seems to have known what he wanted to do. He shows
some conception of unity and of amplification. He has at
least attempted to use the devices of apostrophe and periodic
structure. His difficulty, like Edward's, above, was that he

50. Pp. 33-34.

could not prevent his incidental ideas from clogging his
progress and obscuring his form. He could neither cull them
out nor fit them together. For instance, he gives two reasons why he will 'leue of' (line 24); but one is expressed
in a relative, the other in an adverbial clause, and the two
seem utterly disconnected. Perhaps they were; perhaps one
or the other was an afterthought. But perhaps, too, he conceived of them as parallel. This difficulty is most obvious
in the overweighted second sentence, which is periodic. Between each of the main connectives he has interposed a breath-
taking length of by-thoughts which, as phrased, cannot possibly be brought into relationship with the period as a whole;
for they are in a chain of sub-dependence or in a formless
heap of prepositional phrases.

These difficulties with structure disappear when the
same man begins translating.[51] In the passage which follows, the periodic connectives 'right . . . right soo' (lines
1-2) and 'so . . . that' (used three times, lines 9-10, 15,
21-24,) are not merely a frame for any number of interjected
parts; they knit the sentence together. In one construction
or another, there are relatively as many detailed statements
here as in the prologue, and except for the verbals there is
no greater variety of construction. Yet each statement is so
constructed as to show its logical relationship to the others;
and there are fewer subordinations. For instance, in the description of the saint's ecstasy (lines 14-19), there is a
shift to short principal clauses, steadily increased in length.
In fact, variety in construction has also produced variety in
length and in rhythm:

> Right as oure lorde graunted to his spouse, this holy
> mayde, a syngular lyuyng as touchyng her body, ryght
> soo he vysyted her soule wyth grete mereuylous comfort-
> es of reuelaciones. Fyrst fro the grete haboundant
> 5 graces with-in her come that bodely strengthe ᵽat she
> had aboue kynde. Wite ye right wel ᵽat fro the tyme
> that this holy mayde had I-dronke of oure lordes syde
> the drinke of lyf, as it is rehersid afore, so many
> grete graces were haboundant in her, ᵽat ofte-times,
> 10 as it had be in maner contynyabul, she was occupyed in
> actuell contemplacion; and her spyryte was lowyd to
> our lord so that for the more parte she bylefte wythout
> felyng in her bodely wyttes. Soo that, as it is rehers-

---

51. There are some examples of confused construction in the
Life. But these occur only when the translator has parted
from his Latin text. The translation is examined in detail
in Chapter V, p. 110.

ed in the fyrst party, her armes were founde ofte-tymes
15 soo styf in tyme of suche actuell contemplacion, that
rather they sholde breke thenne bowe; her eyen were all
closed, her eres herde none noyse, were it neuer so
grete, and her bodely wyttes for that tyme were sequest-
red fro her owne werkynge. This sholde be none merueyle
20 to noman, yf they wolde take hede to at syweth. Oure
lorde began to bee soo homely with her and brennyd her
soule wyth soo moche haboundante fyre of loue, not oonly
in pryuy places but also in open places, as well stond-
yng as goyng, that she, the whiche hadde thyse grete
25 graces, by-knewe it playnely to her confessour she coude
fynde none wordes for to telle expressly the grace that
she felte.[52]

Though the translation is not always so close as those
quoted before, the description of the English will apply equally well to the Latin. Within some of the sentences there have
been transpositions, paraphrases, omissions, or insertions.
The most considerable change is the paraphrase of about thirty
words of Latin (lines 8-11 below) into fifteen of English, ending with the neat phrase 'rather . . . breke than bowe' (line
16). Yet apart from length, even this sentence is structurally
correspondent to the source; and the rest of the passage is
equally or more so:

Right as oure lord graunted to his spouse, this holy
mayde, a syngular lyuyng as touchyng her body,

Sicut singularem modum vivendi concesserat Dominus
sponsae suae, quantum ad corpus illo in tempore;

right soo he vysyted her soule wyth grete merueylous
comfortes of reuelaciones.

sic profecto mentum ejus magnis et admirandis revelat-
ionum consolationibus visitabat:

Fyrst fro the grete haboundant graces with-in her come
that bodely strengthe þat she had aboue kynde. Etc.

inde siquidem procedebat supernaturalis ille vigor corp-
oreus, ex abundantia scilicet spiritualium gratiarum

Noveris igitur, lector, quod ex quo virgo Deo dictata
potaverat de Salvatoris latere potum vitae, tanta super-
abundavit in ea gratiae plenitudo, quod quasi continue

---

52. Part II, chap. vi; p. 265. 11.4-24.

in actuali contemplatione occupabatur; et spiritus ejus
5 tam fixe suo inhaerebat et omnium conditori, quod part-
em inferiorem et sensitivam, pro majori parti temporis,
relinquebat absque actibus sensitvus. Haec, ut in prima
parte tactum est, millies sumus experti, nos, qui vid-
imus et manibus contrectavimus brachia ejus ita una cum
10 manibus ejus esse, quod frangi ossa potius potuissent,
quam de loco cui adhaeserant removeri, dum illi contemplatione actuali vacabat, oculi clausi erant ex toto,
aures nullum quantumcumque magnum sonum percipiebant,
et omnes sensus corporei proprio acta pro tunc erant
15 privati. Nec mirum cuiquam debet esse, si attendantur
cum diligentia quae sequuntur. Coepit enim Dominus ex
tunc non tantum in locis secretis, utprius consueverat,
sed etiam in patentibus, palam et familiariter se ostend-
ere sponsae suae, tam eunti quam stanti; tantumque ignem
20 sui amoris in ejus corde accendere, quod ipsamet, quae
divina haec patiebatur, fatebatur suo confessori, se
plane ad exprimendum quod sentiebat nulla vocabula in-
venire.[53]

    If the Latin text of the translator was something like
this one, he has made twelve changes of his own choosing besides those naturally called for in any Anglicization from
Latin. Yet the influence of the source upon the structure of
the translation appears in every sentence and in the division
of the sentences. With his Latin prose to guide him, the translator would seem never even to have met the difficulties of selection and structure which vitiated his own writing in the
prologue.
    Most of Caxton's original work — to move toward the
end of the century — is in his prologues and epilogues. With
very few exceptions these are in the typical manner observed
above: the tone both personal and commendatory; the exposition
patterned upon cause and effect; the structure hypotactic, very
loose, often highly complicated. In his first dozen or so prologues, down to about 1480 or 1481, Caxton could not handle
this style any better than Edward of York or the translator
of St. Katherine.[54] But most of those written in his last
ten years show a fair degree of control over structure; though

---

53. Pars II, cap. vi, p. 907, B - C.
54. See Robert R. Aurner, Caxton and the English Sentence.
University of Wisconsin Studies in Language and Literature,
XVIII (1923), 23-59. The best edition of Caxton's original
writing is by W. J. B. Crotch, The Prologues and Epilogues
of William Caxton. (EETS os 176) London, 1928.

they are always loose, they are usually clear and even.[55]
     Caxton never gained a sure sense of structure, how-
ever.[56] When, like the translator of St. Katherine, he
ventured to try any unusual cast of rhetoric, his lack of
resources became evident. In translating the Curial, as we
seen, Caxton wrote a prose which was quite adequate for the
rhetoric of medieval epistolography. A declamatory appeal
to the knights of England, part of his original epilogue to
The Ordre of Chivalry[57] was written in the same year as
the Curial, 1484; and like the Curial it was an attack on
manners. But here, in his own writing, he impaired the effect by frequent inattention to the requirements of the form.

> O ye knyghtes of Englond where is the custome and
> vsage of noble chyualry that was vsed in the dayes/
> what do ye now/ but go to the baynes & playe atte
> dyse And some not wel aduysed vse not honest and
> good rule ageyn alle ordre of kynghthode/ leue this/
> leue it and rede . . .

It is just possible that the sudden shift in construction was
not blind, but an awkward attempt at a sort of dialyton, a
separation for emphasis. However, a few lines below, after
a roster of the heroes, the same surprising break in structural sequence is repeated:

> Allas what doo ye/ but slepe & take ease/ and ar al
> disordred fro chyualry/ . . .

It seems more likely that Caxton was merely indifferent about
his constructions; or, perhaps, that he changed the construction whenever his mind took a new turn.[58] A more certain
example occurs in the very next sentence:

---

55. Caxton's own prologue to The Book of the Kynght of the
Towre (Crotch, op. cit., p. 86-7) compares very favorably with
the prologue which he translated from the French. The firmest
and most praised of them all, however, the prologue to Trevisa's Polychronicon (Crotch, op. cit., p. 64-67) was, as I in-
tend to show in a separate publication, a translation from
either a Latin or a French version of Diodorus Siculus.
56. The prologue to The Royal Book, written as late as 1488,
is obscured by frequent sub-dependence and anocoluthon.
57. Crotch, op. cit., pp. 82-84.
58. A suggestion of Leon Kellner's to explain the frequency
of anacoluthon in Old and Middle English writing. Historical
Outlines of English Syntax, New York, 1892, p. 9.

> J wold demaunde a question yf J shold not displease/
> how many knyghtes ben ther now in England/ that haue
> thuse and thexcercyse of a knyghte/ that is to wete
> that <u>he</u> <u>knoweth</u> his hors/ & his hors hym/ that is to
> saye/ <u>he beynge</u> redy at a poynt to haue al thyng
> that longeth to a knyght/

This disregard for structural form may be seen in
Caxton's prologue to <u>Caton</u>, written the year before he translated his <u>Curial</u> and containing, here again, a somewhat similar attack on manners.[59] 'O whan I remembre the noble
Romayns,' Caxton begins, and presently cites Cato, 'auctor
and maker of this book.'   He then continues:

> <u>And</u> <u>as</u> in my Jugement it is the beste book for to be
> taught to yonge children in scole/ & also to peple of
> euery age it is ful conuenient yf it be wel vnder-
> standen/ <u>And</u> <u>by</u> <u>cause</u> J see that the children that ben
> borne within the sayd cyte//encreace/ and prouffyte not
> lyke theyr faders and olders/ but for the moost parte
> after that they ben comen to theyr parfight yeres of
> discrecion/ and rypenes of age/ how wel that theyre
> faders haue lefte to them grete quantite of goodes/ yet
> scarcely amonge ten two thryue/

From the punctuation, it seems that 'And as' and 'And by cause'
are parallel members of a long period, the end of which, however -- the effect of the cause -- is never reached; Caxton
appears to have forgotten how he began the sentence. It may
be that he meant 'And as' to be completed in 'it is full con-
uenient,' with a pause after 'age,' and that 'And by cause'
may be paraphrased 'All the more so because.'   But even then
this surprising informality in so rhetorical a passage can
only be put down to inadequate habits of composition.
     The prologue to the <u>Curial</u> itself provides another
sharp contrast with the translation. Though it is not in the
same style, it is one more example of an original writer's
failure either to reduce the number of his interposed ideas
or to take care with the constructions of them.

> Here foloweth the copye of a letter whyche maistre
> Alayn Charetier wrote to hys brother/ whyche desired
> to come dwelle in Court/ in whyche he reherseth many
> myseryes & wretchydnesses therin vsed/ For taduyse
> hym not to entre in to it/ leste he after repente/
> like as hier after folowe/ and late translated out

---

59. Crotch, <u>op</u>. <u>cit</u>., p. 77.

of frensshe in to englysshe/ whyche Copye was delyuer-
ed to me by a noble and vertuous Erle/ At whos Instance
& requeste I haue reduced it in to Englyssh.[60]

Merely because they offered the readiest way, Caxton allowed
three which-clauses to follow in sequence, with no concern
over similarity of function or over the connection between
'wrote' and 'For taduyse.' When he was ready to say 'translated', he blithely clapped in on as another modifyer, leaving form and logic to anyone who might care to reshape the
long mass.

　　　Perhaps this brief, informal jotting of a prologue
cannot fairly be forced into contrast with the translation
it precedes. But in the prologue to Cato and the epilogue
to The Ordre Caxton was trying hard in a style and a vein
somewhat like that of the Curial. Yet his case appears to
be the same as those of Edward of York and the translator of
St. Katherine. All these writers seem to need the guidance
and discipline of their sources to maintain any complexity
of form with surety. They apparently have not yet enough
tradition or experience of prose composition behind them.
At the same time the increased firmness in the same men's
translated prose was clearly due to the corresponding firmness in the sources. In other words, it was produced by
close translation.[61]

　　　Translation -- close translation of prose -- should
be constantly realized for what it so obviously is, a specific manner of composition. The form of prose so composed
is peculiarly influenced by the prose of the source. In the
various examples taken from early English it was this process which provided the writers with at least their structural technique, an element of prose so basic that variations of
it produce variations of style: Caxton has been seen writing

---

60. Crotch, op. cit., p. 89.
61. Alois Brandl, reviewing Mr. Chambers' essay (Archiv für
das studien der n.sp., CLXIII (1933), 267-9), has called attention to a similar contrast between the original writing and
the translation of King Alfred: 'Dabei kann man Alfred bei
aller hochachtung fast nur als Übersetzer nennen, und wo er
einmal aus eigenem schöft, wie in der berühmten Vorrede zum
Gregorius, baut er so lange und umständliche Perioden, in die
er sich mühsam verstrickt, dass er enge Schülerhaft gegenüber
lateinischen Vorbildern, namentlich Epistolographen, seiner
zeit verrät.' (p. 268.)

in at least two different ways beside his own.

Under these conditions, translated prose must, for historical purposes, be considered apart from original prose. As long as the main body of the sources remained of the same general nature -- as it did until about 1520 -- [62] the main body of the translations remained so as well. But toward the end of the fifteenth century original prose underwent important changes in structure. Chief interest in the practice of translation during the preceding period lies in the possibility of its having partly caused these changes. To describe the differences in English original prose between the opening and the closing of the fifteenth century, and at the same time to indicate what habits of composition account for the differences, is the next step in determining the historical place of translation.

---

62. H. B. Lathrop, Translations from the Classics from Caxton to Chapman, Madison, 1933, pp. 15-29.

Chapter Two

THE ORIGINAL PROSE OF THE TRANSITION

To describe a piece of prose mainly or only in terms of its structure -- a liberty taken in the preceding chapter -- may give a misconception of its total effect. Often enough early English prose which is structurally crude has a sweetness of rhythm or a pungency of diction which is its most characteristic trait. Historically, however, the limitation has a good basis, for it was the structural quality of this prose which changed most -- a change which it is the purpose of this chapter to analyze.

'Structure' itself is not a very narrow term. At its broadest it should include the disposition of all units of the context. At one end, it involves the first of the two classic divisions of rhetoric; at the other, when the unit considered is only the single phrase or word, it involves pure linguistic. Neither extreme can be disregarded. Yet historically, once more, there is good reason for dealing mainly with relatively small units. For the greatest difficulties and the greatest changes in early English prose appear in the arrangement and expression of the common patterns of thought: cause and effect, likeness and difference, attendant circumstance either in time or in condition, relative importance, etc. The sequences thus to be built may be of only two ideas -- two clauses or phrases, or even single words -- or of several, amounting to a length about equivalent to a modern paragraph. The sentence is the mean unit here, but the real basis of the matter is the combination of small units or the sentence-members into the full periods of thought.

It is because of its inadequacy in this respect that much medieval prose has for modern readers the effect of naïvete. The cast of its thoughts is so unvaried or so random, or the thoughts themselves seem so unselected, that we incline to call it primitive, forgetting that twentieth century psychology has released a somewhat similar prose which we call stream-of-consciousness. The difficulty of pre-Tudor prose writers can scarcely have been their unawareness of the nature of the thought-relationship within any

given sequence or period. In fact, it is possible that to
them there was no 'difficulty' or 'inadequacy' at all: the
modern judgement may be based only on a change of usage.
Yet that very change was begun within the latter end of the
medieval period itself; and while even usage may be judged
for its degree of sophistication, the main interest lies in
the fact of the change.

For that matter, the expression of thought-relationships is less a matter of usage in the absolute sense than
of the habits which lie behind it. An important kind of
habit is that associated with a sense of form. In the passages from Caxton's original writing quoted in the last chapter, a most conspicuous trait is the inconsistency of the
structure in respect to sheer logic. Thus 'Alas what do ye
but sleep and are all disordered' violates rational expec-
tancy to the point where form can scarcely be felt longer to
exist. Again, in the following passage from an early sermon,
not even the standard device of numbered division has im-
parted enough form to counteract the break caused by the
shift of constructions:

> first, in busynesse of getynge and dightynge of mete,
> afterward in the lust and delite in etynge, and the
> thridde, whan thei recorde how wele thei beth fed.[1]

Asymmetrical coordination and other constructions inconsistent with logic were of common occurrence in Middle English,
and not only in prose. In poetry, where they are equally
frequent, they cause no disruption of form; formal observ-
ances of other kinds are sufficiently conspicuous. But
prose, by nature relatively amorphous, needs the presence of
an abstract quality of logic in order to develop in any sub-
stantial degree an effect of artfulness. There was little
literary prose in Middle English before about 1350, and it
was not at all widespread until well into the fifteenth century. Yet before the end of the century the eliminiation
of illogical usages had already begun. The change may therefore have partly resulted from a perception of the ineptitude
of such usages when they appeared baldly in prose of literary
purpose; also from a perception of the superiority in this
respect of prose which is relatively freed from them.

.1. MS. Harley 45, fol. 142, v.   Quoted by G. R. Owst,
Literature and Pulpit, pp. 147-8.

CONSISTENT CONSTRUCTION: THE CHANGE

OF USAGE IN PROSE

Considerable connection can be shown between certain concrete usages like asymmetrical coordination and a broader kind of usage which may be best described as habit of composition.

Until 1460 or 1470, the Middle English prose writers appear to have lacked the habit of associating pattern of thought with pattern of expression or form. Whether or not they perceived the full pattern of thought from its beginning, their attention to the form did not embrace the whole but was habitually concentrated only upon the part immediately under expression. In respect to form, their basic unit for composition in prose was the single statement, approximately the single construction or sentence member.

The part of this habit in illogical combinations of constructions may be seen in the use of the pleonastic pronoun, not as figure of speech but redundant after an inserted sentence-member:

but the erle forasmoche as he was made by auctoryte
of the parlement, he wolde not obey the pryue seale. [2]

This is a small ineptitude, with slight if any effect upon the sense or the structure. Its interest lies in the reflection it gives of the writer's psychology of form. After inserting even so short a sentence-member he forgot the nature of his original construction. 'The erle' was retained as a thought, as the use of a pronoun shows. But the form of the final statement was conceived only in terms of itself; and the writer, feeling obliged to provide a subject for his verb, did so with a redundancy that was not at all conscious.[3]

Another frequent usage of the time, the synthetic verb -- ellipsis of the subject -- though exactly the opposite of pleonasm, was often the result of inattention to the form of the whole sequence of thought. Examples may be found at random in the earliest original English chronicles:

---

2. An English Chronicle, edited by J. S. Davies, Camden Society no. 64, London, 1856, p. 79.
3. Similar examples are in Kellner, Historical Outlines, p. 183, cf. ibid., pp. 67-8.

>And in the vj yere . . . went the Erle of Salusbury,
>with a grete retenewe of men of armys and archeris,
>by comaundement of the Kynge and of alle the Coun-
>seile of Engelonde, & made hym the Leftenaunt or
>alle the partyes of Fraunce . . . forto distroye the
>Kynges enemyes . . . And so he departid . . . . [4]

>And from thens she was brought to Westmynstre, and
>þere was hir terement holden and doon rially; and
>þere buryed in the chapell of oure Lady.[5]

>And in this same yere . . . a seruant þat was with a
>man of Hakney, ij myle from London, come with his
>mayster to London, and bought vitayle and must for
>dignte, forto sende hoom to his wife, for she was
>grete with childe, And the fals creature, when he
>come hoom slewe þe wife . . . .[6]

In the first of these the Earl did not make himself lieuten-
ant, any more than in the other two it was the 'interrment'
which was buried or the servant who bought the food. The
synthetic verb is in part a relic of the time when an inflec-
tional ending made the subject clear. But verbal inflections
never had the power to identify the subject from among two
or more nouns when person and number were the same. In each
case quoted, the ambiguity has come because the writers composed the form of their sentences by short units. The subjects of the statements about buying or burying or making --
that is, the thought-relationships of the statements -- were,
of course, clear in the writers' minds. But at the moment of
constructing the statement, there was no regard to the form
of any outside part of the sentence. [7]
    Asymmetrical coordination has a more important effect
upon the form of prose. In his study of this Middle English
usage, Mr. Urban Ohlander gives a psychological explanation
of it which implies the habit of composing by short units:
'In ME., which was more unhampered by grammatical and stylistic inhibitions, asymmetrical coordination has a wider scope
. . .. Whereas a reasonably careful modern writer avoids dis-

---

    4. The Brut, ed. by F. Brie, Part II (EETS o s 136), London,
1908, 'Continuation D,' p. 434, 11.15-21.
    5. Ibid., 'Continuation G,' p. 471, 11.3-5.
    6. Ibid., p. 474, 11.29-33.
    7. See also W. J. F. Roberts, 'Ellipsis of the Subject-pro-
noun in Middle English.' London Medieval Studies, I,i (1937)
107-15. Mr. Roberts gives many examples, all earlier than
the fifteenth century.

turbing asymmetries either by choosing symmetrical expressions from the beginning or by revising what he has written, a ME. writer was seemingly not so scrupulous in that respect, the latter's language reflecting rather the spoken language of his times. Thus it may happen that when the writer gets to the second member, he is forced to give this an asymmetrical form because there is no other symmetrical expression available, unless, of course, he revises the first member to bring it into conformity with the second. In other cases the second member's assuming an asymmetrical shape may be due to the writer's confusing mentally the actual form of the first member with a synonymous expression which determines the form of the second member (blending, 'contamination').'[8]

In the following excerpt from an English sermon of about 1400, the basic structure is a sequence of coordinations. Aside from the adjective clauses there are only three verbal constructions of subordinating type. Yet two of these are used asymmetrically.

> For he [the great nobleman] wold be callid manly and worchypfull; and also in holdyng of grete festes, feding riche men. And the pore man stondythe at the gate with an empti wombe. He may rather have a knoc then a crust of brede. And so these riche men will feede them that hathe no nede; and he that hathe nede schall go with-owte. Then commythe mynstrells and cowrtyers, and thei schall have grete yftes. And there gothe ther expences a-wey, be-cawse thei wold be magnyfyed, and to bere theire name a-bowte of grete worchype.[9]

The writer of this appears to have had a pattern present in his mind, a pattern of short equal blocks of thought. But lacking a consciousness of the grammatical cast of the blocks,

---

8. _Studies in Coordinate Expressions in Middle English_, Lund, 1936, pp. 114-16. 'Blending' implies a certain vague regard for preceding units, but a regard which takes no account of the written form.

9. MS. Lincoln Cath. Libr. A.6.2, fol. 21v. Quoted by G. R. Owst, _Literature and Pulpit_, p. 311. (For the date of the sermon, see Owst, _Preaching_, p. 201. n.1.) The ambiguous use of the pronoun 'ther' in the last sentence, a confusion often observed in early prose, may have been caused by the same habit as were 'blending,' the synthetic verb, and other constructions which imply a referent not written in the text but only vaguely present in the writer's mind.

he simply added any thought he wanted in the most convenient construction at hand. Thus to him 'becawse' did not introduce a new clausal form, but was simply a connective between thoughts, and 'to bere' represented only the same connection repeated; his pattern had nothing to do with mechanics of expression.

     Here again the disruption is more in form than in clarity of meaning. But when a writer with the same psychology used a greater variety of constructions, the sense itself must sometimes have been seriously obscured at least to a reader if not to a listener, usage notwithstanding. A good instance may be had, this time from secular literature, in the very opening page of Lydgate's The Serpent of Division.

> Whilome, as olde bookis maken mencion, when tholde
> noble famous citie of Rome was most shyning in his
> felicitie and flowring in his glory, — liche as it
> is remembered in bookis of olde antiquyte — the
> prime temps of his fundacion, whenne the wallis
> were reised on heithe bi the manly & prudent dili-
> gence of Remvs and Romvlus; fro þe which tyme þe
> citie stood vnder governaunce of kyngis, tyl at the
> tyme Tarquyne soone of Tarquyne the prowde, for his
> outragious offence doone vnto Lucresse wife to þe
> worþy Senatour Callatyne . . . pvnysshing of whiche
> trespace by the manly pursuite of Collatyns kynrede
> and ful assente of all the Senate the name of kyngis
> ceased in the citie of Rome for evur more, and all
> the Roial stokke of þe forsaide Tarquyne was pro-
> scripte & put in exile.[10]

     Here it is hard to trace even any pattern of thought. Before he has gone very far Lydgate himself seems to have forgotten what he started out to say. Certainly he paid no attention to how he started to say it. Still, the basic procedure of composition here can be seen to be the same as in the sermon just quoted. The only difference is that Lydgate has cast his successive blocks of thought in subordinating rather than coordinating constructions. Some of these may have been considered demonstrative rather than relative ('fro e which tyme'; 'in pvnysshing of whiche trespace').[11] But it is plain from the uncompleted con-

---

10. Edited by H. N. MacCracken, New Haven, 1911, p. 49, 11.1-11.

11. See T. Reul, The Language of Caxton's 'Reynard the Fox,' Université de Gand, Receuil de Traveaux, no. 26, Gand, 1901, pp. 69-70.

structions at the opening that Lydgate had very little awareness of the connection between syntactical form and logic of
thought.

Anacoluthon, sometimes obscuring the sense, sometimes
only the form, is frequent in Middle English prose. It is
found more often in complex or hypotactic structure than in
paratactic, the reason no doubt being that there was less
chance for misfitting when the constructions were all the
same. Any writer using a variety of constructions was likely
to overlook the requirements of logic. This was true not only
of secular writers who pretended to no especial education in
rhetoric, men like Edward of York at the beginning of the century or Caxton toward the end. Anacoluthic sentences are to
be found in the usually careful prose of Reginald Pecock, one
of whose literary ambitions was that his works be translated
into Latin.[12] Two examples appear within three pages of
The Book of Faith.[13]

> and the iie is this, setting not bi forto folowe
> the determynaciouns and the holdingis of the chirche
> in mater of feith; and that for as myche as thei
> presupposen as what may be sufficiently provid and
> wherto thei alleggen witnessing of Seynt Austyn in
> his book of Baptym aȝens Donatists, that the chirche
> may erre in determynyng articlis for feith; wherfore
> foloweth that the labour . . . shulde be the profit-
> ablist labour . . . etc.

> . . . it is not ynouȝ that the seid bokis be writen . . .
> and that the bokis schulde opene to hem that thei
> erren; but tho bokis musten be distributed and delid
> abrood to manye, where that nede is trowid that thei
> be delid: and that the seid erryng persoonys take
> longe leiser, forto sadli and oft overrede tho bokis,
> unto tyme thei schulen be wel aqueyntid with tho
> bokis, and with the skilis and motivis therynne writ-
> en, and not forto have in oon tyme or ii tymes a liȝt
> superficial overreding or hering oonly. Forwhi . . .
> oold custom . . . wole make . . . etc.

Structure inconsistent with logic is to be found, though
rarely, in Fortescue:

---

12. Folower to the Donet, ed. by E. V. Hitchcock, (EETS o s
164) London, 1921, p. 64.
   13. Edited by J. L. Morison, Glasgow, 1919, pp. 114-116.

> With wich desire God was gretly offendyd, as wele
> for thair folie as for thair vnkyndnes; that sith-
> yn thai had a kynge, wich was God, that reigned
> vppon thaim politikily and roialy, and yet wold
> chauge hym for a kynge, a verray man, that uolde
> reigne vpon hem only roialy.[14]

The following sentences are from a letter of 1487, apparently carefully written by a Prior who was interested in ob-
taining financial redress for his priory:

> And also the seid Annes that was hys wyf lyved more
> thanne xxx. wynter aftir hir husbonde, and was in
> singuler trust with her husbonde, and one of his
> executours, and wele knowen in this cuntre, a wo-
> man of vertuos lyvyng and disposicion, and of goode
> discrecioun and conscience, and knew hir husbondes
> mynde and last will as wele as ony lyvyng creature;
> she witnessed alway that it was hire husbondes last
> will to have this perpetuall messe . . . . etc.

> And in asmoche as ꝫe be of our cuntre and speciall
> frendes to our monastery, and longest acqueyntyd
> with you, that makith me and all my brethren the
> more bolde to schewe this our mater and interest
> unto you . . . . etc.[15]

        Sentences thus illogically composed continue to ap-
pear well after the end of the fifteenth century.[16] By
that time, however, and for at least twenty years before
1500, the tendency appears to have greatly lessened. Thirty-
four pages from John Fisher's Treatise concernynge the Seuen
Penytencyal Psalmes, published in 1509,[17]show no instances
of anacoluthon whatever, and only three of asymmetrical coordination. Fisher often used the synthetic verb, but only
twice in the pages is the subject ambiguous. In about six

---

14. The Governance of England, c. 1475, edited by C.
Plummer, Oxford, 1885, pp. 109-10.
  15. John Bonwell to ---. Dated the Second Henry VII.
From the Paston MSS., edited by James Gairdner, The Paston
Letters, Westminster, 1895, III, 331, 332-3.
  16. See e.g. Thomas More's, De quatuor novissima, 1522,
ed. by W. E. Campbell, The English Works of Sir Thomas More,
New York, 1931, I, 469-70; and the Dialogue concerning Tyndale, ibid., II, p. 25.
  17. Edited by John E. B. Mayor, The English Works of John
Fisher, (EETS e s XXVII) London, 1876, pp. 200-233.

thousand words from the latter pages of Robert Fabyan's
Chronicles, published in 1516 but written by 1504, there are
only two instances of anacoluthon, two of asymmetrical coordination, and three of the ambiguous synthetic verb.[18]
More significant, a London chronicle written about 1485
shows, in about the same length, only one instance of anacoluthon, three of asymmetrical coordination, and none of
the ambiguous synthetic verb.[19] The London chronicle is a
significant example not only because of its early date but
because of its obscurity; it is found only in manuscript and
is likely to have been the work of an average writer of the
time.
        The prevailing 'correctness' or logical consistency
in the sentence structure of early sixteenth century prose
has been often remarked, and the explanation given for it has
been the revival of learning.[20] It is true that the function -- and the importance -- of logic in English syntax
might be learned by the study of Latin. Pecock probably, and
very likely Fortescue, isolated cases in the fifteenth century, achieved the prevailing correctness of their English
sentence structure by placing it in direct analogy with that
of Latin. But it has been observed above that logical inconsistency was apparently connected with the habit of composition by short units of thought. The tendency of syntactical
usage toward correctness may therefore have resulted not so
much from an analytical understanding of the science of grammar as from a broadened sense of form, a growing habit of
planning the expression to fit the whole of a sequence of
thought. That such a growth was taking place may be seen
from other changes in fifteenth century prose which do not
involve the correctness of the structure.

---

18. Edited by Henry Ellis, London, 1811, pp. 622-625, 667-
673; date by Fabyan, p. 681.
    19. Brit. Mus. Cotton MS Vitellius A XVI. Ed. by C. L.
Kingsford, Chronicles of London, Oxford, 1905, pp. 150-162,
169-178, 189-193; date intro. p. xv-xviii.
    20. L. Kellner, Historical Outlines, p. 9. J. A. Gee, The
Life and Works of Thomas Lupset, New Haven; Yale University
Press, 1928, pp. 181-197.

THE BROADENING OF THE UNIT OF COMPOSITION:

NARRATIVE STRUCTURE.

      Until after the middle of the century, _exempla_,
chronicles and other narrative types were almost invariably
characterized by an elementary simplicity of structure. A
rather extreme example will best make plain the basic nature
of the habit that led to composition of this sort. The following allegory, written about 1425, was part of a warning
to 'halu þe sonday:'

    Therwith cometh in pride & sittith him in þe middle
    of alle, and þan he beginneth to boste & ruson him
    self of many þinges þat he hath not, ne kowde, &
    alle saien it is sooth. Then couetise herith þat,
5   & þan cometh he in boldely, & he cherith þam alle,
    and anoon he bi ginneth for to bargen, and þen
    lacketh not gret o us & sweringes and an is ich of
    þam abowte to begyle oþer. Then cometh in lechere,
    and he lokuth al abowthe þe hows, & þen he settith
10 him downe on þe benche, and þen beginneth he to speke,
    & bringe in oolde storius of wemen & of lustus, &
    ribaldy, & faste he rusith himself of olde synnes,
    and alle lau en, & been glad to here his prechinge.
    Than cometh in glotone þe stuard of þat howsolde, &
15 he cherith þam alle, & bidith þam sitte stille & be
    mery and glad, so þat noon of ȝow go hoom bot it be
    so he be sad, or a staf in his hoonde for fallynge.
    Than slowthe herith þis maundement, þat is þe march-
    el of þat halle, & þen he ouerloketh þam alle. And
20 þen he chargeth Udulnes to cheren þam alle, & to
    sitte stille, and þat þe cuppe, be not empte no tume.
    Than at þe laste ende comith in wrath & he bringeth
    with him enuye, & rekunneth þer acunthes, for þat he
    is tresureer of þat howsoolde, he chargeth þat noon
25 of hem parte from oþer in charite, & loke he saith
    wen þat euer ȝe com togedur þat noon speke good of
    oþer, ne of ȝowre neibures. And þen saide þai alle
    Amen.[21]

---

21. A Middle English Treatise on the Ten Commandments. Edited by J. F. Royster, Chapel Hill, 1911, p. 22; for date
and originality of composition, Introduction p. iv, vii.

These tavern manners are charming to the imagination. But the expression of them has only the appeal of the naive. There is a minimum attempt to distinguish any one statement from the other for its relative value in the picture. Each new part is laid side by side with the last. To use the standard classifications of thought-relationships, there are, in nearly three hundred words, only one construction to indicate cause (line 23), one of result (line 16), one of concession (line 16) and three of attribute (lines 3, 14, 18). Except once (line 26), even time-relationship is expressed by no other means than coordination. There are only two series of subordinate phrases, each shifting into asymmetrical coordination (lines 17, 21). But the best indication of the habit of composition by short units alone is the sudden shift, in the very middle things, from the third to the second person and back again to the third (lines 15-17). Clearly one form of expression carried little influence in the writer's mind when he came to the next; but each successive idea was constructed separately in its turn, being set down in the form which most readily or habitually fell to mind in connection with the context. There was no more combining than was inevitable in common speech; no attempt to arrange the parts. Apparently there was no pre-conception of a structural form.

This flat narrative structure, with its unvaried form imparting no perspective to the context, appears to have been the rule in original English prose before about 1470 or 1480. It is characteristic of the exempla, original or freely translated, as in Mirk's Festial (about 1400)[22] or Jacob's Well (1420) [23]. It is prevalent in private records and registers -- when they are not written in standard legal forms -- such as The Brewers First Book (1422) [24] and The Coventry Leet Book [25]; and it is almost universal in the earliest original English chronicles. Malory's Morte

---

22. Edited by Theodor Erbe (EETS e s XCVI), London, 1905.
23. Edited by Arthur Brandes (EETS e x CXV), London, 1918.
24. A Book of London English, 1384-1425. Edited by R. W. Chambers and Marjorie Daunt, Oxford, 1931.
25. Edited by M. D. Harris (EETS o s 134), London, 1907. See e.g. the complaint against the iron workers, dated 1435 (pp. 180, ff.). This opens with a long hypotactic sentence closely imitating the standardized legal form in French, which is used frequently in the same book. But as soon as it becomes necessary to describe the iron-workers' peculiar practices, the sentence-structure changes to parataxis.

Darthur, 1469, was so written, both in the passages where he
may have been under the influence of a source, and in those
where he is very far indeed from any known source,[26]
     It was at about the time of Malory's book that the
structure of narrative prose began to grow more sophisticated.
The change is best measured in the chronicles, more and more
of which during the second and third quarters of the century
were written in original English prose.[27] The earliest known
certainly to be without French or Latin source are three of
about 1435.[28] From then until about 1460 there are at least
eight separate compositions.[29] All eleven of these chronicles are characterized by a structure essentially the same as

---

     26. Edited by Sommer, London, 1894. For the sources see E.
Vinaver, Malory, Oxford, 1929, Appendix II, 'The Sources of
the Morte Darthur,' pp. 128-155; also appendix III, pp. 155-189.
     27. The material considered in each chronicle includes only
that which is not closely copied from some earlier one, that
where the composition is the compiler's own. It also includes
only passages in continuous narrative, however brief, and ex-
cludes those which merely itemize names or events. Starke,
Pop. Engl. Chroniken, has observed the difference in sentence-
structure (pp. 86, 135), but has not emphasized it or traced
it chronologically.
     38. Harley MS. 3775, ed. C. L. Kingsford, Eng. Hist. Lit.,
pp. 292-95. Brut D, in several MSS, ed. Fr. Brie, The Brut,
Part II (EETS o s 136), London, 1908, pp. 394-439; date in
Kingsford, op. cit., 118, 132. Cotton, Julius B II, ed.
Kingsford, Chronicles of London, Oxford, 1905, pp. 79-97;
date and composition, ibid., viii-ix.
     29. Cotton MS. Vitellius F ix,(1439) ed. N. H. Nicholas and
E. Tyrrell, A Chronicle of London, London 1829, pp. 101-112.
Date and composition in Kingsford, Chron. of Lond., p. xiii.
     Harley MS. 565, (1443-4) ed. Nicholas and Tyrrell, op.
cit., pp. 112-133. Date in Kingsford, Chron. of Lond., p. x.
     'Brut F', (1446) ed. F. Brie, op. cit., p. 456-90.
Date in Kingsford, Engl. Hist. Lit., p. 92.
     Hatfield MS. 281, (1450) ed. Kingsford, 'A Continuation
of 1446-50', Engl. Hist. Rev. XXIX (1914), 513-5.
     Cotton MS. Cleopatra CIV, (1446-50) ed. Kingsford, Chron.
of Lond., p. 135-45. Date and composition, ibid., ix-x; 313.
     Cotton MS. Vitellius A XVI, (1450) ed. Kingsford, Chron.
of Lond., only to folio 102, r., pp. 153-4; date, ibid., p. xvi.
     Arundel MS. 19, (1452) ed. Kingsford, Engl. Hist. Lit.,
pp. 297-8; date, ibid., p. 297.
     'Bale's Chronicle', (1461) ed. R. Flenley, Six Town
Chronicles of England, Oxford, 1911, pp. 114-153; date, ibid.,
p. 70-1.

that illustrated above from the religious treatise.

Of the eight more written in the next decade, however, only four are characterized throughout by paratactic
structure.[30] Two others, though in the greater part so, have
a great many passages in hypotaxis.[31] And in two, hypotaxis
is as characteristic as parataxis is in the earliest chronicles.[32] Of the seven between 1475 and 1504 (Fabyan's),
only one is paratactic [33], one is mainly so but in many
parts hypotactic [34], and five are hypotactic throughout.[35]

---

30. 'Short Chronicles', (1465) ed. Jas. Gairdner.   'Three
Fifteenth Century Chronicles, Camden Socity, n.s., v. 28, 1880.
Date and composition, intro. ii, v.

'Record of Bluemantle Pursuivant', (1471-2) ed. Kingsford, Engl. Hist. Lit., pp. 379-88; date, p. 379.

'Gregory's Chronicle', (c. 1470) ed. Jas. Gairdner, Historical Collections of a London Citizen in the Fifteenth Century, Camden Soc., n.s. 17, 1876; date, Kingsford, Chron. of
Lond., pp. xii-xiii.

Cotton, MS. Julius B. I. (c. 1461), ed. Nicholas and
Tyrrell, A Chron. of London, pp. 133-141.

31. 'Brut, G.' (the same as 'Caxton's Chronicles'), after
chapter 259.   Ed. Brie, op. cit., pp. 528-53; date, Kingsford,
Engl. Hist. Lit., p. 119.

'Capgrave's Chronicle', ed. F. C. Hingeston, Rolls Series I, London, 1858; date before 1464, ibid., p. xxi.

32. 'Davies' Chronicle' (1459), ed. J. S. Davies, (Camden
Soc. no. 64)' 1856. Date and composition, Kingsford, op. cit.,
pp. 122, 128-9. Chronicle of the Rebellion in Lincolnshire, in
1470', ed. J. G. Nichols (Camden Soc. no. 39, 'The Camden Mis-
cellany', I) 1847.

33. MS. Gough London 10, ed. by R. Flenley, op. cit., pp. 153-
64.

34. John Warkworth's Chronicle (continuation, 1483), ed. J. O.
Halliwell-Phillips (Camden Soc. no. 10) 1839; date, ibid., xxiii-
iv, where Warkworth states 'is wretyn a remanente lyke to this
forseyd werke, i.e.,[Caxton's Chronicle]'.

35. Cotton MS. Vitellius A XVI (1485), ed. Kingsford, Chron.
of Lond. folios 102-140, pp. 154-192; date, ibid., p. xvii.

Cotton MS. Vitellius A XVI (1496). Ibid., folios 140-
160, pp. 192-211; date, ibid., p. xvii.

'The Great Chronicle,' (1485); never edited (Starke, op.
cit., p. 41); an account of the style and passages of some length
given by Starke, op. cit., pp. 86-9.

Cotton MS. Vitellius A XVI (1503), ed. Kingsford, op. cit.,
pp. 211-258; date ibid., p. xvii.

Fabyan, 'The Chronicle of England and France' (1504), ed.
H. Ellis, London, 1811; date, ibid., p. 681.

Most of the chronicles were anonymous. Only two authors of
those signed, Capgrave and Fabyan, had any known position as
men of letters; and the whole group appears to represent the
average in literary ability through the seventy-five years.
  If the shift from parataxis to hypotaxis were the
whole matter, the chroniclers might be thought merely be-
lated. For hypotaxis was common in some forms of prose especially in religious writings, from the earliest times. To
realize the significance of the change in the chronicles it
is necessary to remember that the composition of narrative is
peculiarly likely to follow colloquial habits. The readiest
way to express an action is by a simple declarative sentence;
and a sequence of events often seems to speak for itself, ap-
pearing to need little variety in the form. Yet in narrative
as in other forms of prose, the use of hypotaxis indicates a
tendency to combine, to inter-relate. That this tendency became strong enough among the chroniclers to overcome the natural habit -- and, apparently, the established tradition --
of uniformity in structure is in itself a certain indication
that the unit of composition was broadening.

THE BROADENING OF THE UNIT IN COMPLEX STRUCTURE.

  Considering the peculiar nature of narrative, the very
attempt of the chroniclers to utilize a variety of constructions is significant. A distinction must be made, however,
between the attempt and the ability.
  It is not the complexity -- or length or even logical
correctness -- of the single sentence that is important, but
the presence of a plan for the whole sequence of thought.
Thus in the following excerpt from a 'sermon on the passion,'
which Mr. G. R. Owst dates late in the fifteenth century, the
sentences are short and the constructions simple, but obviously they are chosen and arranged for rhetorical antithesis.

    Christ is oure moste special frende, and we be to
    hym worse then the jewys were. He is passyng
    lovyng to us, and we wchewe to him grete unkyndnes.
    He schewythe to us obediens, and we schewe to hym
    disobediens. He is ever to us gracius and good,
    and we be to him wickyd and ungentill.[36]

---

  36. MS. Linc. Cath. Libr. A.6.2, Fol. 130, quoted from G. R.
Owst, Preaching in Medieval England, p. 347; date, p. 347 and
p. 201, n. 1.

Whether simple or complex, original prose of the fourteenth and of all but the late fifteenth century was commonly handled in units no broader than those realized in the earliest chronicles. The main bulk of it is the work of religious writers. The one conspicuous structural design was repetition, often itemized or numbered and often running on through long passages:

> But summe techen here children jeestis of bataill-
> is, and fals cronyclis not nedful to here soulis.
> Summe techen novelries of songis, to stire men to
> jolite and harlotrie. Summe setten hem to nedeles
> craftis, for pride and coveitise; and summe suff-
> ren hem in ydlenesse and losengerie, to breden
> forth strumpatis and Þeves; and summe wiÞ grett
> cost setten hem in lawe, for wynninge and worldly
> worschipe, and here to costen hugely in many weis.[37]

Wycliffe usually wrote without much hypotaxis and without the use of constructions for ornament or effect. In the follow-ing typical passage, aside from substantive clauses, only one principal clause has more than one subordinate member; all of the subordinate parts are indicative clauses except three (to shew at . . . ; boÞe in office . . . ; Þe depperst place in helle):

> And summe Þenken a greet evidence, Þat if Þe Pope
> canonise Þis man, Þanne he mut nedis be seint in
> Hevene. But trowe Þei Þis men Þat wolen. Hel Y
> woot Þat Þese popis may erre and synne, as Petre
> dide, and ჳit Petre dremede not Þus, to shewe Þat
> men ben seintis in Hevene. But it mai falle Þat
> manie men Þat ben canonisid by Þes popis ben depe
> dampned in helle, for Þei disseyven and ben disse-
> eyved. Afferme we not as bileve, Þat if a man be
> chosen Pope, Þan he is chosen to blis, as he is
> here clepid 'Blessederste Fadir'. And many trowen
> bi Þer werkes Þat Þes ben depperst dampned in helle.
> For Þei chargen hemsilf as ypocritis, boÞe in off-
> ice and in name; and so Þei sitten in Þe firste

---

37. Of Wedded Man and Wifis, from Wyclif, Select English Writings, ed. H. E. Winn, Oxford, 1929, p. 107, ll.12-20. For an entire sermon composed on this basis, see one of about 1400, published by Homer G. Pfander, The Popular Sermon of the Medie-val Friar in England, New York, 1937, pp. 54-64. For the pre-valence of the practice of amplification by simple enumeration see G. R. Owst, Preaching, pp. 312-3; 321-9.

> place here, and at þe laste day of dome þei schulen
> be in þe laste place, þat is, þe depperste place of
> helle. Holde we us in bondis of bileve, þat stondi
> in general wordis and in condicionel wordis, and juge
> we not here folili. But we mai seie bi supposal, þat
> we gesse þat it is so; and whoever haþ more evidence,
> his part shulde sunner be supposed.[38]

Variety of length is used in the second sentence, but the only
construction which brings attention to the thought it expres-
ses is the imperative, 'afferm we not . . . Hold we us . . .
. . . and juge we not'; and here the first two parts of what
may have been intended for a series are so separated as to
lose the needed effect of antithesis. The passage is effec-
tive, and bears the flavour of a strong personality behind it.
But that is due to the vigor of the thought; Wycliffe shows
little awareness of the possibilities of structural form.

Many writers of the period, it is well known, used not
only complex structure but even structural devices for ornament. What most clearly indicates that they, too, worked mainly by the short unit is their habit of unselective insertion.
Often apparently a sentence member was simply a spontaneous addition to the author's thought; it was therefore placed immediately after the particular member which suggested it to his
mind, and it was constructed only according to the relationship between it and the member preceding, not between it and
the sentence or the period as a whole. Thus the position of
the clause or phrase in the sentence and the type of construction employed do not seem determined by any pattern of structure or by any essential modification of thought.

Richard Rolle least often offends in this way, and
most frequently uses structure for effect.[39] But he has many
passages which illustrate the tendency to work in short units:

> For þat þou has forsaykn þe solace & þe ioy of þis
> world, & taken þe to solitary lyf, for gods luf to
> suffer tribulacion & anguys here, & sithen com to
> þat blys þat neuer-mare blynnes; I trowe treuly
> þat þe comforth of Ihesu Criste, & þe swetnes of
> his loue, with þe fire of þe holy gast, þat purges
> all syn, sall be in þe, & with þe, ledand þe, &
> lerand þe how þou sall thynk, how þou sall pray,
> what þou sall wyrk; so þat in a few ȝers þou sall

---

38. Þe Chirche and hir Membris, Ibid., p. 124, 11.30-125, 1.9.
39. See Antonie Olmes, Sprache und Stil der englischen Mystik
des Mittelalters, in Studien zur Englischen Philologie, Heft
LXXVI, Halle, 1933, pp. 47-55; 66-85.

haue mare delyte, to be by þi nane, & speke till
þi luf & to þi spows Ihesu Crist, þat hegh es in
heuen, þan if þou war lady here of a thowsand worldes.
[40]

After the very first clause, Rolle begins adding. As far as
'for Gods luf to suffer . . . here,' the thought holds
steadily enough forward toward the idea expected after 'For
that . . .' But the 'sithen come . . .' alliteration not-
withstanding, amounts only to an after-thought attached to
the preceding clause, and diverts the flow of the sentence.
Then after passing the main clause, he begins a succession
of short phrases, the form and number of which he has determined by nothing except the successive thoughts which came
to him: Thus he adds up three subjects for 'sal be in þe,'
inserting after the last one a modified which is really a
by-thought; and again, the series of three _how_ clauses can
follow from no preceding idea but the one in 'lerand', which
in turn is simply the second of two ideas further modifying
or enlarging the three subjects.
       The prose of Rolle is in many respects to be closely
associated with verse. He tended to build in series of very
short, roughly even phrases, frequently with alliteration or
rhyme. At the same time the ornamental designs of his
English sentence members can only occasionally be identified
with those standard types which he used for the _cola_ of his
Latin prose.[41] However this may be, when his long sentences are read for their poetry rather than for their structure, the frequency of the pause and the lack of unity are
easily forgotten.[42]
       This explanation cannot be made, however, for the
structural qualities of the later devotional prose. In
Hilton, the sentence members are longer and irregular. Usually he uses not more than two, very often only one subordinate part for every principal clause. But whenever the
idea in one subordinate clause suggests another, he uncritically fits it in. Thus he allows himself to wander a   con-

---

40. The _Form_ of _Perfect Living_, MS. Cambridge Dd. V. 64.
Ed. C. Horstman, _Yorkshire Writers_, London, 1895, 10.
   41. Olmes, _op. cit._, pp. 66-72; 79-81.
   42. The lyrical aspect of Rolle was the one most success-
fully cultivated by his followers. See the two _Meditations
on the Passion_ (Horstman, _op. cit._, I, 83-103); _A talkyng of
the love of God_, (ibid., II, 345-366); or the various versions of Don Jon Gaytryge's _Sermon_, printed as prose by G. G.
Perry (EETS o s XXVI) 1889, pp. 1-14 and as verse by T F.
Simmons and H. E. Nolloth (EETS o s CXVIII) 1901.

fusing distance between 'And if' . . . and 'þan' and between
'Wha-so . . .' and 'he', in the first and last long sentences
of Chapter 70 of the <u>Scale of Perfection</u>:

> And if þou be nogth styrd agaynes þe persone be
> angre or felle cheer outward ne be na pryue haat
> in þi hert for to despyse hym or deme hym or forto
> sette hym at noght, & þe mare schame & vilany he
> dos to þe in word or in dide, þe mare pete or com-
> passion þou has of hym as þou wald of a man þat war
> out of his mynd, and þou thynkis þou can nogth fynd
> in þi hert forto hate hym, for luf es swa gud in
> it-self, bot pray for hym and helpe hym and desire
> his amendyng, nogth anly with þi mygth als ypocrytes
> can doe, bot þi affeccyon of luf in þi hert: þan has
> þou parfyte charyte to þi eeuenristen. . . . .

> Wha-so wenes an hym-self to be a parfite folower
> of Ihesu Cristis techyng & his lifyng as sum men
> wenes þat þai be, in als mykel as he preches & tech-
> ys & es pouer of werldly gud as Crist was; & can
> nogth folow Crist in his luf & charyte for to lufe
> his euene-cristen, lyke a man, gud and ille, frend-
> es and faees with-outene fenyg, flateryng, dispisynge
> in hert, angrines & malencolius reprouynge: southly,
> he bigilis hym-self.[43]

Only the widely separated complements give evidence that the
relationship of the whole has been planned. But as much evidence might have been put in a marginal note. Though the pattern of thought was vaguely foreseen at the beginning, the whole
pattern of the structure was not. All the intermediate parts
are really separate units.

     Loose connective devices such as <u>if</u> . . . <u>þan</u>, <u>who-so</u>
. . . <u>he</u>, <u>as</u> . . . <u>so</u>, <u>more</u> . . . <u>than</u>, <u>where-as</u> . . . <u>there-
fore</u>, etc., were the chief ones employed by original writers
well into the fifteenth century. In between the two semi-cor-
relative words would be thrown any number of sentence members
in any type of construction.

     It was this form of disregard for the structure of
the whole which was so frequent a cause of anacoluthon.
Nicolas Love, writing in 1410, thus explains the naming of
his book, in a passage of it which is not translation.

> And so for as moche as in this book ben conteyned
> dyuerse ymaginaciouns of cristes lyf, the which lyf

---

43.   Ed. C. Horstmann, <u>op</u>. <u>cit</u>., I, 104-5.

fro the bygynnyng into the endyng euermore blessed
and with outen synne, passynge alle lyues of alle
othere seyntes, as for a synguler prerogatyf may
worthely be cleped the blessed lyf of Jesu Crist.
The whiche also be cause that it may not be fully
discryued as the lifes of othere seyntes, but in
a maner of lickenes as the ymage of a mannis face
is schewed in the mirrour, therfore as for a perty-
nent name to this book it may skilfully be cleped
the mirrour of the blessed lyf of Jesu Crist. [44]

Another excerpt from a sermon of about Love's time,
probably Lollard [45], not only illustrates anacoluthon
caused by indiscriminate insertion; it is as well a good
example of the failure to cast and arrange constructions,
even when a variety of them is under command, with attention to the nature or pattern of the thought. In the first
-- the anacoluthic -- half of the passage below the preacher
cites a number of worldly practices from which Christ ab-
stained; then, claiming that modern prelates indulge in them,
he cites the same practices again, though in modern form. In
other words, his thought pattern is of extended antithesis.
He has used ten or twelve different kinds of construction.
But he has never used correspondence of construction to identify the successive correspondences of thought.

There, also, as Crist hadde never house of his owne
bi title of worldeli lor[d]shipe, to hile in his
heved, ne greet multitude of proude araied meyne,
but 12 seli pore men, withoute ʒemen or pagis, to
whom we reden he servede ofter than ever we rede
thei servede him, whiche also never rood at greet
araie, nether he, nether his meyne, but ones sem-
peli on an asse sadelid with his disciplis clothes,
-- prelates, that ben now-a-daies, hav many dyverse
castellis and maners, as rial as the kynge him selfe,
to chaunge whanne so evere hem likith for to take
diverse eiris, withynne araied as realli with cost-
li clothes of gold and selk and in multitude of other
iewellis bothe of selver and of gold; in all maner
housis office as thouʒ it were in Salamons temple,
and so greet multitude of meyne of Knyʒtes, squyers,

---

44. The Mirrour of the Blessed Lyf of Jesu Christ, ed.
L. F. Powell, London, 1908, pp. 9-10.
45. Owst, Lit. and Pulpit, p. 284, n. 2.

> ȝemen and gromes, myche more nyseli disgisid than
> any seculer lordis meyne.[46]

Though the structure here is hypotactic, it might as well
have been paratactic; for, with a few exceptions, the form
of each expression means nothing in respect to the relationships of thought. There is, as in Hilton, the broad frame
of the complements ('There, . . . as Crist . . . — prelates'); but in between, the constructions are little more
than haphazard. In short, variety or complexity in the constructions is no indication of a broad sense of form.

    The chaos, the welter of phrases which characterize
the so-called aureate style can likewise be in great part
traced to the habit of composing by narrow units. A fine
though brief specimen from Lydgate has been quoted above.
It takes a longer passage, one where the chain of sub-dependence stretches far out of sight, to show how little relationship these writers felt between the form of the part and the
form or the meaning of the whole. The following one is from
the <u>Boke</u> <u>of</u> <u>Noblesse</u>, written late in the third quarter of
the century:

> In profe wherof how and in the first yere of the
> reigne of king Harry the sixt, at whiche tyme his
> seide uncle toke uppon hym the charge and the name
> of Regent of the roiaume of Fraunce, that had the
> 5 victorie at the bateile of Cravant, where as at
> that tyme Thomas Montague the noble erle of Salis-
> burie, the erle of Suffolke, the marchalle of
> Bourgoine, the lord Willoughebie, withe a gret power
> of Phelip the duke of Bourgoine is host, holding
> 10 the partie of the said Johann, regent of Fraunce,
> duc of Bedford, withe the eide and help of the
> trew subgettis of this lande, had the overhande of
> the ennemies assembled to the nomber of .ix.ML.
> Frenshemen and Scottis at the said bataile of
> 15 Cravant in the duchie of Bourgoine. Where there
> were slayne of the ennemies to the nombre of .iiij.
> Ml., beside .ij.Ml. prisonneris take, of whiche
> gret part of them were Scottis, the erle Bougham be-
> ing chief capitein over them. Which late before
> 20 were the cause of the male-infortuned journey at
> Bougée, where the famous and victorious knight Tho-
> mas duc of Claraunce, youre nere cousyn, for the

---

46. British Mus. MS. Add. 41321, fols. 100–101. Quoted
by G. R. Owst, <u>Lit</u>. <u>and</u> <u>Pulpit</u>, p. 283.

right of Fraunce, withe a small company of his side,
with the Scottis to a grete nombre there assembled
25 among hem in the feelde, was slayn, withe many a
noble lorde, baron, knightis, squyres of Englond,
that never so gret an overthrow of lordes and noble
bloode was seene in so many daies as it was then.[47]

Almost every statement is in a subordinate construction.
Yet the pattern is basically paratactic, a mere string or
juxtaposition of ideas. Nothing better reveals the vague-
ness of the accord between thought and form than the shift
to the plural in the third of a series after 'many a . . .'
('many a noble lorde, baron, knightis, squyres . . .'). It
is possible that this writer was simply under the fascination of subordinating connectives and constructions, which
he used with an intent toward ornament, often without thought
of their significance to the meaning. In any case, he has
not been able to manipulate them into broader units of composition. Just as with the writers whose constructions were
predominantly principal clauses, there is here a certain
progress of thought. But also as with them, there is no
realization of the relation between periods of thought and
the pattern of the constructions.

By the fourth quarter of the century a change in
this respect had begun. Again it can easily be measured in
the chronicles. Until 1460 or 1470, it will be remembered,
all chronicles were written with an extreme simplicity of
structure, but in that decade there appeared four with complex structure, of which two are so characterized throughout.
These two, 'Davies' chronicle' and especially 'The Chronicle
of the Rebellion in Lincolnshire'[48] though never so loose as
the passage just quoted from the Boke of Noblesse, seldom
show any real firmness. Anacoluthon is frequent in both;
and the typical mark of the small unit, long insertions constructed in sub-dependence, is present on almost every page.

But in a London chronicle of no later than 1485[49],
the change has already appeared. The thing to be especially
noticed here is the marked improvement in the use of complex
structure. But to illustrate likewise what the evolution
from simple structure meant in terms of the writers' habit

---

47. Edited by J. G. Nichols, for the Roxburghe Club, London,
1860. I have altered Nichols' punctuation by starting new
sentences at 'where,' line 15, and at 'which,' line 19, for
these pronouns are apparently demonstratives.
48. See note 32 in this chapter.
49. Note 35, in this chapter.

of composition, it will be well to compare an early and a
late version of the same story. About 1465 the opening
events of Jack Cade's rebellion were written as follows:

> And than the comynes of Kent a rose and hade chosen
> hem a capteyne the whiche namyd hym sylfe John Morty-
> mer, whose very trew name was John Cade, and he
> was an Iresheman; and so he come to the Black hethe
> withe the comynes of Kentt. And the kynge with all
> his lordis made hem redy with all her power for to
> with stonde hem. And the capteyn hiryng that the
> kynge was comynge, and so the nyght a fore the capt-
> eyne with drwe him and his peple; and so the xviij
> day of June the kynge toke his wey taward the Blacke
> Hethe. And Sir Umfrey Stafford, knyght, and John
> Stafford, squyer, with her peple went in the fowarde,
> and they were slayne and myche of her peple. And
> the kynge came to the Blacke Hethe with his lordys.
> [50]

In the account written in 1485, the same length, about 140
words, covers only half the same events. But there is no
waste; the story is given circumstance and connection:

> Item, this yere was a grete assemble of the comon-
> es in kent, which came downe to blak heth in June,
> and ther made their feld, abidyng there vij daies.
> Wherof when the kyng herde, beyng at leiceter, he
> assemblid his lordes; and cam in all haste agayne
> the Kentisshemen, and at his comyng sent dyuers
> lordes to theym to knowe their Entent. And when
> these lordes came to their Capeteyn namyd Jak Cade,
> otherwyse Mortymer, cosyn to the Duke of York as
> the saide Capitayne named hym self, he seid he and
> his people were commen to redresse many poyntes
> wherby the kynges subgettes and comons were grev-
> ously wrongid; but his fynall purpoos was to robbe,
> as after it shall appere. Wherfore the kyng and
> his counsaill, seyng the dowblenesse of this Capi-
> tayn, the xviij day of the said moneth addresid
> his people toward theym; but whan the kynges peo-

---

50. 'A short English Chronicle,' ed. J. Gairdner, <u>Three
Fifteenth Century English Chronicles</u> (Camden Soc., n.s. no.
28) 1880, pp. 66-67.

    ple cam to the blak heth the Capitayne was goon.
    Wherfore it was agreed that Sir Humfrey Stafford,
    knyght . . .[51]

Here, in the 140 words, there are eight principal clauses,
not eleven, as in the earlier story. There are fourteen
subordinate verbal expressions; in the earlier there are
only four. Principal clauses are juxtaposed with and as
connective only twice in the later, eight times in the
earlier. The difference in use of connectives is striking.
In the first story, and so, used three times, introduces a
statement of result only once, and then it is redundant and
grammatically asymmetrical ('the capteyn hyring . . . and
so with drowe him'). In the story of 1485, the thoughts
are grouped into periods, in which time, cause, purpose, attribute and circumstance are accurately expressed by the form.
    That logical perspective could thus be given to the
total group of statements is, of course, evidence that the
writer constantly took account of more than the statement
which happened to be under his pen. From the standpoint of
structure, more important evidence of this is found in the
use of suspended constructions, which occur in three of the
sentences. Instead of making this construction a frame for
the insertion of any number of statements, incidental or important, the writer here has twice interrupted with only one
sentence-member; in the one case where there are three, two
of them are appositives. The passage shows no high literary aim. But that only indicates more significantly that
composition by larger units of thought had become habitual
to its author.
    Fabyan probably thought of his great chronicle as a
literary work. An analysis of his account of Jack Cade,
however, could be made in the same terms applied to the
anonymous passage of 1485. In fact, the opening sentence of
Fabyan's prose here is paratactic -- perhaps under the influence of some older chronicle which he used as source.

    And in the moneth of Iuny this, the comons of Kent
    assemblyd them in grete multytude, and chase to
    theym a capitayne, and named hym Mortymer, and
    cosyn to the duke of Yorke; but of moste he was
    named Iak Cade. This kepte the people wonderously
    togyder, and made suche ordenaunces amonge theym,
    that he brought a great nombre of people of theym
    vnto the Blak Heth, where he deuysed a bylle of

---

    51. Cotton MS. Vitellius A XVI, ed. Kingsford, Chron. of
Lond., p. 159.

> petycions to the kynge & his counsayll, and shewyd
> therin what iniuryes and oppressions the poore
> comons suffred by suche as were aboute ye kynge,
> a fewe persones in nombre, and all vnder coloure
> to come to his aboue. The kynges counsayll seynge
> this byll, disalowyd it, and counsayled the kynge,
> whiche by the vii. daye of Iuny had gaderid to hym
> a stronge hoost of people, to go agayne his rebell-
> ys, and go gyue vnto theym batayll. Than the Kynge
> after the sayd rebellys had holden theyr felde vpon
> Blak Heth vii. dayes, made towarde theym. Wherof
> herynge, the capitayne drewe backe with his people
> to a vyllage called Seuenok, and there enbataylled.[52]

Through his book as a whole, Fabyan tends to overuse
the participle, especially as absolute. But it is always a
device for differentiating the relative value of the statement so cast, never for unselective insertions. Fabyan has,
at the same time, a wide variety of constructions. Here, for
instance, are four different means of expressing cause, taken
from Fabyan's 'tragedyous hystory' of Richard III:

> Thanne began the longe couert dissymulacion, whiche
> of the lorde protectour had been so craftly shadow-
> yd, to breke out at large, insomoche that vpon the
> Sonday folowyng at Paulys crosse . . . was there
> shewyd openly . . .

> Thenn, soone after, for fere of the quenes blode
> and other, whiche he had in iolousy, he sent for a
> strength of men out of the North.

> Wherof herynge, the foresayd Banaster, were it for
> mede of the sayd rewarde, or for the fere of los-
> ynge of his lyfe and good, discoueryd the duke vnto
> the sheryffe of the shyre.

> Kynge Richarde than ledynge his lyfe in great agony
> and doubte, trustynge fewe of such as were about
> hym, sparyd nat to spende the great treasour.[53]

Each of these sentences illustrates as well Fabyan's careful
use of the suspended construction. In the last two, the
parallelism of the insertions is typical of his sureness in
matching structure with thought.

---

52. *The New Chronicles of England and France*, ed. H. Ellis,
p. 622-3.
    53. *Ibid.*, pp. 669, 670, 671.

There are, then, two respects in which the late fifteenth century chroniclers indicate the broadening of the unit of composition. First of all, the very change from a simple and uniform to a complex and varied structure reflects a tendency to combine and inter-relate. Since the natural tendency of narrative is the other way, it is likely that those who made this first change had decided for the importance of form, both as an end in itself and as a means of expressing the variety which had always existed among the different parts of a thought-relationship. Complex structure had been used before -- and was at first used by the chroniclers -- without a realization of the accord needed between thought and form. Thus the second and more important change was toward accuracy in this accord. Inconsistencies of logic became practically eliminated. Sentence-members were seldom constructed without reference to their fitness and proportion in the period as a whole.

Rare before the third quarter of the fifteenth century, these traits are well established in the prose of the early sixteenth. They are characteristic in the work of outstanding figures like Fisher, More, Tyndale, or Lupset [54], and likewise in that of writers who were anonymous or relatively obscure, the 'Translator of Livius'[55], the author of A Manifest Detection[56], or John Bourchier[57] and Simon Fish[58].

The structural qualities of the prose of this period have been described by Mr. J. A. Gee [59] and, less analytically, by Professor J. P. Krapp [60]; there is no need to

---

54. For the editions of Fisher, More and Lupset, see notes 17, 16, and 20, in this chapter. For Tyndale I have used Doctrinal Treatises and Introductions and An Answer to Sir Thomas More's Dialogue, both ed. by Henry Walter (for the Parker Society) Cambridge, 1848 and 1850; also S. L. Greenslade, The Work of William Tindale, London, 1938.
55. The First English Life of Henry V, ed. C. L. Kingsford, Oxford, 1911.
56. Ed. by J. O. Halliwell (Percy Soc., Vol. XXIV), London, 1850.
57. Prologue to the Chronicles of Froissart, ed. W. Parker (Tudor Translations, no. xxvii), London, 1901. Prologue to Arthur of Little Britain, ed. by E. V. Utterson, London, 1814.
58. A Supplication for the Beggars, ed. F. J. Furnival (EETS e s XIII), London, 1871.
59. Op. cit., pp. 191-97.
60. The Rise of English Literary Prose, New York, 1915, pp. 80, 100, 107, 167, 414-15.

take up each writer again. Between Tyndale and More or between the Translator of Livius and Simon Fish, there are, of
course, a great many differences of style. But for the present study the important comparison is between their prose
and that in corresponding genres of fifty or more years before. It is not only the religious prose that suggests such
a comparison; The Life of Henry V or A Manifest Detection can
be compared to the early chronicles [61]; Bourchier's prefaces
to Caxton's [62]; or Fish's attacks on prelates to the attacks
on manners in the early sermons [63].

Naturally there appear a great many semblances in the
writer's interests, in the acuteness or confusion of their
observations, in the naturalness or pomposity of their tone,
and even in the devices which they used for disposition. But
in one quality there is a constant difference. In structural
form the earlier prose appears naive, the later is plainly
matured.

---

61. The Translator of The Life noted most of his own additions in the margin, and all of them are indicated by the
editor; see, e. g., pp. 92-3.
62. Bourchier's prologue to the Chronicles of Froissart, in
fact resembles Caxton's prologue to the Polychronicon in too
many respects to be original. Each is probably a translation
from some version of a prologue by Diodorus Siculus. See
note 55 in Chap. I, above.
63. Owst, Lit. and Pulpit, 'The Preaching of Satire and Complaint,' Chaps. V, VI, VII, pp. 210-470.

Chapter Three

TRANSLATED PROSE: THE QUANTITY AND THE PROVENANCE

The preceding discussion of the changes in fifteenth century prose has not taken account of the translations. The reason for this has been shown in Chapter I: the structural nature of a prose translation is likely to be determined by the source. Thus the basis of the discussion, the writers' habit of composition by narrow or broad units, cannot be applied to translated work. The same man, it has been seen, may write in one way by himself and in another as translator.

In the examples of this difference studied in Chapter I, the influence of translation was always in the direction of maturity: that is, of composition by broad units. Obviously in each of these cases the writer of the source had reached a stage of maturity which was still more or less beyond that of the translator when he had to write without guidance. If these examples are altogether typical the century through, from Edward of York to Caxton, it is possible that English writers may have learned much from the structural composition in the foreign originals. More important, translation may have provided fifteenth century England with a body of prose which in this important respect was more advanced than the native prose. If a large amount of such prose had been accumulating through the century, it must have affected the critical concepts, conscious or unconscious, of both writers and readers. When, in the latter half of the century, the native prose began gradually to acquire breadth and firmness in the common structural units, a considerable influence toward the change could be assumed to have come from a widespread practice of translation.

This depends, of course, on the typicality of the examples just referred to. There could have been little influence if the common procedure of translation was not something like the close adherence practised by Edward of York, Lady Margaret and the others studied in the first chapter. For a second condition, most of the prose thus translated must have possessed the structural qualities found in Le Livre de la Chasse, the Imitatio Christi, etc. And further, the sheer quantity of such translation would have had to be large; if the writing and especially the reading of it had been relatively infrequent, it is not likely to have had any general effect upon critical standards or upon common habits of composition.

The proportion of translated prose to original prose appears to have been extraordinarily high. During the hundred and thirty-odd years between 1400 and, say, the death of Berners or the appearance of Elyot, it probably was higher than in any other period of English literary history. To decide the proportion by actual count would, of course, be impossible, even if all the texts could be found and examined. For one thing, translators often saw no reason to state that their English was not original [1]; and there are several familiar pieces of fifteenth century prose which for various reasons cannot even be stated surely to be translation or original writing [2]. Some very definite indications of the proportion, however, may be had by an analysis of the English printed books between 1475 and 1500.[3]

Aside from cook books, indulgences, grammars, etc.[4], we have seventy-four fifteenth century printed books in prose. Five of these I have not identified.[5] Of the sixty-nine others, only eleven were written originally in English; two were redactions or compilations in great part from foreign originals [6], and fifty-six were translations. Moreover, of

---

1. F. R. Amos, Early Theories of Translation, New York, 1920, pp. 43-46. And see the section on theory in Chapter IV, below.

2. Capgrave's Life of St. Augustine (ed. by J. J. Munro, EETS o s CXL, London, 1910, intro., pp. vi, ff); parts of Lydgate's The Serpent of Division (ed. by H. N. MacCracken, New Haven, 1911); John Russel's Boke of Nurture (ed. F. J. Furnival, Roxburghe Club, 1867, intro., p. vi).

3. The following references are to E. Gordon Duff's Fifteenth Century Books . . . etc., Oxford, 1917. References for date and other information on all translations cited in this chapter and later are given in a bibliographical list of translations and sources, Appendix A; chronological list follows separately.

4. I have also excluded the Fifteen Oes.

5. They are The Contemplation of Sinners, Duff no. 106; the Contemplation of the Shedding of the Blood of Jesus Christ, Duff, 107; Death-Bed Prayers, Duff, 112; the Doctrinal of Death, Duff, 126, and the Rote or Mirrour of Consolation, Duff 364-5. These may be translation or original, contemporary or much older. It will be observed that they are all religious tracts.

6. The Chronicles and Le Morte Darthur.

the eleven original books, five date from before or about
1400, one no later than 1405; there is none from then to
about 1470, and there are only five written during the period
of printing.[7]
        Fifty-six translations to eleven original compositions
in the English prose first chosen for printing is certainly a
significant proportion. True, it would probably be less un-
even if books copied in manuscript during the same period
were counted as well; for the translations of a single printer,
Caxton, accounted for twenty-five of those printed. Yet Caxton's method of creating prose works for the press was popular.
Not only were many of his translations reprinted by others[8],
but his successors employed the same method well into the next
century. Robert Copeland, Henry Watson, and Andrew Chertsey
did at least fifteen volumes of just such work for Wynkyn de
Worde and others. Lord Berners, last of the translators of
voluminous medieval material, though by no means a publisher's
hack, is only the best-known representative of a widespread
activity. Whether or not one discounts some of the proportion
because of Caxton's work, the important generalization still
remains: when the early English printers looked about for
books to publish, what they found usable in prose was largely
translation.

    7. The original writings of before 1400 are: The Abbey of
the Holy Ghost, preceded by the Charter, Duff, no. 1-2 (Fifteenth Century Facsimiles, Cambridge Univ. Press, 1907) in
part a translation (Hope Emily Allen, Writings Ascribed to
Richard Rolle, New York, 1927, pp. 335-43); The Chastising
of God's Children, Duff, 85 (no modern edition, but see H. E.
Allen in M. L. R. XVIII (1923) 1-8); Hilton's Scale of Perfection, Duff, 203 (no modern edition; parts in C. Horstmann's
Yorkshire Writers, I, 104-6); Mirk's Festial, Duff, 298, et
seq. (EETS e s xcvi, 1905) also in part translation; and
the Quatuor Sermones, Duff, 299, et seq. (for the Roxburghe
Club, 1883). Dives et Pauper, Duff, 339-40, is of about 1405
(see H. G. Richardson in Notes and Queries, 11th ser., IV
(1913) 321-3). There is none other till the three sermons and
the two devotional tracts of Richard Fitzjames -- the Sermo
die Lune . . . etc., Duff, 151 (Fifteenth Century Facsim., Cambridge Univ. Press, 1907) -- and of Bishop Alcock -- the Sermon
pro episcopo puerorum, Duff, 15-16, the Spousage of a virgin
to Christ, Duff, 19-20, and the Mons perfectionis, Duff, 12-
13-14, the Sermon on Luke VIII, Duff, 17-18 (none of Alcock's
in modern edition).
    8. Before 1530, twelve of them had been re-issued by other
printers at least once; his Golden Legend had six reprintings,
the Book of Good Manners, five, and the Paris and Vienne three.

Indeed, the choice of the printers appears to indicate the proportion of translation before their time. The fifty-six translations printed, like the eleven original writings were not all contemporary. Besides five of doubtful date, some of which may have been very old [9], there were sixteen definitely to be dated no later than 1470. Five of these were of the fourteenth century [10]. That is, dividing the printed books of prose into those written at about the time they were printed, and those in existence before any printing began, we find among the older ones only six original writings, but at least sixteen translations[11].

At the same time, these older books were not odd pieces taken up at haphazard. Wide popularity is easily demonstrated for the fourteenth century translations of Chaucer and Trevisa and for the Mandeville. Nicholas Love's Mirrour of the early fifteenth appears on the evidence of wills as the most popular single book of the century[12]. The wide circulation of The Three Kings of Cologne is attested by the state of the nine manuscripts extant; they fall into definite groups of three states of revision, so that there must have been many interlinking versions now lost[13]. There are

---

9. They are The Revelation . . . to a Monk of Evesham (Eynsham); the Miracles of Our Lady; the Treatise against the pestilence (Canutus); the Revelations of St. Elizabeth of Hungary; and the Rule of St. Benet.   (All of these I have listed, however, as dating from the time of printing.)

10. Of these I have listed only Trevisa's Polychronicon (Higden). The others are Trevisa's translation of Bartholomaeus Anglicus, Duff, 39-40, Chaucer's Boethius and prose Canterbury Tales, Duff, 47 and 87-88-89-90; and the Mandeville, Duff, 285-286. The eleven books of 1400-1470 which were printed are so designated in the chronological list, Appendix B.

11. I am not counting Le Morte Darthur of before 1470 or the Chronicles. The latter were composed of a translation made after 1377 and of new matter added at various stages up to 1461 (C. L. Kingsford, English Hist. Lit., pp. 114-115). Note that the proportion in the older books is about the same as the whole proportion if Caxton's translations are not counted (eleven to thirty-one).

12. See Miss Margaret Deanesley, 'Vernacular Books in England in the Fourteenth and Fifteenth Centuries,' M.L.R. XV (1920), 353-5; also Miss Deanesley's The Lollard Bible, Cambridge, 1920, p. 321, 342.

13. C. Horstmann, intro. to his edition of the Three Kings, EETS o s LXXXV, 1896, p. v.

known six manuscripts of the Pilgrimage of the Soul, a book
also frequently cited in wills[14]. The evidence of numerous manuscripts likewise shows the popularity of the original
writings printed. I take from Wells' Manual the mention of
fourteen 'and others' for Hilton's Scale of Perfection[15],
of 'at least' nine for The Abbey of the Holy Ghost.   There
are five of The Chastising of God's Children[16], and six of
Dives and Pauper.[17] There is, then, good reason to believe
that the twenty-six older books of prose, original and translation, were well-known ones which the printers picked out or
were commissioned to edit for the same reasons that they picked
out Chaucer, Lydgate or Gower[18].
        They did not, of course, include all the prose in wide
circulation. But so far as prose composition during the fifteenth century is concerned, it is significant that all the
older original writings date from about 1405 or earlier; that
there is a gap in the list from the first few years of the
fifteenth century to the last quarter. For of the older translations in print, four date from the first quarter of the century, three from the second quarter, and four from the third
[19]. The proportion in the older books chosen for printing --
roughly of three translations to one original -- may well be
representative of that in all the English literary prose during the first three quarters of the fifteenth century.
        Remaining throughout the century within the old cul-
tural tradition, this rapidly growing literature of translation was taken almost altogether from French and medieval
Latin. Caxton's Reynard the Fox of 1481 was from the Dutch.
But this was the only English translation from any modern
language other than French until about 1501, when, it is
thought, John von Doesborch, printer of Antwerp, began to

---

14. Miss Deanesley, 'Vernacular Books,' as above, p. 342.
    15. And see Miss Deanesley, 'Vernacular Books,' as above,
p. 355.
    16. Hope Emily Allen in Mod. Lang. Review, XVIII (1923), 1.
    17. H. G. Richardson, Notes and Queries, 11th ser., IV
(1913), 322; H. G. Pfander, Library 4th ser., XIV (1923),
301; and H. G. Richardson, Library, 4th ser., XV (1934), 31,
and see especially 33.
    18. For further evidence of Caxton's taste in selecting
from among the older books and of his responsibility to his
patrons, see A. T. P. Byles, 'William Caxton as a Man of
Letters', Library, 4th ser., XV (1934), 1-25; and H. B.
Lathrop, 'The First English Printers and their Patrons',
Library, 4th ser., III (1922), 69-96.
    19. See the chronological list of translations in Appen-
dix B.

play for the English market with books drawn from German and
Dutch[20]. Nor did the classical languages furnish much
material. There was nothing whatever from Greek; in fact,
except for the Alexander and perhaps the Aesop materials,
which are a long way removed indeed, Skelton's five books of
Diodorus Siculus are the only prose of even ultimate Greek
origin. There was just one direct translation from classical Latin, John Tiptoft's Tullius de amicicia, and only
three of indirect classical provenance[21].

But medieval Latin, of course, was no new language.
Even the average writer of it had the advantages of a syntax
which had long been adapted to refinements of thought. That
is, not only did he possess a wide variety of constructions
for expressing different relationships and for facilitating
the style, but more important, he found it only traditional
and normal constantly to employ them. Moreover, the medieval
practice in rhetoric demanded much use of structural pattern,
not only for expression but for ornament[22]. The members
of the periods were carefully assimilated, the most frequent
and obvious pattern being to repeat or balance the syntactical
types in accord with paralleled or antithetical thoughts.
Further ornament of structure was secured by repetition of
sounds, alliterative, rhymed, etc., often in intricate patterns, and by cadencing the close of the members with a pre-
scribed type of cursus. Ornaments of thought, the tropes,
especially those requiring the aid of syntax, as the simile,
the antithesis, the apostrophe, etc., made integral the importance of structure in such writings [23]. In short, a
translator working from an original in Latin had before him
a practised language, one in which the sentence-structure

---

20. See Robert G. C. Proctor, Jean von Doersborch, for
the Bibliographical Soc., 1894. Modern editions of three
of von Doesborch's books are listed in C.H.E.L., II, 547.
Virgilius, as possibly, though doubtfully, of French origin,
I have included in the appendix.

21. Cicero's de Senectute, probably by William of Worcester
about 1470; the last six books of Ovid's Metamorphoses, and
a version of the Aeneid, both by Caxton, the Ovid found only
in manuscript. Caxton's French sources had been much altered
from the classical originals.

22. For general reference see Edward Norden, Die Antike
Kunstprosa vom vi. Jahrhundert v. Chr. bis in die Zeit der
Renaissance, Leipzig, 1898, et seq., II, 748-63; C. S. Baldwin, Medieval rhetoric and poetic (to 1400) interpreted from
representative works, New York, 1928.

23. Good examples of this rhetoric are the Curial and the
Imitatio Christi, quoted in Chapter I, pp.5 and 10.

presented a variety of members always inter-related and
often highly patterned.
        French prose, though a relatively new medium, had by
the fifteenth century acquired at least the stability of an
art form[24]. The history of its structural composition
during the century and a half before 1400 seems to have
been something like that of English from 1350 to 1500. At
first French prose was normally paratactic, simple in structure[25]. Later, by the middle of the fourteenth century,
hypotaxis appears to have been frequent, both in exposition
and in narrative[26]. It was still used loosely, largely
put together member by member. But inconsistent constructions, even in the many over-complex sentences, are very
rare indeed. The habit of a variety of constructions had
been acquired, and their grammatical or logical relationships were understood without effort[27]. By about 1400
many original French prose writers show considerable ability at arranging syntactical parts to overcome the effect
of looseness. For instance, in the prologue to Les Faits
d'Armes, written by Christine de Pisan about 1410, the tendency toward bulkiness is usually counteracted by varying
the constructions on eacy new occasion of lengthy insertions
or additions, and by avoiding subdependence[28]. In the following sentences, which open the prologue, the use of parallelism and other devices for confining the verbs to a single
predicate, is fairly adroit:

---

        24. For early French sentence-structure see Fr. Brunot,
Histoire de la Langue Francaise, Paris, 1898, I, 353-7; for
brief descriptions of French prose through the XIIIth and
XIVth centuries, W. von Wartburg, Évolution et Structure de
la Langue Francaise, Leipzig, 1934, pp. 119-121; and Albert
Douzat, Histoire de la Langue Francaise, Paris, 1930, pp.
488-9.
        25. An example in exposition, L'image du Monde, has been
quoted and described in Chapter I, above p. 12. An example
of similar structure in narrative is the prose Merlin, translated into English about 1450; see Appendix A.
        26. Examples quoted in Chapter I are Le Livre de la Chasse,
above, p.22, and Les Quatre Fils Aymon, above, p.13.
        27. In the French prose used by English translators I have
seen only one case of anacoluthon and only two of asymmetrical
coordination: Livre du Chevalier de la Tour (Appendix A, 'La
Tour Landry'), Chapter I, p. 5; Livre de la Chasse (Appendix
A, 'Gaston III') Chap. XV, p. 81, XXXVI, p. 147.
        28. Only once in the prologue is subdependence continued
for more than three sentence-members.

Pource que hardiment est tant necessaire a.haultes
choses emprendre que sans luy jamaiz emprises ne
seroient, ycellui mest conuenable a cest present
oeuure mettre sus, aultrement veu la petitesce de
ma persone que ie congnois non digne de traittier
de si esleuee matiere ne losasse neis seullement
penser, quoy que hardiesce face a blasmer quant
elle est folle. Moy, nonne mene par arrogance en
folle presempcion mais admonestee de vraye affec-
tion et bon desir des nobles hommes en loffice dez
armes, suis enortee apres mes autres escriptures
passees, sy comme cellui qui a ja abastu plusieurs
fors edifices est plus hardy de soy chargier dedi-
fier ung chastel ou forteresce quant garny se sent
de conuenables estoffes en ce neccessaires, dentre-
prendre a paroler en ce present liure du treshonn-
eure office darmes et de cheuallerie, tant es choses qui y conuiennent comme es droitz qui leur sont
appartenans, si que le declairent les loys et diuers
aucteurs, ainsy qua propos Iay assemble les matier-
es et cuillies en plusieurs liures pour produire en
mon intencion ou present volume.[29]

    A description of the French used by English transla-
tors must include the French writings translated from Latin.
The looseness of the French sentence structure tends to disappear under the influence of the Latin original Syntax is
employed in more of its varieties, and the order of parts is
more consciously manipulated, in order to fit the members
together as they had been in the Latin. Devices appear
which imitate the Latin without violating French idiom and
which knit together the period and heighten the style[30].
    Two examples of translated French prose have been
quoted and described in Chapter I, above[31]. Another such
book later translated into English by Earl Rivers, the
Cordiale, is worth citing for further illustration; a short
sequence, however, will be enough:

---

    29. Royal MS 19 B xviii, fol. 1 _r_. Quoted from A. T. P.
Byles edition of Caxton's translation; see Appendix A,
'Pisan.'
    30. The influence of translation on early French writing
is remarked by Brunot, _op. cit._, I, 356.
    31. pp. 8 and 10.

Isti sunt quattuor rote currus animi vehentes eam ad eternam solutem Ista sunt quattuor incitamenta incitantia spiritum hominis vt spretis omnibus mundanis ad suum redeat creatorem.	Ce sont les quatres roes du chariot de lame qui la portent a leternelle gloire de paradis. Et sont cy les quatre esmouuemens resveillans lesperit de lomme affin que toutes choses mondaines meprisees il sen retourne a son createur.[32]

French prose, then, while not yet of so much maturity as Latin in its structural composition, was, by 1400, considerably ahead of English, both in the sense of style with which its variety of constructions was manipulated and especially in the accuracy and correctness of the grammatical or logical relationships. French as well as Latin was a likely influence upon the course which English prose took in the fifteenth century. But the stronger influence would be expected to have come from Latin.

It is, therefore, interesting to find that Latin was far predominant either as direct or ultimate source of the fifteenth century English translations. In several cases where texts are not available for comparison the source of an English translation cannot be decided between the Latin original and a known French translation from the Latin. Of the certain cases, fifty are from Latin and fifty from French, prose or verse[33]. But at least seventeen of these French sources are themselves translations from Latin; and there are twelve more cases where the source of the English was either Latin directly or a French translation from Latin. In other words, among the 112 English translations involved, perhaps fewer than thirty-three were from a source in original French, but at least seventy-nine were directly or indirectly from Latin.

The high proportion of translation in the sheer quantity of fifteenth century English prose would alone suggest its literary importance during this period of transition. The nature of the prose translated was of a sort likely to have influenced the writing of English prose in the very direction it took after the middle of the century; that is, in the growing habit of composing common patterns of thought with atten-

---

32. French from a print by C. Mansion, Bruges, 1476, fol. 2, r.: Latin printed by Quentell, Cologne, 1492, fol. 1, v.
33. Only two certainly, possibly three are from French verse (Appendix A, 'Guillaume de Deguiliville'); only one from Latin (Appendix A, 'Coarsinus').

tion to the structural form of the whole pattern. The action of an influence in this respect, however, is clearly a
matter of many details. Several examples of translation
from throughout the century have shown how tangible the influence could be -- how closely the structure of the source
was often followed in English. But it is important to determine the prevailing practice of the many translators --
as many as can be got at through available texts -- and to
observe what resulted from the many small operations naturally involved in translation.

Chapter Four

THEORY AND PRACTICE

No accurate conception of the typical procedure in prose translation can be drawn from the small body of critical comment by the translators themselves. That is not only because so few of them had anything to say. When the statements in their prologues are reconsidered after a collation of their work with its source, they are found to be insufficient and usually misleading. There was no literary standard in the modern sense, one that condemned as plagiarism any unacknowledged translating and set up a rule of artistic fidelity to the original avowed.

Perhaps there was more of this than there had been during the fourteenth century.[1] But the increase of obligation appears principally in the matter of acknowledgement. A fifteenth century translator frequently states what he is doing; sometimes he names the author translated, even with encomiums. Acknowledgement is perhaps the rule by the time of the early printers, and it is common from the earliest part of the century.[2] Yet books keep appearing throughout the century which, like the older Ywain and Gawain or the Abbey of the Holy Ghost, only modern reference has made known as translation.[3]

---

1. F. R. Amos, Early Theories of Translation, pp. 43-46.
2. Early examples are Edward of York's Master of the Game, c. 1408; Love's Mirrour, c. 1410; The Pilgrimage of the Soul, 1413; Secreta Secretorum, c. 1420; The Life of St. Elizabeth of Spalbeck, c. 1430.
3. Examples are the Three Kings of Cologne, the Art of Dying, and The Alphabet of Tales of the early part of the century; the Merlin, the Book of La Tour Landry, and Ponthus and Sidone of the middle years; and the Revelations to a Monk of Evesham, Salomon and Marcolphus, and Melusine, of the latter part. Many of these must have been so well known that the translator could have had no thought of passing the book off as his own.

Fidelity to the content of the originals is not readily to be disputed, because apparent differences might easily have come from an altered copy of the source. However, though there are more than in the century before, cases are still rare where a translator has designated or even admitted his alterations, either of omission, addition or variation. Nicholas Love was explicit indeed in the following little preface to his Mirrour of the Life of Christ:[4]

> Attende lector huius libri prout sequitur in Anglico scripti quod vbicunque in margine ponitur litera .N: verba sunt translatoris siue compilatoris in anglico praeter illa que inferuntur in libro scripto, secundum communem opinionem, a venerabili doctore Bonauentura in latino de meditacione vite christi. Et quum peruenitur ad processum et verba eiusdem doctoris inferitur in margine litera .B. prout legenti sunt siue intuenti istum librum speculi vite christi lucide poterit apparere.[5]

So much precision, I believe, is unique throughout the century, although other writers have made some references to their own changes. The translator of the Saints' Lives in Douce MS 114, Elizabeth of Spalbeck, Mary of Oignies, and others, stated in two different prologues that in his work he would be 'neiþer puttynge to nor doynge awaye any clauses þat schulde chaunge þe substaunce of þe story, but oþerewhile leuyng legeauns and auctorites of holy writte, þat wolde be ful dymme to vndirstonde, if þey were turnyd in to englisshe withoute more declarynge of glose.'[6] Capgrave is no more specific in the Prologue to his Life of St. Gilbert: 'which lyf I haue take on hand to translate out of Latyn rith as I fynde be-fore me, saue sum addicionis wil I put þertoo which men of þat ordre haue told me, and eke othir þingis þat schul falle to my mynde in þe writyng which be pertinent to þe mater.'[7] Caxton both explained the composite nature of his Golden Legend, and in it and in the Mirrour of the World, he made it obvious when he was insert-

---

4. If, indeed, Love did not simply take or adapt this preface from the Frenchman Galopes; see Appendix, Bonaventura.
5. Edited by Powell, p. 10.
6. P. 107; a similar statement precedes the Mary of Oignies, p. 134.
7. EETS o.s. CXL, p. 62.

ing short excerpts of his own[8].

On the other hand, Edward of York, a translator who names and praises his French author, said nothing when he omitted two-thirds of that author's material, or when he inserted several whole chapters of his own. The same man who confessed the omission of certain citations from the Life of Elizabeth of Spalbeck, tacitly cut out whole pages from the interior of the text[9]. Of the various books entitled 'Revelations of St. Birgitta,' none gives the full text as it was then known in England, but all are simply assortments[10]. And the Disciplina Clericalis omits long portions from within the individual tales[11].

In short, there was no stability of practice. One translation may reproduce accurately the contents of its source, another may give only excerpts. Both apparently would have been considered simply as books written in the English language; they would have been judged as translations only by a person who knew the source well enough to regret the exclusion -- or inclusion -- of particular passages.

The same attitude must surely have prevailed toward the finer matter of fidelity to the style of the source. Two translations of well-known books, Atkinson's Imitation of Christ and Barclay's Jugurthine War, both made shortly after the close of the fifteenth century, show what an English writer could do if he chose. Both are in the aureate style, florid, expansive; and in each case the style is the product of the translator, who used the phraseology or ornament of the original when he wanted it, but who showed no obligation to reproduce it whenever he could.

---

8. W. J. B. Crotch, Prologues and Epilogues of William Caxton (EETS o s CLXXVI) 1928, pp. 72-76; 56. In three others of his comments, Caxton promises to keep to the contents of his sources: his Jason was translated 'not chaungyng the sentence, ne presumyng to adde ne mynusshe ony thing otherwyse than myne auctor hath made in Frenssh.' (Crotch, p. 33); in the Reynart (I haue not added ne mynusshed.' (p. 62); of the Fayttes 'I hope to almighti god . . . that it shal not moche varye in sentence fro the copye receyued of my said souerayn lord.'(p. 104).

9. Collation by G. H. Gerould, Anglia XXXIX (1916), 357.

10. See W. P. Cumming in EETS o s CLXXVIII, pp. xvi-xxii; xxix-xxxi.

11. In his edition, Mr. W. H. Hulme gives a running collation with the Latin tales, pp. 12, ff.

Atkinson adds little ideas of his own:

Quis te magis impedit et molestat quam tua immortificata affectio cordis? Bonus et devotus homo opera sua prius intus disponit: quae foris agere debet. Nec illa trahunt eum ad desideria vitiosae inclinationis sed ipse inflectit ea ad arbitrium rectae rationis. Quis habet fortius certamen, quam qui nitetur vincere se ipsum? Et hoc deberet esse negotium nostrum, vincere vidlicet se ipsum, et quotidie se ipso fortiorem fiere; atque in melius aliquid proficere.	who resisteth and letteth a man more than his owne sensuall affeccion? we rede of many Emperours & conquerours that conquered kyngdoms and empyres, and yet neuer ouercame ne subdued theymselfe, for that is one of the moste victorious conquestis where man perfytely ouercometh hym selfe. This shulde be our daylyle batayle to stryue with our selfe, and the more vyctoryes the soule hath of the bodye the more stronge it is, and more apte to encrease and to growe in grace.[12]

But Barclay almost writes a new Sallust:

Bellum scripturus sum, quod populus Romanus cum Iugwitha, rege Numidarum, gessit,	In this worke I purpose to wrytte of the warre, which the Romaynis had and executed agaynste the tyrrany [of] Iugurthe, wrongfully vsurpyng the name of a Kynge ouer the lande of Numidy. Many causes moueth me by writinge to commend this warre to per-
primum quia magnum et atrox variaque victoria fuit	petuall memory. First for that in the same was foughten at many tymes with greate multitude of men on eyther partie, with moche cruel murdre and variable victorye; the Romaines sometyme, sometyme the Iugurthius preuaylying in
dehinc quid tunc primum superbiae nobilitatis obviam	victory. Furthermore bycause that fyrst at this batayle; and from thens forward the

12. Latin, I, iii, 37-48; English, p. 155, 27-35.

itum est.   commen people of Rome matched
                                       with the princes, resistynge
                                       their pryde.[13]

The freedom used by Atkinson and Barclay must not be taken
as typical of the process of translation employed during the
fifteenth century. But it does indicate that during the
hundred years of translating which preceded these two writers, there had not yet been formed any sense of a translator's responsibility to the style of his source.
       Comment on style by the prose translators is very
scarce. I have found it only in Caxton and in two religious
translators of the first half of the century. Caxton often
talks of his inability to produce other than 'symple' and
'rude' English. His concern for his own style shows that he
felt no obligation in this respect toward his source. In
perhaps his last prologue, written for the _Eneydos_ of 1490,
he considers with some self-confidence his choice of English
'termes,' taking no account of any duty toward the 'fayr and
honest termes and wordes in frenshe.' Then, growing apolo-
getic, he regrets that, unlike the great Skelton, he cannot
put a style of his own into a translation[14]. Instead, he
says, 'I haue but folowed my copye in frenshe as nygh as me
is possyble.'[15]
       This following of the copy in French is the impor-
tant thing in Caxton's comment. His concern for his own
style was probably due to his fascination with aureate diction, his 'termes,' which he came to find in conflict with
the need to be plain. As theory it is of interest only in
that he assumes the right to independence from the style of

---

       13. Sallust, _Iugurtha_, V, 1. English, Chapt. i from Ewald
Flügel, _Neuenglisches Lesebuch_, Halle 1905, p. 307. Barclay
printed the Latin beside his translation in order, for one
thing, that 'by the same they shall haue some help toward
the vnderstandyng of latyn.' See H. B. Lathrop, _Translations
from the Classics_, Madison, Wisc., 1933, pp. 81-4.
       14. I have collated Skelton's translation of the Prologue
to Diodorus Siculus with its source, Poggio's Latin translation. While by no means so free in respect to content as
Barclay's _Sallust_, it follows the style far less than Atkynson's _Imitation of Christ_, being in fact a tremendous explo-
sion of aureate phrases. English, Corpus Christi Coll. Camb.
MS. 357, fol. 4, _r_; Latin from a print at Venice, 1476, pp.
a ii, _v._ -a iiii, _v._ (see Appendix A).
       15. Crotch, _Prol_. and _Epil_., pp. 107-110.

his original. He never really took that right himself. If
he was thinking chiefly of diction in his reference to the
'polysshed and ornate termes' of Skelton, it is possible
that he was thinking of phraseology in his 'folowed the
copye.' Certainly that phrase describes his actual method.
The literalness of his early work is notorious. I do not
have available a French text for the Eneydos, but the Four
Sons of Aymon, of 1489, is only a year earlier. A long passage from this collated with the source has already been
quoted in Chapter I[16]. It shows that in his later translating, as well as in his earlier, he makes the phraseology
of the French original the basis for his composition in
English. 'Accordyng to the coppy whyche he [the patron]
sent to me I haue folowed as nigh as I can,' he says in the
Prologue[17]. And as the collation shows he was able to
follow very closely indeed. Down to the very prepositional
phrases, he simply used the French construction and the
French order for every sentence member except three.

     Such a following of the copy was possible only when
the source was French. The difference between Latin and
French in this respect is the important matter in the comments of the two religious translators. They seem at first
glance to show real concern for the reproduction of at
least certain aspects of style. The translator of the
Saints' Lives in the Douce manuscript, noted above for his
care about omissions, says in his 'apologe of the compilour':

> As seint Jerom þe holy doctour seiþ in a bibul þat
> he made: hit is harde to turne a language into a
> noþer worde for worde, but oftentymes hit byhouiþ
> to leue & take diuerse wordes þat are propur to
> on tunge and not to a noþer: wherfore þis englysche
> þat foloþ heere, is turnyd oute of latyn, to þe
> worschip of god & edificacyone of deuoute soulles
> þat are not leeryd in latyn tunge, and þerfore þe
> wryter, þat is but symple-letrd, neiþer can ne
> purposis to folowe þe wordes, but vnniþis and wiþ
> harde þe sens . . . '[18].

The same idea is amplified in Oure Lady's Mirrour, a translation, with elaborate commentary, of the Birgittine service
for Sion Monastery. The author, perhaps Thomas Gascoigne[19],

---

16. Above, pp. 13-15.
17. Crotch, op. cit., p. 106.
18. Anglia VIII, 107.
19 J. H. Blunt, Introduction to his edition of the Mirrour
(EETS e s 19) London, 1873, pp. viii-lx.

says in his second prologue:

> Yt is not light for euery man to drawe eny longe
> thynge from latyn into oure Englyshe tongue. For
> there ys many wordes in Latyn that we haue no
> propre englyssh accordynge therto, And then suche
> v wordes must be turnyd as the sentence may beste
> be vnderstondyd. And therfore though I laboure
> to kepe bothe the wordes and the sentence in this
> boke as farre as oure language wyll well assente:
> yet some tyme I folowe the sentence and not the
> wordes as the mater asketh. There is also many
> wordes that haue dyverse vnderstondynges; & some
> tyme they ar taken in one wyse, some tyme in an
> other, and some tyme they onay be taken in dyuerse
> wyse in one reson or clause. Dyuerse wordes also
> in dyuerse scryptures; or set & vnderstonde some
> tyme other wyse then auctores of gramar tell or
> speke of. Oure language is also so dyuerse in yt
> selfe, that the commen maner of spekyng in Englysshe
> of some contre can skante be vnderstonded in some
> other contre of the same londe . . . I am not wyser
> then was seint Hierome that in the drawying of holy
> scripture from other langage in to latyn sayth how
> he was compellyd at eche boke to answere to the
> bak-bytinge of them that depraued hys laboure. [20]

The principle -- or formula -- stated in each of the
prologues is the same: 'not word for word but meaning for
meaning, by the authority of St. Jerome.' It probably appeared more often in translators' apologies than the number
I have seen would indicate. It even occurs, St. Jerome and
all, in connection with a metrical translation. [21]
    Two meanings might be read into the principle: either

---

20. Ed. by Blunt, op. cit., pp. 7-8
21. The Life of St. Agnes by Osbern Bokenham, ed. by C.
Horstmann, Heilbronn, 1833, p. 119, 11. 675-683. It is interesting that Chaucer put it the other way, promising to
follow 'bothe . . . wordes and sentence' in his Prologue to
the Life of St. Cecilia (Cant. Tales, ed. Robinson, VIII
(G), 78-84). One fifteenth century prose translation,
Richard Misyn's The Fire of Love, has in the prologue: 'The
whilk boke in sentence ne substaunce I þink to chaunge'
(11. 7-9). But sentence and substaunce are practically
synonymous (N.E.D.) For Misyn's practice, which was absurd-
ly literal, see below, pp. 96-99.

a warning that the ensuing translation was to be very free; or, if the translation turns out to be close, a sincere apology for whatever slight alterations in form the difference in language made necessary. In the latter sense it would seem to reflect a real sense of duty toward the source. But taken either way it would be misleading. For the translators' apologies were practically meaningless. The principle they state had become a commonplace.

The source of the Birgittine Service is not available, but if the translator in the Douce MS. were taken to be apologizing for his freedom with the style of his source, his statement would seem strangely inconsistent with his practice in translation. The four Saints' Lives there are not new compositions like Atkynson's, stating the thoughts of the Latin sources but expressing them as the translator chose. The form of the expression in them has been closely adapted from that in the Latin originals. The order both of words and of members has been re-arranged, and the language remains native English in grammatical construction. Yet with one exception, underscored below with a solid line, the division of parts or members in the English is throughout that of the Latin. In no case is there a change in the logical relationship between the members as expressed in the syntax. And in all but eight cases — underscored with a broken line — the English construction is the exact syntactical equivalent of the Latin; two of these eight, þat is to saye and it is to witte, possibly a third, a good while, are simply a matter of idiom. The passages paralleled are the beginnings of Chapters I and II of the Elizabeth of Spalbeck, a fairly plain composition in the Latin. In view of the number of his omissions, the translator seems to have followed his 'word' more faithfully than his 'sentence.'

Porro in provincia Leodiensi prope quoddam famosum et solemne monasterium virginum, filiarum beati Bernardi primi claraevallensis abbatis, quod vocatur Erkenrode, per sex aut septem leucarum distantiam a Leodiensi civitate remotum, est [var. erat] quaedam puella nomine Elizabeth, in cujus virginia puritate misericors et miserator Dominus,	In þe province of Leody bisyde a famous abbey of Nunnys of cistens ordir þat is called Herkenrode, sex myle or seuene fro þe cite of Leody, þere was a mayden þat hyght Elizabeth, in whom our mercyful lord hath schewed merueilous

mirificans misericordias
suas, fidei nostrae
manifestissima docu-
menta necnon et passionis
suae miracula
multipliciter et mirab-
iliter suscitavit, ut
incredulos ad fidei
firmitatem, peccatores
ad poenitentiam, in
gratos ad gratiam,
duros et obstinatos
ad pietatis et devot-
ionis affectum accer-
sat et invitet, immo
quasi cogat invitos.
Quae quidem mirabilia
Domina opera
cum audissem, ego
frater Philippus de
Claravalle, circa partis
illas officium visi-
tationis exercens
non credebam narrant-
ibus, donec ipse veni
et vidi oculis meis,
et probavi quod di-
midia pars mihi non
fuerat nuntiata....

Media siquidem nocte
surgit
ad confiteneum mirifice
principia passionis
Domenicae,
videlicit quomodo
captus extitit et dis-
tractus et impiorum
manibus crudelissime
pertractus. Illud tamen
non aestimo praeter-
mittendum quod tam
hac quam aliis horis
antequam surgit
rapitur
et in eodem statu in
quo rapitur
non modico spatio

miracles of his blissed
passyone,

þat maye stir alle
cristen pepil to
deuocyone.

þe whilke merueilous
werkes of our lorde
whan I dan Philippe
of Clareualle, herde,
what-tyme þat I
visityd howses of myn
ordre in þat countrey,
I gaf no credens to
hem þat tolde me, til-
tyme þat I come my-
selfe and sawe and
proued þat I hadde
not herde þe halfe....

At mydnyȝhte, soþely,
sche rysep, to knowleche
wonderfuly þe
begynnynge of oure
lordes passyon, þat is
to saye, how hee was
taken and drawen hyder
and þyder full cruelly
wiþ wicked mennes
handys. Neuerþeles it
is to witte
þat booþ þis oure and
oþer oures, she is
rauesched, or she ryse
fro his bedde, and
sche abydeþ in the
same staat þat sche
is rauisched in a good
while, alle starke as

ut imago quaedam	an ymage of tree
ligni aut lapidis, sine	or stoon, wiþ-outen
sensu et motu et	felynge or mouynge
flatu, tota rigida	and brethe,
perseverat,	
ita quod de ipsa	þat no þinge maye
nihil tangi aut moveri	be touchyd or stiryd
potest, nec etiam	of hir, not as mykel
minor digitus,	as hir litil fynger,
quin tota machina	but if alle the body
moveatur.	be moued with-alle.
Post quem raptum,	After the whiche rau-
	eschynge, as turnyd
quasi ad se reversa,	agayne to hir-selfe,
surgit et exit de	sche ryse vp and
lecto velociter,	goth oute swiftly
	of hir bedde, and
et incedit per cameram	walkiþ in here chaumbyr
suam mirabili	with a meruylous and a
et composito gressu,	mannerly goynge, as
angelica ut creditur	as hit is trowed, with
manu ducta.	aungeles ledynge. [22]

There is no alteration of style here which seems to
require an apology. There has been some re-arrangement,
especially of words and sometimes of sentence-members, in
order to make the English native in grammatical construction.
But that is all -- except, strangely, for the omissions from the
content, further evidence that the promise to follow meaning
by meaning was merely a convention.
     Thus this translator, and no doubt that of the Bir-
gittine Service too, so far as they were sincerely concerned
with their inability to reproduce the style of the original,
could only have been laboring under a confused notion of
style. Some such confusion may possibly have arisen from an
exaggerated respect for the syntactical details of the source,
when they found it hopeless to bring Latin into English without some re-arrangement. As translators of religious books
they may have felt themselves affected by something of the
same attitude which the Wyclyffite translators of the Bible
tried to face. There was an association, partly superstitious,

     22. English in Anglia VIII, 307-08. Latin, Vita, 2-3, p.
363, 11.7-17; p. 363, 1.38- p. 367, 1.8.

of the exact thought with the exact form of expression, even
with the exact number and order of words[23]. Sacred writings,
if translated at all, must, then be as literal as possible.
Purvey, writing about 1395, maintained that 'the best translating is out of Latin into English, to translate after the sentence, and not only after the words.' But surprisingly enough
he found it necessary to explain why Dominum formidabunt adversarii ejus should be rendered, 'by resolution,' the adversaries
of the Lord shall dread him; this was his revision of the Lord
his adversaries shall dread from the earlier Bible[24].

However, it is more probable that the two translators
quoted were merely cultivating prologue manners. The same
apology and the same inconsistency of practice is to be found
in the translation of Boethius by Jean de Meung[25]. By the
fifteenth century 'meaning for meaning, not word for word' had
become one of the things a French translator might be expected
to say no matter how he treated his source[26]. Nothing better
reveals the conventionality of the formula than its use in the
English translations of the Ship of Fools. Jacob Locher put it
in the prologue to his Latin Stultifera Navis, of 1497, itself
a translation from German; and from him it twice came into
English, once in Alexander Barclay's translation, and again in
Henry Watson's translation of Drouyn's French translation of
Locher. Locher wrote, and after him Barclay:

Nolim tamen arbitretur	But concernynge the
fidus laboris	translacion of this
nostri lector: verbum	Boke: I exhort ye
nos verbo minus	readers to take no
reddere (vt Flaccus	desplesour for yt it
ait) Sensus enim	is not translated

23. See Amos, Early Theories of Translation, pp. 56-59; and
e.g., Thomas Palmer's De translatione sacrae scripturae in lin-
guam Anglicanam, printed by M. Deanesley, The Lollard Bible,
pp. 418-431, pp. 426-9.
24. Chap. XV of Purvey's 'General Prologue,' in A. W. Pollard,
Fifteenth Century English Prose and Verse, Westminster, 1903,
pp. 194-5.
25. James M. Cline, 'Chaucer and Jean de Meung,' Eng. Lit.
Hist., III (1936), 170-181. Mr. Cline goes too far, however,
in his generalizations upon medieval practice in translation
(pp. 179-181).
26. P. H. Larwill, La Théorie de la Traduction au Début de la
Renaissance, München, 1934, pp. 8-21.

duntaxat notasque	word for word accordinge
vernaculi carminis	to ye verses of
simplici numero	my actour. For I have
latine transtulimus.	but only drawen into
	our moder tunge, in rude
	languages, the sentences
	of the verses . . . .[27].

Note that in Locher, Flaccus has replaced Jerome. In Watson,
Flaccus remained:

> Nevertheless thynke not you lectours that I haue
> worde for worde dyrecte and reduced this present
> boke out of Frensshe in to our maternall tongue
> of Englysshe ['redige ce present livre dalamant
> en latin'], for I have only (as recyteth Flaccus)
> taken entyerely the substaunce of the scripture . . .
> [28]

It will be observed from the French inserted above that
Drouyn kept to Locher but that Watson blandly altered the
text to fit his own case. Translated prologues were frequent, and if the prologue translated were already the prologue to a translation, we have second-hand theory, if not
mere ornament[29].
    There are less irregular uses of the formula in early
sixteenth century English prologues. Lord Berners thus apol-
ogizes for his translation of Froissart, in a part of the prologue which is clearly of his own composition[30]:

---

27. English from Jamieson, p. 17; Latin in Zarncke, p. 213.
    28. Quoted from F. A. Pompen, The English Versions of the
Ship of Fools, 1925, p. 282.
    29. See the Secreta Secretorum in MS Royal 18. A. Vii (Aris-
totle), ed. R. Steele, p. 3-4. The Pilgrimage of Man of the MS
of Cam. Univ. Lib. presents Deguiville's induction translated
into the first person, with the word English carefully written
for French in the phrase En françois toute mise l'ai (1.23).
Caxton did the same thing with the Prologue to the Game of
Chess (Crotch, Prol. and Epil., pp. 10 and 11, ff.); and see
Caxton's other translated prologues, to the Recuyell (p. 2-3),
the Mirrour of the World (p. 50 ff.), the Order of Chivalry
(p. 80), and Charles the Great (p. 95); to these apparently
must be added the prologue to Trevisa's Polycronicon.
    30. See note 62 in Chapter II, above, p. 58.

> . . . requyrynge all the reders and herers therof
> to take this my rude translacion in gre. And in
> that I have nat folowed myne authour worde by worde,
> yet I trust I have ensewed the true report of the
> sentence of the mater.[31]

Sir Thomas Wyat explained his translation of Plutarch's
Quiet of Mind in practically the same language:

> [This book] I haue made now of late in to our tong
> nat precisely (I confesse) without errour as one
> shulde haue done that had ben of perfite lernyng,
> but after my rudenesse, seking rather the profite
> of the sentence than the nature of the wordes.[32]

Certainly both these men, if taken at their word, would appear overly timid. With his French source, Berners was
able to keep literal to a point which would have delighted
the religious translators of Wycliffe's time. The following first paragraph from Froissart's own prologue shows
how narrowly Berners missed translating word for word:

Affin que les honnour-
ables emprises et nobles
aventures et faits d'ar-
mes, lesquelles sont
avenues par les guerres
de France et d'Angle-
terre, soient notable-
ment registrées et mises
en mémoire perpétuel,
par quoy les preux
aient exemple d'eulx
encouragier
en bien faisant, je
vueil traittier et
recorder hystoire et
matière de grand lou-
ange. Mais ains que je
la commence, je requer
au Sauveur de tout le
monde, qui de néant créa
toutes choses, que il
vueille créer et mettre
en moi sens et entende-

To thentent that the
honorable and noble
aventures of featis of
armes, done and achyved
by the warres of
France and Inglande,
shulde notably be in-
registered and put in
perpetuall memory,
whereby the prewe and
hardy may have ensample
to incourage them in theyr
well doyng, I syr John
Froissart wyll treat
and recorde an hystory
of great louage and
pryse: but or I begyn,
I require the Savyour
of all the worlde, who
of nothynge created
al thynges, that he
wynn gyve me suche
grace and understandyng.

---

31. Ed. by W. P. Ker, p. 6.
32. Facsimile ed. by C. Baskerville, p. Aii, v.

ment si vertueux que ce,
livre que j'ai commencié
je le puisse continuer   that I may continue
et persévérer en telle   and persever in such
manière que tous ceulx   wyse that who so
et celles qui le liront,   this proces redeth, or
verront et orront y puis-   hereth may take
sent prendre esbatement   pastaunce, pleasure,
et plaisance, et je   and ensample. [33]
encheoir en leur grace.

Wyat with his Latin is of course not so literal as Berners;
but as the opening sentences show, he usually forms his
phrases just as strictly after his original:

Serius tuam epistolam   I receyued very late
accepi, in qua me   thy letter, wherin
hortabaris   thou exhortes me
vt quippiam ad te   that I shulde write
& de animi tranquil-   som thyng unto the of
litate scriberum   the quitnesse of mind
& de his quae in Timaeo   and of those things in
accuratiore indigere   Timeus that thou thynkest
tibi enarratione   nedeth more exquisite
videntur. Equidem   declaration. Trewly,
quum Eroti amico   where as Eros my frende
nostro navigandum   was redy to sayle
actutum Roman esset   towardes Rome
literis raptim à   and I had receyued
fundano optimo viro   hastely of Fundanus the
acceptis,   honest man the letters,
nec ideo spacium haberum   & I had not therefore
meo modo incumbendi ad ea   leysar to apply me to that
que optabas,   that thou desyredst, as
                                  I wolde haue done,
nec rursus sustinerem   nor agayne coude I
vacius omnino manibus   suffre the man to
hominem à nobis   be seen sent from me
amissum esse videri   with empty handes,
delecta quaedam de   certeyn chosen thynges
tranquillitate animi   I haue taken forth of the

---

33. English ed. Ker, Vol. I, p. 17; French ed. de Litten-
hove, I, p. 4 (2me rédaction). See G. Schleich, 'Lord
Berners' Froissart-Übersetzung in ihren Bezeihungen zum
Original,' Archiv für das St. der n. Spr., CLX (1931), 34-50;
CLXIII (1933), 205-17; CLXIV (1933), 24-35; CLXIX (1934),
18-25.

ex commentariis con fectis olim nobis decerpsimus.	quietnesse of mynde out of the comentaris that somtyme I made.[34]

There is here the same inconsistency between the apology and the practice as was shown by the translator of the Elizabeth of Spalbeck. None of the translators, fifteenth century or early sixteenth, French or English, really meant anything by their talk of sentence for sentence. The emphasis of their apologies is on the 'rude' abilities of the translator. They were not expressing an attitude concerning the repro- duction of style, but simply a commonplace of humility.

The translators' own theories, and their practice, to sum up, do not indicate that there was any prevailing literary custom to force them to follow their sources, either in context or in form. Since most of the translations are found without critical comment, it is impossible to be sure of this. There was perhaps a growing duty at least to avow any differences of content. And possibly in the religious writings a reluctance to tamper with holy material had more influence than can be determined in holding translators close to the form of their sources. But there was not even, as the case of the Elizabeth of Spalbeck demonstrates, any con- sistency of practice; that is, there appears no correlation between fidelity in content and form. A translator could deal fully and faithfully with the context of his source, and yet disregard the style[35]. Or he could omit or even add matter, and still follow the structure of whatever he took with as fast a literalness as he thought his English language permitted. It is probable that the translator's own judgment, or his patron's, was what decided the pro- cedure.

Considering, then, that respect for religious mate- rial is the only discernible outside influence upon a trans- lator's practice, it is surprising to see how many of them remained faithful to the style of the original. The work of

---

34. English, p.[a iii, r.]; Latin, p. 5. A detailed de- scription of Wyat's over-literal adherence to his source is given by J. L. Wortham, English Prose Style in Translations from the Classics, diss. (unpublished; on deposit in the Princeton University Library), Princeton, 1939, pp. 8-13.
35. The first two-thirds of the Ponthus and Sidoine (Ap- pendix, 'La Tour Landry'); Atkynson's Imitation of Christ, though it has occasional phrases added; Skelton's 'Diodorus Siculus.' I have seen no other certain example of this pro- cedure.

Caxton with his French sources and that of the Douce translator with his Latin, are typical of the others using French
or Latin. Translations from the French could be more literal
than those from Latin; but for both it was the same method
which prevailed, to keep as close as the syntax and grammar
of English permitted -- and sometimes closer than it permitted -- to the sentence structure of the composition under
translation. Such fidelity may indeed have been encouraged
by a school of criticism which has not left enough traces to
be recognized; it may have been due to a personal standard,
a sort of conscience concerning foreign models or an admiration for them; or perhaps it came about in a sense auto-
matically, because of a translator's inability to progress
well otherwise than by throwing himself upon his source.
There were, as will be seen, several interesting exceptions,
and it is they which indicate that freedom of choice existed.
But for whatever reason the choice was made, to depend upon
the composition of the original was the prevailing practice
throughout the fifteenth century.

Chapter Five

THE TYPICAL PROCEDURE: DEFINITIONS AND EXCEPTIONS

I have closely examined, in whole or in part, thirty-eight translations made in the fifteenth century by, probably, thirty-three different translators. Except for parts of three of them, all those observed are alike in this, that the correspondences of meaning for meaning between a translation and its source may be traced by very small units, usually by units equivalent to a phrase or a clause in verbal expression. There are often omissions from the source, and occasionally there are additions; but normally each group of words or <u>colon</u> of the translated prose has been determined in meaning or content -- as distinguished from construction -- by a similar unit in the source.

In parts of the three exceptions mentioned, the correspondences of meaning are so broad, so general, or the rearrangements of and additions to the material are so frequent, that the composition must be called paraphrase or recension, not translation proper. A few excerpts from <u>the English Conquest of Ireland</u> will illustrate:

(Cap. I, p. 226)

Videns itaque Dermit-
ius viribus se undique
destitui, et aversa
penitus fatorum facie,
fortunaeque favore,
jam desperanter affligi,
post multos et graves
impari certamine cum
hoste conflictus,

tanquam ad ultimum
confugiens salutis
remedium tandem tamen
fugae praesidium
navigo destinavit . . .
Fortunam igitur fugiti-
vam sequens, et rotae

(Cap. I, p. 4, 11.15-24)

Macmorgh saw þat
power hym failled,
& euerich half he was
amyde his fomen beset.
he was man of high hert;
and with þe litill power
þat he had, he werrede
as long as he myght:
bot he ne myght nat all-
way all-on ageyns all
the lande folke. he was
so narrowe bilad þat
nedes he most tholl
deth otherþe lond leue;
he saw þat non other
remedy was: he went to
see, and fond ship redy.
and wynde at will, &
passede oure to England

volubilitati multum
confidens. Murchardi
filius, velis sulcant-
ibus aequor, vento
que ad vota spirante,
ad Anglorum regem
Henricum cecundum
auxilium obnixe
postulaturus accessit.

with well few
with hym; and on
this maner he sawct
his lif & lyte lond
& lede & all his other
good.

[At the above point of
omission Giraldus has
a fourteen-line sermon
for tyrants.]

Herby þat men may witte,
þat be a man of neuer so
mych power, bettre hym is
þat hys men hym love þan
hate.

Two words have grown into twenty:·

(Cap. I, p. 228)

(Cap. I, p. 6, 11.17-21)

multasque promissiones,
tam terrarum quam
stipendiorum, multis
inaniter emisset,

& largely he behight
londes and rentes, & Rich
yiftes, if any wer that
hym helpe wold. Bot he
ne fond noon with-al that
such tynge wolde ne durst
vndirtake, till þat the

tandem comes Strigulens-
is...cum eo locuturus
advenit.

erle of Strugoul....com
to hym.

Or the most precise statements appear in vague epitome:

(Cap. III, p. 232)

(Cap. IV, p. 12, 11.3-4)

Ex ictus hujus vehe-
mentia, sedecim annis
post elapsis, dentes ei
molares ceciderunt, et
quod stupore dignius
erat, novi statim suc-
creverunt.

The cry was well
gret on euery syde
for this knyght þat
thus was I-hurt.

Far more often than not, however, the Conquest is
quite close to its source in meaning if not in language;
and this is true of the two other books which are in part
recensions, Capgrave's Life of St. Gilbert and Nicholas

Love's Mirrour[1]. With the exception of these three, none of the thirty-eight books examined as translations contains any considerable passages of recension [2]. Correspondence to the source is normally detailed at least in the meanings.

The differences between the procedure of one translator and another, therefore, are to be described in the extent to which each has reproduced the form or construction of the original units of meaning.

Purvey, in his famous preface to the English Bible, recognized only two main procedures, the strictly literal and the 'open.' For the literal he gives only one example, and it is enough; 'The Lord his adversaries shall dread,' for 'Dominum formidabunt adversarii ejus.' But the many kinds of 'resolution' which he described for the 'open' must be separated and classified on a different basis from his. ' . . . an ablative case absolute,' Purvey said, 'may be resolved into these three words, with covenable verb, the while, for, if . . . and sometimes . . . into when either into afterward, thus . . . after the master read I stood.'[3] By such a procedure he is expressing — by means of equivalent constructions — the same relationship between the two ideas as was expressed in the Latin. Such a translation of magestro legente is not so literal as the master reading, yet it leaves the structure of its little sentence essentially the same as does the closer rendering. But Purvey continues: 'and sometime it may well be resolved into a verb of the same tense, as other be in the same reason, and into this word et, that is, and in English, as thus, arescentibus hominis prae timore, that is, and men shall wax dry for dread. Also a participle . . . as thus, dicens, that is, saying, may be resolved thus, and saith . .

---

1. The nature of each of these three is briefly discussed under the respective listings in Appendix A; the Conquest under Giraldus, Capgrave under Saints' Lives, Love under Bonaventura. For the discussion of translators' practices in the present chapter, the three have been separately classified according to the nature of the large portions in them which are translation proper.

2. Malory's Morte Darthur appears — so far as its sources can be recovered — to be in greater part recension, and I have not included it in my list of translations, Appendix A. See Eugene Vinaver, Malory, Oxford, 1929, Appendix II, 'The Sources of the Morte Darthur,' pp. 128 - 155; also Appendix III, pp. 155 - 189.

3. From Chapter XV of the 'General Prologue.' A. W. Pollard, Fifteenth Century English Prose and Verse, Westminster, 1903, p. 194.

Also a relative, which . . . as thus, which runneth, and he runneth.[4] Here only the individual statements, the units of meaning or content, remain the same; their relationship to each other and to the whole sequence of thought is no longer expressed by the syntax of the English; and the sentence in which they are included no longer will have the same structure as it had in the source.

On the basis of structural form, then, though we can still recognize in Purvey's description two main procedures, they must be differently distinguished. The first is that which retains the original structure of the sentence and the original expression of thought-relationship; this may be done either literally or by finding English equivalents. The second is that which alters both the structure of the sentence and the expression of the pattern of thought.

In regard to the second, the substitution of a paratactic for a hypotactic syntax is the only manner of real alteration described by Purvey. Perhaps thinking it a greater departure than resolution by and, and therefore not to be considered, he neglected to explain that the alteration may work the other way, the sentence being made more 'close' by subordination of originally coordinate members; or that members already subordinate may be retained, but in different hypotactic relationships; as if the magistro legente steti were turned into while I stood the master read, or even his arescentibus hominis prae timore, into fear making men dry. Of course this latter form of alteration makes a real departure from the original, and the more it is practised, the more the translation becomes independent composition. It was, however, occasionally used by all the translators.

With these amendments to Purvey's description, we have roughly all the forms of procedure which appear. They are four, these being two main forms of alteration and two of adherence, and according to these four all the translations examined may be classified. The forms of alteration were either to remove the hypotaxis of the original sentence members, so that they were no longer combined into a larger period; or to apply new or different subordinations, so that the syntactical relationship of the members to each other -- and thus to the period as a whole -- was no longer the same. Translation by either of these procedures is to be called free. The forms of adherence were either to imitate literally not only the sentence structure but many of the detailed syntactical usages peculiar to the language of the source; or to match the sentence-members taken from the source with native English equivalents. By

---

4. Ibid., pp. 194-95.

either manner of adherence every member translated was kept
in the same relationship to the other members and to the
period as a whole, and either manner may be called close.

As Purvey implied, however, the same translators may
-- for brief sequences or for long -- employ now one procedure, now another, and many of the fifteenth century translators did so vary, often changing between one sentence-
member and the next. Equally important as the kind of procedure, therefore, is the frequency with which any one kind
has been used; both of these together determine the degree
of adherence to the source which any translation presents as
a whole.

Of the thirty-eight translations examined, only nine
are free, two having been altered largely into parataxis,
seven occasionally by new forms of hypotaxis. The two in
parataxis, however, are the only ones which have completely
lost the structural character of their sources; the other
seven, though erratic, have normally been patterned upon
their sources in all important respects. Twenty-nine of
the thirty-eight are close. Yet only three of these are
characterized by strictly literal imitation of the syntax
of the sources. As to degree of adherence to the sources,
therefore, only five out of the thirty-eight represent extremes, two of independence and three of slavishness. In
about seven-eighths of the translated prose, the basic structure is derived from the sources and yet the constructions
and word-order have seldom been warped.

That this degree of adherence was so predominant, almost uniform, is the most important fact, I believe, in fifteenth century translation. I have pointed out some of the
more conspicuous effects of the practice in my first chapter,
and in later chapters I shall describe others in more detail.
My purpose at this point is mainly to demonstrate that such
adherence was predominant and how it was practised. Yet a
survey of the translations and the procedures, by throwing
the extremes into contrast with the typical, will help illustrate further not only the manner but also the effects
of close but idiomatic translation. I shall therefore
group the examples according to the four main kinds of procedure distinguished above. But the nature of the typical
degree of adherence will be better realized if the two extremes, the independent and the literal are examined first.

'RESOLUTION' BY 'THIS WORD AND':

THE TRANSLATIONS ALTERED IN FORM.

Many translators, as I have said, used all four
kinds or procedure, each kind, however, to a greatly varying
extent. The first to be described, the substitution of
paratactic for hypotactic syntax, is likely to appear occasionally in translations which are very little altered. In
a collection of the Revelations of St. Birgitta,[5] for instance, absolute constructions are usually handled in such
ways as the following:

<table>
<tr><td>(Lib. I, cap. 2;
Vol. I, p. 5)
Ego sum qui . . .
mortuus fui, & sepultus
Deitate illaesa
permanente</td><td>(p. 1, 1. 14)
I am he that . . .
was beryed,
Þe godhed abydynge
vnhurte.</td></tr>
<tr><td>(Ibid.)</td><td>(p. 1, 1. 23)</td></tr>
<tr><td>Tam etiam eo
defuncto cogitasti
. . . .</td><td>and also after hys
deth whan thowe
thoughteste . . . .</td></tr>
</table>

But now and then the translator will resolve them 'into this
word et, that is, and,' though in isolated sequences of only
two or three members the effect of the parataxis is practically unnoticed.

<table>
<tr><td>(Lib. I, cap. 2;
Vol. I, p. 6)</td><td>(p. 3, 11. 5-6)</td></tr>
<tr><td>Ut mundata citius
ad magnum praemium
peruenias</td><td>that Þow might Þe sonner
be made clene and
come to grete rewarde</td></tr>
<tr><td>(Lib. VIII, cap. 56;
Vol. II, p. 341)</td><td>(p. 92, 11. 5-11)</td></tr>
<tr><td>Cui etiam persuasi,
diu & multos ortationes
. . . legere . . . vt sic</td><td>I conceylled him also
to say longe & mony
prayers . . . Þat so he</td></tr>
</table>

5. Mid-century; Garrett MS.

inaniter prolungando &
occupando tempus,
nullos conquerentes
audiret . . . .
Persuasi quoque Regi
vt ceteris bonis viris
Regni despectis,
vnum super omnes hom-
ines elevaret.

schulde prolonge &
occupie þe tyme in
vayne, & not her
any þat wold compleyn . . .
Also I styrred þe kynge
to live & despice oþer
goodmen of the realme;
& to lyft vp and prefer
oo man above all oþer.

Similar variety of treatment, sometimes involving longer sequences, may be illustrated from the Life of St. Elizabeth
of Spalbeck. The following two sentences both present the
same type of expository material:

(p. 364, 11. 24-29)   (p. 108, 11, 23-29)

Postquam vero sur-
rexit, sicut semper est
induta tunica lanea
ad carnem et superin-
duta candido lineo
vestimento aliquantu-
lum super terram
ultra talares terminos
et mensuram virginiae
longitudinis defluente,
incidit honestissime
per cameram suam
et sine intermissione
eundo et redeundo
utraque palma crebro
ordine se percutit
in maxillis,
clara exinde et con-
corde sonorum constan-
tia resultante

And whanne sche is
vp, cladde as sche is
alle-wey wiþ a wollen
coot next her flesch
and with a whyte lynnen
garement sumwhatly
trailynge on þe erthe,

an sche walkeþ ful
honestly in hir chaumbyr,
and with-out
blynnynge, as sche
goeth and commith
agayn, she swappeþ
hir-selfe vpon þe chekys,
and of hir strokes may
be herde accordaunte
sowne and cleer.

(p. 368, 11. 10-15)   (p. 110, 37-42)

His omnibus longe
Solemnius et mirabilius
quam meae parvitatis
stilus exarare suffic-
iant consummatis,
eadem tabula a se
prius composita et
clausa, tradita
alicui sibi assisenti

Whan all this is doon,
mykel moor solempnely
and moor merueylously
þan I can or maye write:

sche keueriþ and closeþ
þe same tabil,
& takiþ hit to som body
bisyde hir

personae, extendit	and strikeþ forthe hire
brachia ad matrem	armes to her moder
suam et sorores	and to her sostres,
minores se minis-	ȝonger thanne sche, þat
trantes eidem. Quae	serue hir;
scilicet mater et soror-	
es eam susceptam et ele-	and þey take and liftes
vatam a terra deferunt	hir vp from þe erþe
in cubile, illic reclin-	and beriþ and leyeþ hir
antes, eamdem clarita-	in her bedde, and sche
tem vultus . . . spiritual-	schewith to him clernesse
ium verborum dulcidin-	of chere . . . and swetnesse
em sibi mirifice	of goostly wordes.
ministrantem.	

In the first sentence, the translator has condensed the adjective phrases built on _induta_ and _superinduta,_ and matched
the temporal phrase on _eundo et redeundo_ with a clause. But
except for the last member, which has been altered from a
phrase to a principal clause, he has imitated the syntax of
the Latin, thus building up a period much like the Latin,
with whatever perspective of thought, ease of movement, and
variety of expression the original possessed. In the second,
he has re-cast six of the Latin subordinate constructions
into completed clauses joined by _and,_ leaving a period in
which eight members are all expressed alike.

     Resolution into parataxis is not the typical pro-
cedure used in the _St. Elizabeth_ or in the revelations[6]
or in any thirty-eight translations which I have examined,
except two - _The English Conquest of Ireland_ and _The Alphabet of Tales._   In these two it has led to the greatest difference in form between translation and source that is to be
found in any of the thirty-eight. Even when the affinity of
the meanings in the _Conquest_ is very close to the source,[7]
there is seldom much affinity of language. The Latin of
Giraldus is somewhat complex, but the translator has largely
resolved it into simple individual statements:

(Cap. III, p. 232-3)	(Cap. IV, p. 12 - Dublin MS.)
A muris itaque se re-	Thay with-drow ham fro
trahentes, et ad litus	the wallys and wenten ham

---

6. Longer passages which are typical of the _St. Elizabeth_
have been quoted in Chapter IV, above, pp. 76-8; of the
Revelations, Chapter I, pp. 16-20.
     7. The _Conquest_ is in some parts only a recension, see
above, p. 85.

proximum certatim ir- ruentes, naves omnes quas ibidem invenerunt igne statim succende- runt. Navis autem una, quae mercimonii causa de partibus Brittaniae huc advenerat, tritico vinoque re- ferta, anchorarum morsu in portu re- tenta jacebat.	to þe strond and all þe shippes þat þay þer fond, thay settene a-fyr. And .O. shippe þer was, that was I-com owt of Brittayne aftyr cheffar, and was Y-charget with whet & with wynes and lay I-ancred in the hauene:
Quam cum electae juventu- tis pars potior in scaphis remigando veriliter occupassent, anchorarum funibus nau- tarum industria jam praecisis, circo a tergo urgente, navemque in al- tum propellente, non absque magno salutis dispendio, scapharum remorumque praesidio terram iterum vix obtin- uerunt.	the best parte of the englismen wenten with bottes and toke his shippe. þe shippmen werne many, and saw that þer weren bot a few englys in the shippe, & the wynd was of þe lond; they cutte the cable of the ankre, and þe wynd bare the shippe in toward the see: her fellowes saw this, and wenten after with bottys; and vnnethe with rowyng, and with gret peril of all har lyues, þay come ayen to lond.

The English prose is far indeed here from the style of its source. It is as blunt and as laboured as the earliest English chronicles. And it will be observed that the _Conquest_ and the translation like it, the **Alphabet of Tales**, are both narratives and both of the first quarter of the century.

In the **Alphabetum Narrationum** – I have compared only the tales from Petrus Alphonsus – the Latin constructions were already rather easy:

(No. IX, p. 14)	(No. DXXXV, pp. 359-60)
 Perrexit quidam ut vindemiaret vineam. Quod uxor illius videns intellexit illum circa vineam diutius moratur-	Petrus Alphonsis; how some tyme a man went to wede hys vynys, and his wyfe trowid þat he wold hafe tarid long

um et misso nuntio
convocat amicum con-
viviumque parat.
Accidit autem ut domin-
us ramo vineae in oculo
rediret nihil de oculo
percusso videns;

veniensque ad portam
suae domus hostium pul-
savit. Quod uxor intell-
igens nimium turbata
convocatum amicum abs-
condit scorsam et dom-
in suo hostium postea
aperire cucurrit. Qui
intrans et graviter
pro oculo tristis et
dolens iussit cameram
parari et lectum sterni,
ut posset quiescere.
Timuit uxor ne intrans
cameram amicum latitan-
tem videret. Dixit ei:
Quid tantum properas
ad lectum? Dic mihi quid
tibi sit prius!
Narravitque ei totum
ut acciderat.
Permitte, inquit illa,
karissime domine, ut
oculum sanum medicinali
arte confirmen et car-
mine, ne ita eveniat
de sano ut mihi evenit
de iam percusso, quia
dampnum tuum commune est
nobis. Apponensque os
suum ad oculum sanum tan-
tum fovit quousque
amicus a loco ubi ab-
sconditus erat viro
nesciente discessit.
Tandem se erigens:
Modo, inquit, karissime
vir, sum secura ne
simile de hoc oculo even-
iat, quale de altero

and callid her luff
into þe hows.
So þis man happend to
be smyten in þe ee
with a twyste, so þat
he mot not se, & he
mot hafe no ruste þerof
& went home
and when he knokkid
at þe dure
þe wyf was ferde, &

hid hur luff in a
chaumber &
afterward oppynd
þe dure. and hur
husband went in

& wolde hafe gane
vnto þe bed,

and sho axkid hym
what he wold do
at the bed. and he
tellid hur all as it
had happened hym.
and sho bad hym sitt
down & lett hur charm
the hale ee,
þat it happend nott
þe same.

And sho put hur
mowthe vnto þe hale
ee to likk it, vnto
her luff was gone his
way, at hur husband
wist nott. And þan
sho bad hur husband
ryse, & sayd unto
hym: 'Now I am
sekur of þis ee.

evenit. Iam potes, si placet, ad lectum descendere.	And now if you like ye may go vnto your bed and riste you.' And so he did.

The translator has omitted several Latin subordinate members,
[8] but he has written all of those retained (except three
infinitive phrases and the auxiliary constructions) as indicative clauses; and all but nine of the thirty-odd are completed or principal clauses. His composition may be compared
with a later fifteenth century translation of the same tale
out of the Disciplina Clericalis, in which there have been
only two coordinations of originally subordinate parts (cald
and hid; Arise now):

(No. VII, pp. 27-28)

Suche a man went to cut his vyne. Than [MS: that]
his wif seeyng that vndirstode hym to dwelle and
tarie long aboute it and sent a messengier to
cal hir love and lemman, and arraied a feeste.
Forsooth it happened and fil so that the lord
of the vyne smyten with a braunche in the eye,
yeede ageyn anon vnto his house nothyng seeyng
with the hurt eye. Comyng to the gate of his
[house he] knocked at the doore. That the wif
withynfurth [heryng] gretly troubled cald hir
love and hid hym, and after that opened the
doore vnto hir husbonde. Whiche entryng and
gretly sorrowyng for his hurt eye bad array
his chamber and make his bedde, as that he
myght rest hym. The wif dred lest he entryng
the chamber shuld see hir love ther hid and
saide: 'What hastest thow to bedde? First tel
me what is the befalle.' And he told hir what
was hym befalle. 'O diere sir,' quod she, 'so-
effre me that I conferme with craft of medicyne
and charme that it come nat to the hool eye as is
comen to the hurt eye. forwhi thi hurt and damage
is comune to vs both,' settyng hir mowth to the
hol eye til hir love from the place wher he was
hid went his wey and departed, vnwityng the husbond. Than quod she: 'arise now, diere husbond,
for I am sure it shall nat come to the holl eye
that is come to the hurt. Now maistow, if it
please the to go to thy bedde.'

---

8. It is possible that some of the omissions from the basic
version by Petrus are due to the compiler of the Alphabetum
narrationum.

Note the differences made by the use of participles, even when the constructions occasionally are left too literal. The first translation has lost one of the chief character-istics of the Latin, the combination of constructions to cor-respond with relationships of thought. In the second this characteristic has been preserved, the resultant style ap-pearing perhaps unnatural but certainly more sophisticated, more controlled.

THE EXTREMES IN LITERAL TRANSLATION.

The two translations extremely altered in form show little evidence of 'control.' But it is doubtful if the three at the other extreme, the strictly literal, may be said to have any, either. They contain structural patterns which have been transferred from the sources, but other character-istics of the syntax, especially the word-order, have often been transferred, too; not adapted, but adopted. The foreign turns of speech have necessarily been mixed with a high mini-mum of native syntax, and so the constructions and above all the word-order lack both standardization and convenience. To most fifteenth century readers the violations of usage must have seemed not only outlandish and confusing but also point-less, for in themselves they enabled no stylistic effect not possible otherwise. A modern reader receives the impression, and not always falsely, I believe, that this procedure of translation must have been purely and blindly mechanical. Only two translators, both writing early in the second quarter of the century, followed it often enough to characterize their prose.

The Fire of Love and The Mending of Life by Richard Misyn, made in 1434 and 1435 from the Latin of Richard Rolle, are of this sort, and, to a lesser degree, The Pilgrimage of Man, c. 1430. A specimen of Misyn's composition, perhaps more literal than the average run of his work, shows that the English language of the time was at least mechanically capable of copying a great many Latin constructions:

(Incendiam Amoris, Cap. 31, p. 234)	(Fire, Book II, Chap. I, p. 69, 1.39-p. 70, 1.10)
Sed in ueritate uenit in me inuisible gaudium, et realiter intra me con-calui igne amoris qui utique ab istis in-	Bot in treuth in me is cunne un vnsein ioy, & with-in me verraly I ha waxyd warme with fyre of luf, þe qwhilk my hert

ferioribus rebus assump-
sit cor meum, ut iubil-
lans in Ihesu longe ab
interiore armonia in
interiorem euolarem.
Cumque contaminaciones
odirem, et uerborum
vanitates euacuarem,
cibaria quoque superflue
non sumere nec indiscrete
temperare me contendi:
quamvis dicebar domibus
diuitum deditus,
ut bene pascerere, et
in deliciis delectarer.
Sed agente Deo habui
animum aliter ordinatum
ut superna magis saperem
quam suauitatem ciborum,
et exinde equidem.
quoniam solitudinem amare
non cessaui
extra homines saltem
existere elegi, nisi co-
gentibus carnis necessari-
is, successiue solacium
accepi ex ipso quem amaui.

has takyn fro þis lawe
þingis, þat in Ihesu
syngand ful fare fro
vt-ward melody to ful
inhirly I ha flowne.
Qwhen I filthis has hat-
yd & vanite of wordys
cast out & metis in
superfluite not to take
nor vnwisely me to
gouern I haue stryvyne,
þof all of me wer sayd
I was gifyn to riche
howses, well to be fed
& in deletys to lyffe.
Bot god wyrk-and my
sawle I had odyr-wyes
sett, þat rather I sau-
yrd heuenly þan swetnes
of meytt; & be þis cause
certain wyldernes I haue
lufyd
& fro men I chase to
lyfe, þe nedys of body
onely speed,
& so soþely solas I take
of hym þat I lufyd.

The unnaturalness here, however, is due more to the order of
words or of sentence-members than to the imitation of constructions. Note that Misyn did not try to copy such an idiom
as 'dicebar . . . deditus' ('of me wer sayd I was gifyn'). A
comparison of a bit of Misyn's _Mending of Life_ with a later
fifteenth century translation, itself quite close, will indicate the difference in natural effect produced by re-ordering
of words:

(Misyn, Chap. I,
p. 107, 11. 4-13)

He truly þat desires
criste truly to luffe,
not onely with-oute heu-
ynes bot with a Ioy un-
mesured he kestis bak
all þinge þat hym may
lett.
And in þis case nowdyr
fader ne modyr ne him-

(Translation in Worcester
Cathedral MS., pp. 30-31)

Who forsoth desireth
verily to love Crist, he is
nat only without sorow;
also with grete ioye
al thynges that mown
letten hym to come therto
he castith awey.
Also in that cause he ne
sparith fader, moder, nor

self he sparis, no
mans chere he takis,
violence he doys to all
his lettars, & all
ostakyls he byrstis
to-gidyr; Qwhat-euer
he may do, hym þink it
lityll god for to lufe.
ffro vices he flees
als man braynles, & to
wardly solace he lokkis
nott,
bot certanly in god holy
dresyd nerhand his sens-
ualite he has forgettyn.
All inward he is geddyrd,

all in Criste
he is lyfte;
so þat qwhen men se he
als sems heuy,
wondirfully he is glad.

hymself; he settith
bi no faire chiere,
ne violence to all
erthely thyng he bryngith;
al obstaclis hym withstang-
yng he brekith. Whatsoeuer
he may do for goddis love
seemyth hym ful litel.
He fleeth awey fro vices;
to worldly solacis he
biholdith nomore than a
man that is drunke,
dressyng forsoth so highly,
that almost his worldly
wittis he hath lost.
Al his spiritual wittis
inward he hath gadred to-
guyder, al his mynde in
God is lift vp;
so that when men seen hym
weenen that he be sory
than is his mynde in
grete joie.[9]

(Cap. I, p. 609, G)

Qui enim Christum amare vere desiderunt, non solum
sine tristitia sed etiam cum immenso gaudio omnia
quae eum impedire poterunt abiieciet, & nec patri
aut matri, nec sibi ipsi in hac causa parcit. Non
accipet vultum alicuius, violentiam omnibus infert,
obstacula cunctorum frangit. Parum sibi videtur
quicquid facere potest vt Deum amet. Volat a vitiis quasi ibrius, ad ea quae sunt seculi solatia
non respicit: imo in Deum se totum dirigens, pene
exteriores sensus amittit, totus intus collegitur,
totus in Christum elucatur, vt cum videntos illum
contristatum putant, vehementer gaudeat.

In each of these two translations the division, the order, and
even the construction of the sentence-members are practically
the same. But Misyn's word-order makes his prose seem warped,
almost formless; whereas the later translation, even though not

9. So Hulme's copy of the MS. Hulme emends: 'so that when men
seen hym [thei] weenen that he be sory; than is his mynde in
grete joie.' I think it should be: 'so that when men seeyng
hym weenen that he be sory, . . etc.'

always so accurate, is much closer to the stylistic effect
of Rolle.
    The following passage from The Pilgrimage of Man --
less typical of the whole, however, than were the selections
from Misyn -- shows even less sense of style, for without
the poem by Guillaume before one there would often be still
less apparent reason for the stange inversions and separ-
ations.[10]

(Part III, ll.9117-9134, p. 284)	(Part III, cap. iii, p. 138)
En ce point la vielle venir	In thilke poynt I sygh the olde come to ward
Vi vers moi pour moi assaillir	me for to assaile me
'Par Mahomet, dist elle a moi,	and seide me Bi mahoun quod she
Qui est mon dieu en qui je croi,	that is my god in whom i leue
Je t'atendoie. A moi l'aras.	the abod j. Of me thou shalt haue it
Mal i venis, tu i mourras	Eule come thou heere Thou shalt dye heere
Met jus t'escherpe et ton bourdon	Ley doun thi skrippe and thi burdoun
Et fai hommage a mon Mahoun!	and do omage to my mahoun
C'est cil qui sui louee	It is he bi whom j am alosed
Et sage dite et hon-nouree;	and cleped wys and wurthi and wurshiped
Celui sans qui nul n'est prisie	Thilke with oute whom no whit is preysed
En terre ne auctorisee;	in eerthe ne autorised
Celui par qui sont honnourez	Thilke bi whiche ben wurshiped
Mains grans folz et sages clamez	many grete fooles and cleped wise

10. The Pilgrimage of Man is the only prose translation
with a source in verse that I have examined. (Others, not
seen, are: The Pilgrimage of Man in MS. G. 21 of St. John's
College, Cambridge; John Kaye's Seige of Rhodes (Appendix,
Caorsin); and possibly The Pilgrimage of the Soul). It is
quite possible that the nature of the source explains the
presence of un-natural word order.

A li faut que te soumetes	To him it needeth thou submitte thee
Et de le servir t'en- tremetes	and him to serue sette thee
Et puis apres honteuse- ment	and sithe afterward j shal make thee shame-
Mourir te ferai et vilment.'	fullich and vileynes- liche dye.[11]

In Misyn's translations one at least feels a purpose if not a system. Perhaps experimenting with English style, perhaps simply zealous in regard to his materials[12], Misyn was clearly making a conscious effort to Latinize his expres- sion. As the editor of his translations has observed, he sometimes departed from the medieval Latin order of Rolle in order to give his English a classical turn[13]. But in passages from the Pilgrimage such as that just quoted, one can only believe that the translator was working mechanic- ally, thinking of little but his French meanings word by word. In the following sentence he has surely worked blindly:

(11. 1113-16)   (I, xxvii, p. 18)

Or vous diray des II taillans	Now j wole telle yow the tweyne egges
Dont est le glaive dit trenchans,	for whiche the swerd is cleped kervinge
Pour quoi I seul pas ne soulfist	Wher to oo paas alone sufficeth not to telle
Et quel enseignement i gist.	and what techinge lyth ther inne.

And it would seem that the same mechanical reaction accounts for his Gallicisms: as in his 'Eule come thou heere' for 'Mal

---

11. In this as in further quotations from the Pèlerinage de l'homme, I have used Sturzinger's careful text without the parentheses, brackets, and italics by which he marked intru- sions, variants, and emendations.

12. See Chapter IV, above, p. 78.

13. Examples from the passages quoted above:

venit in me :: in me is cunne
Non accipit vultum alicuius :: no mans
   chere he takis
Volat a vitiis :: ffro vices he flees.

See also Harvey's introduction to the edition, pp. xii-xiii.

i venis' (line 9122, quoted above), or in the following:

(ll. 2163;-65-67)   (I, 1v, p. 33)

Quar si cruel est . . .   For it is so cruelle . . .
Que s'il n'estoit   that if there were not
qui le tuast . . .   who to sle it . . .
. . . ne fineroit.   it wolde neuere stinte.

     This translator and Misyn were extreme literalists
far beyond any others I have seen. Apparently any translator working closely, whether from Latin or from French, was
likely now and then to slip into a foreign idiom or word-
order. But only in Misyn's Rolle and in the Pilgrimage has
this happened frequently enough to disrupt the form. In
the others, strict literalness cannot be called a procedure
at all, but an accident; and it is interesting mainly as in-
dicating an occasional relapse into an uncritical or mechanical reaction to the foreign materials.
     The nature of the reaction is best illustrated by
instances where literalness has affected the meaning, apparently unintentionally. The plainest -- and rarest -- examples are the inanities produced by uncritical adherence to a
faulty manuscript. Edward of York wrote:

(Prologue, p. 8)

if they ete well at soper at the leest they han
well defied her nature for they have ete but a
litel.

The French of Gaston de Foix should have been:

(Prologue, p. 8)

se au vespre ils soupent bien, au moins auront
ils au matin corrigié leur nature; quar ils
auront pou mangié.

Edward's manuscript evidently lacked au matin. Again:

(Cap. VI, p. 43)   (Cap. II, p. 11)

. . . elle voit mal. Elle   She (the hare) heþ euel
a grant povoir de courre.   syght and gret fere to
                             renne. [14]

_____

14. J. Lavallée, editor of the French text, notes (p. 43,
n. 1): 'Dans l'édition Verard on lit: paour de courre! Com-

When the same foreign form had two or more different usages and meanings, a translator would sometimes fall upon the wrong one, disregarding the form or the meaning required in English. In Chapter V of his Book of La Tour Landry, Caxton has brought over as a verbal a French infinitive form used strictly as a noun:

(P. 10)	(P. 22)
plus vault une briefve oraison . . . que unes grandes heures et longues et penser ailleurs.	more auayleth a short prayer . . . than a grete longe prayer and and <u>to thynke</u> on other thynges.

Then in Chapter VI he makes nouns out of infinitives used verbally (note, too, that he has mistaken the meaning here of temps):

(P. 14)	(P. 25)
et prendre en soy honeste vie <u>de boir</u> et de <u>mangier</u> es droictes heures, d'entour prime et tierce, <u>et de</u> souper a heure convenable selon le temps.	and to take on her honeste and sobrenes <u>of mete and drynke</u> in due tyme, as aboute the houre of tyerce, at myd day, <u>at souper</u>, at houre couvenable after the tyme.

The translator of the Life of St. Catharine of Siena was once too consistent with his Latin. In the first context below, his rendition of 'ut bene sit tibi' is passable, but a few lines later he used the same English for the same Latin in a different connotation:

(P. 868, F.)	(P. 37, 11. 10-11).
consolabatur, dicens: Eia, ut bene sit tibi, non turberis . . . '	he comforted theym . . . and sayde in Þe maner of that contree, 'A, brother, good day be to the.'

---

prend-on qu'il ait été possible d'éprimer que le lièvre a peur de courir. Cependant cette énorme faute se trouve aussi dans le manucrit de la Bibliothèque Mazarine.' Paul Mylo, who has missed the first example above, lists five others in Das Verhältnis der Handschriften des mittelenglischen Jagdbuches 'Maistre of Game,' Berlin, 1908, pp. 2-4.

(P. 869, A.)   (P. 37, 11. 20-21)

ipsam Lapam redarquabat . .   he blamed hys wyf . . .
dicens: Sine, carissima,   and he sayd, 'suffre, dere
ut bene sit tibi, sine   wyf, that good day be
eum Deus . . . '   to the; for our lord . . .

This translator also has fallen into the difficulty which
sometimes came when two English words were used for one Latin
in a passage otherwise literal:

(869, A.)   (37, 32-35)

tanta erat . . . modestia   [His] softnes in speche
in loquando quod   was so vertuous that
familia tota . . . nec   all his meyny . . . myght not
loqui, nec audire pot-   speke ne here noo
erat sermones indecentes   worde that were not
et inhonestos.   semely or dishoneste.

The translator considered 'not semely' as the equivalent of
'indecentes', but when the single word came to his mind for
'inhonestos' he forgot the new turn he had given his English.
A similar neglect to adjust the two words used for one appears
in the 1450 Imitation of Christ:

(III, lix, 54-5)   (III, lxiv, p. 150, 11.9-13)

Protege et conserve   Defende and kepe þe
animam servuli tui   soule of þy litel seruant
inter tot descrimina   amonge se many perels
vitae corruptibilis.   of þis corruptible lyf,
Ac comitante gratia tua   and, þy grace going wiþ,
dirige per viam   dyrecte hym by þe way of
pacis ad patriam   pes to þe cuntrey of
perpetuae pacis.   euerlasting clerness.

Here the only result is a slight ineptitude in form; but the
same translator fell into ambiguity when he forgot that unin-
flected English often cannot adopt Latin word-order:

(Lib. I, cap. 3, 11.29-30)   (I, iii, p. 5, 11. 3-6)

Taceant omnes doctores,   All maner doctoures
                               holde þei her pes,
sileant universae crea-   & all maner creatures
turae in conspectu tuo: kepe þei her silence
                               in þy siзt; speke
tu mihi loquere solus.   þou to me allone.

These over-literal turns appear occasionally in all
the translations, but, as I have said, they are rare in all
but two. Except possibly in the work of Misyn, most of them
were apparently due to a carelessness which was purely momentary, the Latinisms and the Gallicisms occurring for the same
cause as the inanities. The momentary nature of this carelessness is well illustrated in the Life of St. Mary of
Oignies, where the translator has let himself be misled by
Latin word-order in one sentence-member, then suddenly recovered himself in the next:

(P. 569 D.)	P. 178, 11. 20-22)
sed velut ante se scrib- erentur, dabat ei Domin- us in illa hora quid loqueretur: continuo clamore iubil- ans, nec in cogitando laborabat, nec in disponendo cantum interrumpebat.	but as þuf hadde be writ- en before hir, oure lorde gaf in to þat oure what sche shulde saye: ioiynge with contynuel crye, nor she in þenkynge labored, ne sturbled hir mynde in disposynge and settynge of hir wordes.

The usual procedure of the translators must not be thought
of as an uncritical, mechanical progress from one sentence-
member to the next, with attention only to the construction
in hand, not to the synthesis of the whole. The many quotations which I use from typical pages of their work show
plainly that their close adherence to their sources was nevertheless adaptive and critical.[15]

REVISED FORMS OF SUBORDINATION:

THE SLIGHTLY ALTERED TRANSLATIONS

In translations which are normally furthest from
either extreme, brief sequences done with a free treatment
occur perhaps more frequently than those done with strict

---

15. Of those just discussed, Edward of York is quoted in
Chap. I, above, pp. 22-3; Caxton in Chap. 1, pp. 10-15 and Chap.
VII, p. 149, n. 5; the St. Katherine in Chap. I, p. 26; Chap.
V, p. 110, Chap. VII, p. 159; the Imitation of Christ in Chap.
VII, p. 158; the St. Mary of Oignies in Chap. VII, p. 156.

literalness. One manner of altering the language, the substitution of coordinating for subordinating constructions,
has been discussed above. The second manner, more adaptive
to the form of the source, was the substitution of new or
different subordinating constructions. A plain though brief
example is in Edward of York's Master of Game:

(Prologue, p. 4)	(Prologue, p. 5)
Et au matin à l'aube il faut qu'il soit leve et qu'il aille en sa queste.	And erly in the dawning of the day he mvst be vp for to go to his quest.

The change in construction might be quite thorough, as in
the following sentence from the Revelations of St. Birgitta
(Garrett MS.; 1450):

(Lib. I, cap. 2; Vol. I, p. 6)	(Cap. I, p. 3, l. 7)
Decet enim sponsam cum sponso fatigari laboribus.	It is semely that the spouse labor wyth hyr spouse tyll she be werye.

Here only the thoughts correspond; the idea in laboribus has
been expressed with a verb, that in fatigari with a temporal
clause, the infinitive construction being dropped. Now and
then, as in Caxton's Book of La Tour Landry, even the correspondence of thought may become only general, and for a sentence or two translation changes to recension:

(Chap. X, p. 22)	(Chap. X, p. 34)
et à l'example de l'es- pervier sauvage, par curtoisie vous le ferez franc,	Take a sperhauke ramage and calle hym curtoysly and ye shal make hym come frely to yow;

But note that in his very next words, Caxton is back to his
normal procedure:

si que de l'arbre il vendra sur vostre poing, et si vous lui estiez en riens rudes ne cruelz, jamais ne vendroit.	Ye, fro the tre he shall come upon youre fiste. And yf ye be not curtoy- se but rude and cruel he shall never come.

Coming only rarely and in short sequences, any changes
of the sort just illustrated have a negligible effect upon the

form of the translated prose. In only seven of the thirty-
eight translations examined do they come frequently enough
to characterize the whole composition. These few must be
classified as a separate group; they are of a middle sort,
seldom radically altered but often not perfectly close.
     The translators in this group are often quite with-
out system in their adherence to sources. In one sequence
they alter widely the subordinating constructions of the
original, in the next reproduct them closely. Usually the
sequences affected are quite short ones of two or three
sentence-members; occasionally they extend for several sentences. The changes are large enough so that if constant
they would determine the whole structural character of the
prose. But since they are isolated and infrequent, a
basic correspondence between translation and source is seldom lost. In effect, then, the translator is responsible
for the logic and aptness of construction in a large number
of individual thought-relationships and for the style of a
few complete periods; but for most of his constructions and
for the general structural pattern of almost all of his composition he has followed the guidance of his source.
     Chapter CVI of the anonymous <u>Book</u> <u>of</u> <u>La</u> <u>Tour</u> <u>Landry</u>,
to be dated about 1450, begins with a passage which is typ-
ical of this treatment in translation from French. I have
underscored the minor changes with a broken line, the more
important ones with a solid line.

(Cap. CVI, pp. 206-07)	(P. 142, 11. 8-25)
Je vouldroie que vous	I shall tell you an
sceusiez l'exemple d'un	ensaumple of a knight that
chevalier qui se com-	faught <u>and</u> <u>dede</u> <u>bataile</u>
baty pour une pucelle.	for the <u>loue</u> <u>of</u> a faire
5 Il fust en la court	maide. Ther was <u>duellinge</u>,
d'un grant seigneur	in the contre of a great
un faulx chevalier	lorde a falce knight
qui pria de folle	that <u>required</u> <u>and</u> praied a
amour une pucelle;	fayre yonge mayde of loue
10	<u>for his</u> foule <u>delite</u>;
mais elle n'en voulst	and she wolde not consent
riens faire pour lui,	to his <u>desire</u> for no thinge
pour don ne pour pro-	of beheste, <u>or in</u> <u>any other</u>
messe, ains voulst	<u>wise,</u> <u>but that</u> <u>she</u> <u>kepte</u>
15 garder sa chair nette-	<u>her</u> <u>self</u> <u>in</u> <u>clennesse</u> <u>of</u>
ment.	<u>virginite.</u>
Et quant celui vit ce,	And <u>in despite hereof</u> the
si lui dist	knight thought in hym selff
que il luy nuyroit.	that he wolde do her dis-
20	worshipe and displeasaunce;

Si enpoisonna une
pomme et la luy bailla
pour donner au filz
de leans, qu'elle
25 portoit entre ses bras.
Dont elle la lui donna

et en mourut le filz.
Si dist le faulx
30 chevalier que la pu-
celle avoit eu salaire
des hoirs de l'enffant
pour le faire mourir

35 Sy fust la pucelle
mise en la chemise
pour estre getiée
au feu;
si plouroit et se
40 guermentoit a Dieu

comment elle n'y avoit
coulpe et que ce estoit
le faulx chevallier qui
45 la pomme lui avoit
baillié.

and by treson he enpoysoned
an aple, and gaue it vnto
this mayde to bere it vnto
this lordes sone.

And this yonge woman bare
it forthe vnto this childe,
by the whiche he was enpoisoned. And thanne this untrue
knight accused her, and
saide þat she hadde take and
receyued gret rewarde of the
lordes enemys to enpoison
his childe;
so that this yonge mayden
was dispoiled vnto her smock,
and ordeined forto [be]
brent in the fyre; and she
wepte and made gret lamentacion vnto God, besechinge
hym to be her comfort,
and she was not gylty,
and that it was the
false knight of whom she hadde resseiued the aple to
bere it vnto the childe.

The English writer has made little additions -- 'for the loue
of,' 'in despite herof,' 'and by treson,' etc., besides several doublets; he has expressed certain verbals more graph-
ically -- 'ther was dwellinge' for 'Il fust,' 'accused her
and said' for 'si dist,' etc. More important, he has three
times provided his own construction in place of the one found
in the French: once in 'but that she kepte her self' for 'ains
voulst garder' (line 14-15), again in 'by the whiche he was
enpoisoned' for 'et en mourut le filz' (line 28), and, in the
last clause, 'of whom she hadde ressieued the aple' for 'qui
la lui avoit baillie' (line 44-45); perhaps 'and . . . (was)
ordeined forto be brent,' for 'pour estra getiée au feu' (line
37-38) is a fourth change. An important insertion is the participial phrase 'besechynge hym to be her comfort' following
'made lamentacion vnto God' (line 39-41). (Note that when in
the succeeding dependent member he returns to his source (line
43), he inconsistently adopts its construction.) Nevertheless,
the division of all but minor members, the syntax of almost all
of the members, and hence the basic structure of every period
is determined by the original.

Thus:

>'chevalier <u>qui</u> se combaty <u>pour</u>'
>'knyght <u>that</u> faught . . . <u>for</u>'

>'<u>Il</u> <u>fust</u> <u>en</u> . . . <u>d</u>'. . . chevalier <u>qui</u> <u>pria</u>'
>'<u>Ther</u> <u>was</u> . . . <u>in</u> . . . <u>of</u> . . . a knight <u>that</u> requir<u>ed</u>'

>'<u>Voulst</u> . . . fa<u>ire</u>'
>'<u>wolde</u> . . . <u>consent</u>'

>'<u>dist</u> <u>que</u> . . . nuy<u>eroit</u>'
>'<u>thought</u> . . . <u>that</u> . . . <u>wold</u> <u>do</u> disworshipe' etc.

Note, for instance, that the second time the idea of <u>mourir</u>
is expressed by <u>enpoison</u> (line 34), the French infinitive
construction is kept:

>'pour faire mourir'
>'<u>to</u> enpoison'

Similarly, in the last substantive clause (line 43), though
one construction has been changed, the basis is still the
French 'ce estoit . . . qui' ('it was . . . of whom').
        The translator has continued in this way through most
of the chapter. Then in the second and third periods from the
end of the chapter he has radically reconstructed his source;
while in the last period he has returned and followed it very
closely:

(Chap. CVI, p. 207-08)	(Chap. CVI, p. 143, 11.15-36)
. . . laquelle garda la chemise toute sa vie et prioit chascum jour pour le chevalier qui telle 5 douleur avoit soufferte pour elle. Et ainsi pour pitié et franchise se combat-ist le gentil chevalier, 10 qui en eut v. plaies mortels,	And she resceived it, and kepte hit all her lyue, and praied for hym contyn-uelly, for the gret good-nesse and kindenesse that he shewed vnto her, to suffre deth for her deliuer-ance, and for to respite her dethe and aquite her of all shame and all falce accusacion of treson, and ouercome her ennemie, and made her free for euermore.
15 tout aussi comme fist le doulx Jhesucrist qui se combatit pour la pitié que il avoit de nous	Right so oure lorde Ihesu Crist faught for us for the gret compassion and pitie that he hadde

et de l'umain lignage,
20 qu'il lui faisoit
pitié de le veoir ès
tenebrés d'enffer
et pour ce en souffrist
la bataille moult
25 cruelle et moult penible
ou fust de l'arbre de
la sainte croix; et fust
percée sa chemise en .v.
lieux, ce furent ses .v.
30 douleuses plaies
qu'll receust

35
de son debonnaire plaisir
et franc cueur
pour la pitié
que nous lui faisons.
40 Et
aussi doit tout homme et
femme avoir pitié des
douleurs et des miseres
de ses parens, de ses
45 voysins et des
povres,
tout aussi comme eust
le bon chevalier de la
pucelle,
50 et en pleurer tendrement,
comme firent les bonnes
dames qui plorerent apres
le doulx Jhesucrist
quant il portoit la croix
55 pour y estre crucifié
et mis à mort pour nos
pechiez.

upon all humaigne lynage,
whanne he deliuered us
from the derkenesse of hell
and dampnacion perpetuel,
where as faught for us
by vertu of his glorious
passion, whanne he suffred
for us his .v. woundes
vpon the crosse, and bought
us with his precious blode,
and receiued dethe for
oure redempcion and deliuer-
ance, and fraunchised us
of all thraldome, and
restored us ayen vnto his
ioye and blisse euermore
lastinge; and through hys
mercy, debonairet[e], and
vertu, and for loue and
pitee that he hadde
vnto all his creatoures.
And in this ensaumple
eueri man and woman
aught to haue pitie
and sorw of the disese
of thaire frendes
neighbores, and vpon the
poure creatoures of God,
Right so as the
knight had pite upon the
mayde,
– and to wepe pitously,
as wepte the good
ladyes after oure
lorde Ihesu Crist,
whanne he bare the crosse
to be crucified
and suffre dethe for oure
synnes.

The first two thirds of the English above is practically a recension, the composition and much of the material being original. In the last sentence only the reduction of 'firent les
dames qui plorerent' to 'wepte the ladyes,' and the slight
change from 'estre mis à mort' to 'and (to) suffre dethe' are
the Englishman's own work. (Note the anocoluthon at the end
of the first sentence (lines 7-9): 'suffre dethe . . . for to
respite her . . . and made her . . . '; and the uncontrolled
structure of the second sentence (lines 15-39), first in sub-

dependence, then in parataxis, ending with the improper coordination 'and through.') The book as a whole, though it
varies in this way, is mainly characterized by the kind of
translation found in the first of the two passages quoted,
where the basic structure of the English was taken from the
French.

 An example of the same sort but with a Latin source
is the Life of St. Catherine of Siena, of before 1460. The
quotation from this book, given in Chapter I, above,[16]
represents the average procedure of the translator. But he
is erratic. His opening 250 words were translated with only
two important changes in structure:

(Pars I, cap. i, p. 868, E, et seq.)	(Chap. I, p. 36)
Fuit vir unus in civi- tate Senensi regionis Tusciae, nomine Jacobus, cujus pater vocatus est more illius patriae vulgariter Benecasa: et erat vir ille simplex et absque dolo et fraude,	In the cite of Siene in Italye and of the province of Tuskane ther was a man, his name was James or Jacob, and his fader was callyd in the comyn speche of þe contree Benecasa. This James was symple vertuous, wythout fraude or deceyte to onyman,
ac timens Deum, recen- dnsque a malo. Hic orbatus parentibus, uxorem accepit de civitate sua, nomine Lapam, feminam siquidem omnino alienam a quacumque malitia hominum modenorum quamvis in factis domesticis et familiae satis solertem,	dredynge god and fleyng alle euyll. After the deth of his fader and moder he toke a wyf of the same cyte her name was Lapa: she was a woman wythout euche malyce that is vsed amounge men that ben now in our tyme, all-be-it that she was full besy aboute that longeth to houshold and about menye and seruantes,
prout manifestum est omnibus noscentibus eam cum adhuc vivat in corpore. Hi sic mat- rimonialiter conjuncti,	as it was knowen openly to all that knewe her whyle she lived here in erthe. Whan they bothe were ioyned to-gyder in matrymonye
et in simplicitate unite, quamvis plebeii, rebus tamen temporalibus juxta conditionem propriam	and lyued vertuously in symplycite, suffycient habondaunce they hadde of temperall godes,

16. P. 26.

abundebat, et de satis laudabili popularium genere orti sunt Benedixitque dominus Lapam, et foccunditate ipsam adimplens, tamquam abundatem vitam constituit in lateribus domus Jacobi .viri sui: nam quasi omni anno filium aut filiam pariebat, et saepe gemillos aut gemillas concipit et peperit Jacobo supradicto.	and they [were] bothe of gentyll and commendable byrthe. Our reverend lorde blessyd lapa graciously and fulfilled her plentuously, as an habonduunt vyne in the hous of Jacob, whiche was her husbond: Ffor eche yere almost she conceyued and bare a sone or a doughter, and oftsythes .ij. sones or two doughters.

In the next sentence he suddenly began both to epitomize and to add. But after only thirty-five words he returned to his source:

(Ibid.)

Cujus quidem Jacobi singulares laudes non arbitror fustum omittere, exquo, ut pie creditur, jam ad portum pervenit felicitas aeternae. Refert etenim mihi praefata Lapa, quod tanta fuit aequanimitatis, et ita moderatus in verbo, quod quacumque occasione data turbationis seu tribulationis, numquam verborum excessus procedebat ex ore ejus: imo quando ceteros de familia sua amaricatos videbat et amara verba proferre, mox consolabatur quemlibet hilari vultu, dicens: Eia, ut bene sit tibi non turberis, non loquaris talia, quae non decent nos loqui.	After tyme this Jacob was passed out of this worlde, Lapa, hys wyf, as for a syngular laude and commendacion rehersyd and saide to Mayster Raymonde, the confessour of this holy mayde and vyrgyn and glorious martyr Katheryn, that he was euer of soo lyke dysposycion and soo moderate in worde, that what occasion euer came of trouble or trybulacion, he exceded neuer in speche by hasty ne angrye worde, but whan he saw ony of his myny greued or herd hem speke anterly or bytter wordes, anon he comforted eche of theym with a glad chere, and sayde in þe maner of that contree: 'A, brother, good day be to the, be not troubled, speke not suche wordes which falleth ne semeth not us to speke.

in the indirect discourse which follows 'saide . . . that,'
he has re-stated and altered the construction of two members:
'exceded neuer in speche' for 'numquam verborum excessus procedebat ex ore ejus,' and 'saw greued or herd speke' for
'amaricatos videbat et amara verba proferre.' But even in
these members, as in the others, the structure of the period
after that remains based on the Latin.

In the most altered sequence of any length I have seen
in the St. Catherine there is only one sentence (line 10, below)
where the translator has not followed the Latin division of
sentence-members for all the principal meanings. In three
others (lines 19, 30, 37) the structure has been affected by
the alteration or omission of several separate constructions,
but is still at least roughly similar to the Latin, for each
of the alterations is usually surrounded by parts of which the
construction has been transferred from the source:

(Pars II, Cap. ix, p. 917, (et seq.)	(Part II, Cap. vij, p. 283, 11.6-21)
Erat tunc temporis, scilicet anno Domini MCCCLXX, in civitate Senensi, cives quidam	There was a man dwellyng
5 vocatus Andreas Naddini, divis quidem transitoriis et extrinsecis rebus, sed bonis permantibus et intrinsecis ex toto	in the cyte of Sene, the whiche was called Andrewe, a full ryche man of oute-wardly thynges of the world, but full poure off inwardly heuenly thynges;
10 privatus; nullo Dei tim-ore vel amore fulcitus, omnium quasi detinabatur vinculo peccatorum ac vetiorum: ludo etiam	he was a vicious man for he neyther dred ne loued god,
15 taxilliorum totaliter deditus, Dei et sanct-orum erat blasphemus assiduus, et detestabilis nimium. Hic anno jam dicto,	but an hasarder and a cursed blasphemer of god and his seyntes. Wythin a while afterward
20 qui aetatis suae quadra-gesimus erat, mensi Decem-bri, gravi corporis morbo arreptus, in lectum deceiet; et deficiente	that man was take wyth a syknes and lay done in his bedde soo syke that
25 medicorum auxilio, ad utriusque hominis mortem, juxta cor suum impoenitens, propinquabat. Hoc sentiens proprius	euery man and leche sayde he was (nye) deed. That perceyued his

30 ejus Sacerdos, accessit
eum, monuitque ipsum,
ut ante vitae corporiae
terminum,
poenitentiam ageret de
35 comissis, et domui
suae disponeret juxta
mortem [_var_. morem?].
At ille, qui nec eccles-
iarum visitatur, nec
40 sacerdotum fuerat ullo
tempore vitae suae
devotus, et monitum et
monita ex toto contempsit.
Quod uxor ejus et
45 consanguenci attendentes,
zelo salutis ejus moti
plures utriusque sexus
religionas personas et
Deo devotas accersierunt,
50 ut obstinatum ejus animum
immutarent.
Sed ille nec minis
aeternorum incendiorum,
nec blanditiis divinae
55 misericordiae, ad con-
fitendum peccata sua
potuit quomodolibet
flecti per quemcumque
monentum.

curate _and_ come to
hym, _for_ _to_ comforte
hym that

he sholde shryue and
take penaunce and make
his testament, as the
maner was in the contre.
Whan he hadde herdde how
the preeste counseylled
hym,

he dispysed bothe hym
and his counseyll.
His wyf considered that:
hauynge ȝele and loue
to his soule, she went
after all-maner relygyous
folke, both men and wymmen,
for _to_stere_hym_to God.

But yet for all her coun-
seyll they myght not bowe
hym to confession and
contrycion of his synnes,
neyther with thretinge
of endeles peynes ne wyth
rewardes of endeles ioyes.

Most of the differences come from the re-statement of Latin
circumlocutions. In many parts the texts are quite close.
Note, among the correspondences, the paralleled antithesis
(lines 6-9) and the careful repetition of 'wyth' for the
paralleled Latin ablatives (lines 56-58). On the other hand,
among the changes, the translator's own construction 'but an
hasarder' is consistent neither with his preceding addition
of 'he was a vicious man' nor with his alteration of 'timore
. . . fulcitus' to 'for he . . . dred' (lines 10-14).

The seven translations in this group, in short, are
to be called free only in a relative sense. More often than
those in the large group called close, they contain constructions which were chosen and phrased without the influence of
the source; and perhaps the main interest in them as exceptions, as will be seen in the following chapter, is that they
offer the opportunity to isolate certain manners of phrasing
as the translators' own responsibility. But the translators
seldom proceed far without guidance. The important elements
in their structural pattern are seldom more independent of the
sources than those in a typical close translation.

Beside the Book of La Tour Landry and the St. Katherine, other fifteenth century translations to be classified as slightly altered are three from Latin: The Mirrour of the Life of Christ by Nicholas Love, the Life of St. Gilbert by Capgrave, the Mappula Anglie by Osbern Bokenham, from Higden's Polychronicon; and two from French; the anonymous Ponthus and Sidoine and, as nearly as an available text will indicate, The Buke of Battailes by Gilbert of the Haye.[17]

THE TYPICAL CLOSE TRANSLATION

The great majority of the thirty-eight translations observed are characterized by a minimum of alterations. There are a few exceptions in all; and in many there are omissions. But the strongly prevailing procedure in these was to match the grammatical construction of every sentence-member taken from the source with a native English equivalent. The process may be finally illustrated with typical translations of Latin and French source. The first is from the anonymous Letter Touchynge þe lyfe of Seint Katheryn of Senys, in a manuscript which was written about 1430.[18] I have separated approximately the sentence members, and have underscored with a solid line all the connectives and other words which determine the construction of the member, and with a broken line the two slight differences:

(P. 969, F, et seq.)

Litteras vestras affectuose recepi et attente perlegi

(P. 184–185.)

I haue receiued affectuously 3oure lettris and haue redde hem bisily

---

17. Appendix A: For Love see under Bonaventura; for Capgrave under Saints' Lives; for Bokenham under Higden; for the Ponthus under La Tour Landry; and for Haye under Bonet. The books by Love and by Capgrave, as explained at the first of this chapter, contain portions which are recension. Only about the first two-thirds of the Ponthus belongs in this group; the middle third is very little altered; and the last third is quite close. All of these translations date between 1440 and 1460, except Love's, which is of about 1410.

18. Appendix A: 'Saints' Lives.'

perquas me valde re-
quiritis atque rogatis,

by þe whiche ȝee gretely
require and pray me

ut veridiciam informa-
tionem vestrae caritati
dirigere debeam, etiam
in publica forma,

þat I shulde sende to
ȝoure charite in open
forme trewe informa-
cion

de gestis, moribus, vir-
tutibus atque doctrinis
famosae sanctitatis
Virginis B. Catharinae
de Senis,

of þe dedys, maners, ver-
tues, and doctrines of
famos holynesse of þe
virgin blessyd Kateryn
of Senys,

cujus conversationem ali-
quando merui dum ageret
in humanis,

whos conuersacyone sum-
tyme I deserued while
she lyued,

ut asseritis;

as ȝee sey;

et praesertim occasione
cujusdam querlae

and namely for occas-
yone of a quarelle

factae Venetiis in Epis-
copali palatio

made at Venese in þe
byshopes palys

circa celebrationem festi
sive commemoratione ejus-
dem Virginis:

anens þe hallowynge of
þe feste or commemor-
acyone of þe same Virgin;

quia multi credere nolunt

for many wole not leue

veras esse virtutes

atte þe virtues be trewe

quae de ipsa veridice
praedicuntur.

þat are trewly seyde of
hir.

Verum ut aperte fatear,

Atte I sey openly þe soþ,

facies ipsius Virginis

þe visage of þe same vir-
gyn,

cum omni genere suo

wiþ alle hir kynne,

mihi et omni generi meo
penitus ignota fuit,

was þurghly vnknowen to
me and alle myn,

licet in eadem civitate
Senarum oriundi fulrimus,

þof we were borne in þe
same cite of Senys,

usque ad annum Dom. MCCCLXXVI vel circa.	vnto þe ȝeere of oure lorde a þousand three hundred seventy and sex or þere-aboute.
Nec etiam illo tempore	Nor also þat tyme I,
velut immersus in flucti- bus vitae praesentis,	as drowned in þe floter- ynges of þis lyfe,
ejus notitiam habere ex- optabam:	desyred to haue know- leche of hir;
nisi quod aeterna bonitas,	but þe godnes of god,
quae neminem vult perire,	þat wole no man perysshe
per hanc Virginem animam meam de faucibus inferni liberare disposuit	disposyd to delyuer my soule fro þe pitte of helle þurgh þis virgyne.

Unless it be 'nor . . . I . . . desyred . . . but þe . . .' for
'Nec optabam . . . nisi quod . . .' there is no real alteration
here whatever. For the change of the Latin substantive infinitive phrase, 'veras esse virtutis,' to a substantive clause,
'atte þe vertues be trewe,' does not affect either the meaning
of the statement or the relationship of the construction to the
surrounding sentence-members. The only other differences are in
the word-order, which is completely Anglicized. The correspondence in structure is never broken throughout.

Earl Rivers' translation of the Cordiale, made in 1478,
represents typical treatment of a French source. In this case
the French itself was a close translation from Latin.[19]   I
have indicated correspondences and differences as before:

(Chapt. I, fol. 6, r - 7, r)	(Chapt. I, fol. 4, r - 5, r)
Eclesiaste dist en son septieme chapitre les parolles qui sen suivent:	Ecclesiasticus saith in his seuenth chapiter these wordes folowyng:
Ayes memoire de tes der- nieres choses	Bere wel in thy mynde the last thingis,
et tu ne pecheras jamais.	and thou shalt neuer fal in synne.

---

19.   Chapter III, above, p. 66..

Saint augustin dist aussi
ou liure de ses meditations

Seynt Austin saith in his
book of meditacions,

que plus fort fait a es-
cheuer seulement la sou-
illure de pechie

That man ought rather
haue in fere and eschewe
thabhominacion & filthe_
of synne.

que quelconques craultez
de tourmens Infernaulx.

than any other crueltees
of thinfernal turmentis.

Comme doncques la cong-
noissance des quatre
derrenieres choses

Lo thene how the knowlege
of these four last thingis

et la_frequente memoire
dicelles

and frequentyng the memo-
rye and remembraunce of
them

nous rapelle des pechiez

calleth us from synne

noux acoulpe aux vertus

and draweth us to vertues

et nous conferme en
toutes bonnes oeuvres.

and conformeth us to alle
good werkis.

Pour tant par inspiracion
diuine

Wherfor by the helpe of_
the deuyne insperacion

Jay propose de dire et ra-
conter ung pou de ces
quatre derrenieres choses.

I haue purposed to re-
herse and say a lytyl
of these four thingis.

Cest assauoir quelles et
quantes elles sont,

As which they_be and
what they be

et aussi aucunement de
clairer vne chascune di-
celles singulierement a
par soy,

And also to declare som-
what of euery of hem sin-
gulerly by them self,

Especialement et preci-
eusement tant par les
dictz et auctoritez des
sains

precyously and dignely
by seynges and auctor-
itees of seyntis

comme par exemple et par
clers evidens.

and generally by exam-
ples and seynges of_auc-
torised clerkis.

Il est Icy a noter

It is to be noted

que selon les sains | that after the syeng of_
seyntis

on compte communement | men seye comynly

quil sont quatre derrenieres choses, | ther be foure the last thingis.

comme | And whiche_they be_

il appert clerement par les parolles de saint Bernard ou Il dist ainsi: | it appereth clerly by the wordes of seynt Bernard in_a_sermon Where he seyth

En toutes tes oeuures ayes souuenance de ces derrenieres choses | in_al thi werkes haue remembraunce of thy last thingis

qui sont quatre | Whiche be four

Cest assauoir La mort Le jugement La gehine denfer et la gloire de paradis | That is to wete first Deth bodely Seconde. The day of_ Jugement Thirde The peynes of helle Fourth_the glorie of heuen

Qui est la chose plus horrible que la mort | O what thinge is more horrible than deth

Qui est la chose plus horrible que le Jugement | What thyng is more dredeful and terrible than the day of Jugement

Qui est la chose plus Importable a souffrir que la gehine denfer | What thing is more importable to be suffred than the gehenne and peynes of helle

Et qui est la chose plus Joyeuse que nest la gloire celestienne | And what is a more Joyefull_blysse than celestial glorie.

Ce dist saint bernard ou sermon dessusdit: | Seint Bernard seyde in the same_sermone

Ce sont cy les quatre roes du chariot de_lame | These ben the four wheles of the chare

qui la portent a leternelle gloire de paradis: | Wherof the remembraunce_ bryngeth mannes_soule_ to the euerlastyng glorie of paradys

Et <u>sont</u> cy les quatre esmouuemens resue<u>illans</u> lesperit de lomme,	These <u>ben</u> also foure moeuynges <u>that</u> <u>awake</u> the spirit of man
affin <u>que</u> toutes choses mondaines mesp<u>risees</u>	to <u>that</u> <u>ende</u> <u>that</u> he disp<u>rayse</u> all worldly thinges
Il sen re<u>tourne</u> a son createur.	<u>and</u> retorne unto his creatour <u>and</u> <u>maker</u>.
Il <u>est</u> <u>doncques</u> conuenient et prouffitable	Lo <u>it</u> <u>is</u> <u>then</u> both convenient and prouffitable
<u>quon</u> <u>les</u> <u>ait</u> <u>tousiours</u> en <u>continuelle</u> ramembraunce.	that <u>they</u> <u>be</u> <u>had</u> <u>contynuelly</u> in remembrance.

Rivers was more wordy than his source required, and this accounts for most of the differences marked -- 'fal in synne,' 'haue in fere and eschewe,' 'frequentyng the memory and remembraunce bryngeth mannes soule' for 'qui . . . portent (lame),' etc. Aside from what was probably a mistake, the 'by . . . seynges of auctorised clerkes' for 'par clers evidens,' there are only three alterations: 'by . . . and by' for 'tant par . . . comme par,' 'and whiche they be' for 'comme,' and, more important, 'he desprayse all . . . and retorne' for 'toutes . . . mesprisees il sen retorne.' The 'folowynge' for 'qui sen suivent' and the 'that awake' for 'resuellans,' like the similar equivalent in the translation from Latin just quoted, do not affect the structural position of these sentence-members in the whole sequence. The correspondence of member for member moves just as closely in this passage as in the previous one:

    principal clause :: principal clause

    prepositional phrase :: prepositional phrase

    dependent clause :: dependent clause

    imperative clause :: imperative clause . . . <u>Etc</u>.

    Counting only translations made in the fifteenth century, of the twenty-five with Latin source which I have examined, seventeen have been made according to the procedure illustrated above; and similarly nine of the thirteen with French source. They are as follows:[20]

___

20. When it is other than the title, I have given in parentheses the heading used in my list of translations, Appendix A.

From Latin:

The Goverance of Lordships, anonymous, c. 1400.
(Aristotle).

The Three Kings of Cologne, anonymous, c. 1400.
(Johannes).

Gesta Romanorum in MS. Harley 7333, anonymous, c. 1430.

A Letter Touching St. Catherine of Siena, anonymous,
c. 1430. (Saints' Lives).

The Life of St. Christina, anonymous, c. 1430.
(Saints' Lives).

The Life of St. Elizabeth of Spalbeck, anonymous,
c. 1430. (Saints' Lives).

The Life of St. Mary of Oignies, anonymous, c. 1430.
(Saints' Lives).

The Life of St. Jerome, anonymous, c. 1440. (Saints'
Lives).

The Revelations of St. Birgitta in the Lambeth MS.,
anonymous, c. 1450. (Birgitta).

The Revelations of St. Birgitta in the Garrett MS.,
anonymous, c. 1450.

The Imitation of Christ, anonymous, c. 1450. (Thomas.
à Kempis)

The Polychronicon, anonymous, c. 1450. (Higden).

Disciplina Clericalis, anonymous, c. 1460. (Petrus).

The Mending of Life, anonymous, c. 1460. (Rolle).

The Revelations of St. Birgitta in the Garrett MS.,
anonymous, c. 1470.

Solomon and Marcolphus, anonymous, printed 1492.

The Seven Wise Masters of Rome, anonymous, printed
1493. (Rome).

From French:

> The Master of Game, by Edward of York, c. 1410.
> (Gaston III, Phoebus).
>
> Merlin, anonymous, c. 1450.
>
> Cordiale, by Earl Rivers, 1478.
>
> Godefroy of Boulogne, by Caxton, 1481. (Heraclius).
>
> The Mirrour of the World, by Caxton, 1481. (Vincentius).
>
> The Book of La Tour Landry, by Caxton, 1484. (La Tour
> Landry).
>
> Curial, by Caxton, 1484. (Chartier).
>
> The Four Sons of Aymon, by Caxton, 1489. (Aymon).
>
> Melusine, anonymous, c. 1500. (John of Arras).

The thirty-eight translations altogether examined were chosen largely on the basis of ready availability of texts.[21] Since such a basis makes the selection fairly random, it is likely that the proportion here found between close and altered translations, about three to one, is representative of fifteenth century practice. The thirty-eight translations are probably the work of thirty-three different translators. In the absence of any critical standard an English writer was free to treat his sources as he liked. It is therefore not surprising that so few of them — only two — tried to translate with an unnatural literalness. But it is surprising that equally few chose to recast thoroughly the structural form of their sources; especially when these two, both early in the century and both working with narrative, always merely simplified the constructions. All the twenty-nine others, or seven-eighths of the translators, preferred to follow the basic structure of almost every sentence they translated; and three-fourths of the twenty-nine followed in almost every detail, altering their sources only enough to Anglicize their language. The importance of the translators' preference lies in the effects of such a procedure upon the prose thus composed.

---

21. They include, I believe, all for which there are modern editions of both translation and source.

Chapter Six

THE EFFECTS OF CLOSE TRANSLATION:

I -- CONSISTENT CONSTRUCTION

In Chapter One, using a few examples from throughout the fifteenth century, I have described in some detail the effects of close translation upon the structural form of prose thus composed. But since in Chapter Two the analysis of original prose was made with the sentence member taken as the unit of composition, a rapid generalization of the effects may here be made in the same terms.

When all of the sentence-members of the source were retained and all were translated into equivalent constructions, the parts of the English sentence were fitted together with the same correctness, that is, the grammatical or logical consistency between constructions, which had appeared in the source. Another result, equally obvious, was that the small units and the sentences were combined into whatever larger patterns or periods the original writer happened to have composed in. Precisely this is what happened in a very high proportion of fifteenth century prose works. For the translators' activities were of wide extent; and their typical procedure was to translate closely.

Naturally there were exceptions, not only among translators but in the work of any one translator. Aside from extreme cases, these exceptions are without much importance in regard to the broader combinations of structural units. The translators of the _Life_ _of_ _St._ _Catherine_, of the _Ponthus_ or of _La_ _Tour_ _Landry_, for instance, frequently made small alterations but seldom greatly modified the typical form, of their originals. In regard to the more specific matter of consistent constructions, however, the exceptions are interesting. When examined in detail, they may give some important indications of the translators' habits of composition and of the effect their work had upon those habits.

It must not be inferred from the accumulated number of examples to be used in the following discussion that the translated prose was highly 'incorrect' syntactically. The great bulk of it was accurately written in this respect, whether the translation was close or altered. But, once more, there were exceptions.

It is difficult to say whether the inconsistencies
of construction which appeared were due to the same cause
as that found in original prose, the habit of composing by
short units, the clause or the phrase; or whether they resulted only from a certain tendency of the translator to
relapse into mechanical and uncritical use of the source.
The authors of the sources, Latin or French, were themselves a negligible cause. Accepting the textual criticism
of the various modern editors, I have seen only one case of
anacoluthon and only two of asymmetrical coordination which
must be attributed to the original writer. Only two texts
are involved, and both writers, Gaston III and Geoffrey
de la Tour Landry, were fourteenth century French. Edward
of York, translator of Gaston III, and Caxton in his La
Tour Landry both uncritically transferred the constructions
into English. But it is interesting that the anonymous
translator of the earlier English La Tour Landry, a writer
unusually frequent with inconsistent constructions, revised
the French to make it consistent[1].

Mechanical adherence to some inanity in a corrupted
source has been observed in studying the procedure of the
translators; as, for instance, when that great hunter,
Edward of York, allowed himself to write that hares are
afraid to run[2]. There are examples of inconsistent construction which almost certainly were due to an unthinking
reaction to whatever in the source met the translator's eye.

The following asymmetrical coordination appears in
the mid-fifteenth century translation of the Polychronicon:

(Vol. III, pp. 399-401)

Alexander beenge of xij yere in age, ioyed to be
conversante amonge hostes and armes, usenge to
ride and exercisede the actes of chevallry.

The Latin of Higden should correctly have read:

(Vol. III, p. 400)

Alexander jam factus annorum duodecim, inter exer-
citus et arma versari gaudebat, equis insiliens
ut miles se exercebat.

---

1. Asymmetrical coordinations: Livre de la Chasse, XV, p.
81 :: Master of Game, XII, p. 42; Livre, XXXVI, p. 147 ::
Master, XXXII, p. 92. Anacoluthon: La Tour Landry, I, p. 5
:: Caxton's translation, I, p. 6; the correction in the
translation of 1450, I, p. 4, 11.23-4.
2. Chapter V, above, p. 101.

It is practically certain that the Englishman saw 'equis insiliens et miles se exercebat,' and so proceeded to translate literally.
        The following huge sentence from Caxton's transla-
tion of the Faits of Christine de Pisan goes very well until
its impossible ending:

        (Fayttes, p. 7, ll. 2-15)

        And by cause that this is thyng not accustomed &
        out of vsage to wymen, whych comynly do not entre-
        mete but to spynne on the distaff & occupie
        theim in thynges of houshold, I supplye humbly
        to the said right hie offyce and noble state of
        chyualrye that in contemplacion of theyr lady
        mynerue born of the contree of grece, whome the
        auncyents for hir grete connyng reputeden a god-
        desse, the whiche fonde, lyke as olde wrytyngis
        sayen and as I haue other tymes sayd And also
        the poete boece recyteth in his boke of clere &
        noble wimmen and semblably recyten many other,
        the art & manere to make harnoys of yron & steel,
        whiche wyl not haue ne take it for none euyl yf
        I a woman charge my self to treat of so lyke a
        matere . . .

The French constructions need only be summarized:

        Et pource que cest chose non accustumee . . . Ie
        supplie . . . audit . . . office . . . que en
        contemplacion de . . . minerue . . . laquelle
        troua, selon que dient les anciens . . . sy comme
        . . . ay dit et que . . . le recite . . . bocace
        . . . et semblablement le recitent autres, . . .
        lart . . . de faire le harnois, . . . quilz ne
        veuillent avoir a mal se moy femme . . . etc.

Caxton, hurrying along through the complex sentence of
Christine, read the two words quilz, combined in elision,
as the single pronoun quels, and mechanically put it down
in his English as whiche. Of course the logic of constructions could have been troubling him little as he
worked on this passage -- he has also neglected to insert
a connective in the preceding series ('et que . . . le
recite . . . bocace' :: 'and also the poet boece recytheth').
Yet it is possible that the quilz of the Royal MS. actually was written quels or lesquels in the MS. which Caxton
used; and the que of the series above may have been omitted.
Caxton similarly mistook the combination quilz for a rela-

tive pronoun in his Book of La Tour Landry; and here the
earlier translator appears to have done the same. Caxton
wrote:

> (Chap. V, p. 23)
>
> Thenne ye shall fynde in many places and especially
> in the legende . . . of holy wymmen which made her
> beddes . . . hard . . . and laye thereon for to
> slepe the lasse . . . for to wepe ofte and many
> tymes to wake for to entre in to prayers and in the
> seruyce of god, wherin they held hem day and nyght.

And the earlier English translator:

> (Chap. V, p. 7, 1. 31-p. 8, 1. 1)
>
> As ye may see in holy legendis of . . . holy women
> that made her beddes . . . etc.

The French was:

> (Chap. V, p. 8)
>
> dont vous trouverez en plusieurs . . . legendes . . .
> des saintes dames . . . qu'ilz faisoient leurs litz
> . . . etc.

Faulty coordinations probably due to a mis-read or
mis-written source may be illustrated from The Pilgrimage of
Man and from the 1450 Book of La Tour-Landry:

(Pél. de l'homme, 11. 5081-6.)	(Pilg. Man, II, ii, p. 77)
Or sui je, disoie je, homs	Now j am a man quod j
Qui semble estre I champions	that seemeth a champion
Qui en moi ne sai nul mehaing	For mayme wot j noon in me
Ains sui de touz mes membres sain,	but am hool of alle lymes
Qui pour porter sui assez fais	and that am maad ynough
et ceste meschine et son fais.	to bere both this wenche and hire berdene.

The English writer has considered semble as third person,
and has read que (for) for qui, which so far made good sense;

but in the last relative clause, which he plainly coordinates with the first, he has read Qui correctly and translated literally, with the result that in the English no two
members of the original French series of three are in the
same construction, and the last one is inconsistent with
any of those preceding. In the case from the La Tour
Landry it was probably a matter of omission from the MS. of
the source:

(Livre de La T. L., V, p. 11)	(Book, 1450, V, p. 8, ll. 7-12)
et pour ce, belles filles, dictes vos heures de bon cuer et devotement sans penser ailleurs,	And therfor, good dough-tres, saithe your matenis and praiers withoute thinking saue only of God, deuoutly and with good hert; and that ye saie hem fasting;
et gardes que vous ne desjeunes jusques a ce que vous ayes dictes vos heures de bon cuer; car cuer saoul ne sera ja humble ne devote. Apres gardez que vous oyez toutes les messes que vous pourrez ouir, car grant bien de Dieu vous avenra . . .	for a full stomake may not be holy & perfit-ely humble and deuoute. And after, herithe all the masses that ye may, for gret profit and good ye shull haue . . .

Here the English is much altered, most of all perhaps in
the offending clause; but with the abruptness of the construction in the second imperative meaning and the correctness of it in the third, it is likely that gardes had
dropped out of the French copy.

The omission of one word from the source may make
the translator's expression thoroughly anacoluthic. A very
plain instance occurs in Chapter I of the English 'Froissart.' Berners wrote:

(P. 18)

Trouth it is, that I who have entreprised this boke
to ordeyne for pleasure and pastaunce, to the whiche
alwayes I have been inclyned, and for that intent, I
have folowed and frequented the company of dyverse
noble and great lordes, as well in Fraunce . . . as
in diverse other countries, and have had knowledge
by them, and . . .

Froissart had written:

> (2me rédaction, p. 5)
>
> Voirs est que je qui ay empris ce livre à ordonner,
> ay par plaisance qui tousdis à ce m'a encliné,
> fréquenté pluseurs nobles and grans seigneurs, tant
> en France comme . . . en autres pays, et ay eu la
> congnoissance d'eulx; si . . .

Having missed the second ay, Berners began to lose himself
and he knew it; but instead of revising he has tried to
catch up again by inserting 'for that intent.' It is likely that a quite similar difficulty will explain the following anacoluthon in Capgrave's St. Gilbert:

(P. viii*, right, top)	(P. 87, ll. 26-32)
processu ergo temporis, volente Domino dilatare semen, quod ipse semin-averat in illis primis hujus vitae parentibus: multi divites et nobiles Angliae, comites et barones, videntes et approbantes opus quod inchoavit Dom-inus, et quae sequeren-tur bona praevidentęs, fundos et praedia, possessionesque plurimas sancto patri optulerunt.	Thus be processe of tyme, be þe wil of our Lord God, þe seed which he had sowen be þe first faderes of þis weye, many rich men, noblemen of Ynglond, þat is to seye, Erles, Barones, and oþir, seyng and approuyng þis wirk wheech God had be-gunne, and seyng be-for what goodnesse was dispos-ed aftir, offred many possessiones to our fader Gilbert.

Capgrave has left þe seed without any verbal to complete it;
yet every construction he has used can be accounted for if
we assume that he followed literally a source from which
dilatare was missing. As for mechanical transference of
manuscript corruptions, observe that in the same clause
Capgrave evidently read viae for vitae and used it as he
read it.

Now with so many very plausible instances of incorrectness due to mechanical translation from a faulty original, it is tempting to attribute to a similar cause the
errors of construction which occur in a translation normally very correct. For instance, there is only one occurrence
of anacoluthic expression in the 1450 Revelations of St.

<u>Birgitta</u> of the Garrett MS.[3]:

(P. 11, 11. 31-34)

Therfore wete ye well that he dyeth displesabley
and euyl that lyuyng dissolutly dyeth in wyll to
synne, <u>and</u> <u>while</u> <u>he</u> <u>that</u> forth goyng in the worlde
desyrith to lyffe longer and can not thanke God.

This cannot be explained from the source without violence
to the Latin:

(IV, xl; Vol. 1, p. 374)

Ergo scito, quod ille moritus contemptibiliter &
male, qui dissolute vivens moritur in voluntate
peccandi, <u>qui</u> habens mundi processum optat ut
longius vivat, et nescit regratiari Deo.

Yet not only is the blunder in this translator's work unique,
but his ability to handle such a series of constructions with
understanding is amply demonstrated elsewhere. For example:

(i, i; I, 88)   (9, 5-10)

Membra eorum . . . abscin- Her membres . . . shall be
denter ab eis, &   kytt of and descended
disiungenter,   from him
sicut murus destruendus,   as a wall that is dys-
vbi non relinquitur   troyde, <u>wher</u> no stone
lapis super lapidum,   is lyfte vppon other,
nec caementum adhaeribit   ne <u>wher</u> morter clevyth
lapidibus.   to the stones.

(VIII, lvi; II, 339)   (P. 88, 11. 8-11)

Ista etiam Iustitia   þis ryght-winess is also
est in Deo, quod omnes   in God, þat all þat ar
qui sunt super terram   apon erth first hope
primo sperunt firmiter   seurly tho thinges þat
ea quae non vident, &   they see nott, & þat
credant Ecclisie Dei   they beleve to the church
& sancto Euangelio.   of God and to the holy
Deinde diligant   gospel. And forther-more
eum super omnia . . .   <u>that</u> they love God
                            above all thinges . . .

---

3. I have collated only fifteen pages (1-11; 89-93). For
the rest I rely upon the notations of irregularity made by
the editor, Mr. W. P. Cumming (pp. 125-28).

One suspects, therefore, that some corruption has crept into
his copy of the original.

There is of course no limit to the number of cases
which sufficient emendation or corruption of the source will
not explain.   Probably if we knew exactly what the English
writers had before them we should find a large number of instances where the same translators have departed from what
they saw in their source in order to correct it.   Though
scribal error in the source must always be considered, the
clear cases of structural incorrectness due to it are rare.
Even when a case appears certain, the most interesting aspect of it is the blind or mechanical reaction of the
English writer.

Though anacoluthon and asymmetrical coordination are
practically absent from French as well as Latin, the synthetic verb was, in these inflected languages, naturally frequent.   In the French of <u>c</u>. 1400 the usage existed where the
inflection conveyed the change of subject:

> (<u>Livre</u> <u>de</u> <u>La</u> <u>T</u>. <u>L</u>., p. 13)

> . . . et entra en une garderobe, ou sa femme estoit,
> le clavier et deux varlets, et man<u>goient</u> et rigol-
> <u>oient</u> tellement que . . .

> (<u>Ibid</u>., p. 21)

> et quant Dieu vit leur abaissement et leur humilite,
> il eut marcy d'eulx; sy fur<u>ent</u> sauvés.

> (Gaston III, <u>Livre</u> <u>de</u> <u>la</u> <u>Chasse</u>, VI, p. 45)

> Lièvre tient voulentiers un pays, et se elle a
> compagnie d'un autre ou de leurs enfans, ya ou
> cinq ou six, james autre lièvre estrange, fors
> que celle de leur nature, ne laisse<u>ront</u> aprochier. . .

But it was also used where the change is not clear:

> (<u>Livre</u> <u>de</u> <u>La</u> <u>T</u>. <u>L</u>., III, p. 8)

> Et ne demoura gaires que <u>un</u> grant <u>roy</u> de Grece
> la <u>fist</u> demander à son pere <u>et il</u> luy donna <u>et</u>
> <u>fust</u> depuis bonne dame et de notte . . .

> (<u>Ibid</u>., VI, p. 14)

> . . . Dieu l'en guerredonna et lui donna un bon
> chevalier riche et puissant <u>et</u> <u>vesqui</u> avecques

luy ayse et honnorablement.
(The subject of <u>vesqui</u> is <u>elle</u>, five lines above.)

(Gaston III, <u>Livre de la Chasse</u>, p. 85)

<u>elles</u> portent neuf sepmaines ou pou plus leurs
cheaulx <u>et</u> nais<u>sent</u> aveugles.

In the verse Pélerinage de l'homme the usage is common in all
circumstances:

(ll. 231-3)

Vi une dame en ma voie
Qui de sa biaute me fist joie.
Fille sembloit d'empereeur . . .

(ll. 249-50)

Courtoise fu, ce me sembla,
Quar premiere me salua . . .

Mout sont ore d'acrocheteurs . . .
Qui, se aperceeus estoient,
A soudre au roi mout aroient

The diversity of practice in the French writers appears to
have confused the English translators. Sometimes they transferred the synthetic verb into a similar English construction.
They would do this when the French inflection had left no
ambiguity in the original:

(Caxton, <u>Book of La</u> T. L., VI, p. 24.
Cp. <u>Livre de La</u> T. L., p. 13, as above.)

he entred in to his gardrobe, where as his wyfe was
with his clerk and two of his seruantes, and <u>etc</u>.
and <u>played</u> so that . . .

(<u>Book of La</u> T. L., (1450), IX, p. 13, 1. 31-2.
Cp. <u>Livre de La</u> T. L., p. 21, as above.)

and whanne God sawe her humblesse he had mercy on
hem and <u>were</u> saued . . .

but also when the change of subject was not implied in the
original construction:

(Book of La T. L. (1450), p. 6, 11. 23-27;
Cp. Livre, III, p. 8, as above.)

And not longe after a kinge of Grece wedded her
And was continued a good woman and a deuote.

Again:

(Book of La T. L. VI, p. 9, 11. 21-2.
Cp. Livre, VI, p. 14, as above.)

and therfore Jod gerdonethe her and gave her a
rich knight and a puissant and leued long togederes.

One instance of the construction in La Tour Landry has
caught both the earlier translator and Caxton:

(Livre I, p. 6)

. . . tout le vray bien . . . vient de lui [Dieu]
et de la grace de son saint esperit et si donne
longue vie . . . comme il luy plaist.

(Book, 1450, I, p. 4,   (Caxton, Book, I, p. 17)
11. 25-7)

. . . all the verray good   al the very wele . . . com-
. . . comithe of hym only   ethe of hym and of the
and of none other And   grace of his hooly spyr-
yeuithe long lyff . . .   yte and also gyuethe long
                                 lyf . . .

        On the other hand, a French synthetic verb was often
correctly analysed. Caxton got the daughter distinguished
from the king of Greece:

(Chap. III, p. 20)

And it was not long after that a grete kyng of
grece desyred and demaunded her of her fader to
haue her in maryage, and her fader gafe her to
hym. And she was after a good lady and deuoute . . .

Other examples:

(Caxton, Book of La T. L., VI, p. 25
Cp. Livre, VI, p. 14, and the Book of 1450, VI, p. 9)

And therefore . . . god rewarded and gafe to her a
knyght . . . and she lyued with him well . . .

(Edward of York, Master of Game, II, p. 12.
Cp. Livre de la Chasse, VI, p. 45, as above.)

The hare abideþ comonly in oo contre and if she
haue felowship of anoþer . . . no strange hare
shal þei neuvere suffre come dwelle in hure
marchesse . . .

(Ibid., XII, p. 46, Cp. Chasse, p. 85, as above.)

They beren here whelpes ix wekes or more, þe
whelpes byn blynde whan þe ben welpede.

The translator of The Pilgrimage of Man usually analyses correctly the many synthetic verbs in his source. Both he and
Edward of York, in fact, appear to have maintained a certain
alertness for the construction in French, or rather to have
developed a mechanical reaction to it. For they frequently
analyse the verb when the pronoun logically is redundant:

(Livre de La Chasse,
I, p. 22)

(Master of Game, III, p. 21)

Les cerfz, quand ilz sont
près des hautes montain-
nes, descendent quant ce
vient au temps du ruyt
ès plaines.

The hertes þat bene in
greet hilles, whane it
comme to Rutsome tyme,
þei come adoun.

(Ibid., I, p. 22)

(Ibid., I, p. 21)

Biche qui porte faons
à matin quant ira
. . .

And þei which beren
calves, in þe mornyng
whan she shal go . . .

(Pél. de l'homme, 9503-06)

(Pilg. Man, III, xvii, p. 144)

Mont sont ore d'acroche-
        teurs . . .
Qui, se aperceus estoient,
Asoudre au roi mout
        aroient.

Manye ther ben now of
accrochers . . .
that if thei weren aper-
ceyued thei ouhte haue
ynowth to doone to paye
ayen to the king

(Ibid., ll. 671-4)

(Ibid., I, xv, p. 11)

Ce fu moyses qui passer
Fist Ysrael parmy la
        mer,

that was moyses that made
israel to passe thorgh
the see,

Qui de la verge qu'il tenoit	that with the yerde he held
Passage bon fait leur avoit.	he made hem good passage.
(Ibid., 11. 1279-81)	(Ibid., I, xxxi, p. 20)
Moyses quant m'ot escoute	Moyses whan he hadde herkened me
le biau glaive a engaine,	he shethede the faire swerd
Les clefs liees . . .	and bond faste the keyes . . .

In each instance above, the redundant pronoun occurs after a
subordinate clause which has intervened between the subject
and the verb; the translators, working in these passages
simply from clause to clause but alert to the requirements
in English of a French synthetic verb, have improperly analysed
the verbs in the principal clauses which follow. The English
synthetic verb in the fifteenth century, like the French, may
be called a relic of the older, more inflected language; and
the pleonastic pronoun was also a characteristic of the earlier language[4]. In the fifteenth century translations, however, both constructions are so rare as to be conspicuous;
and my surmise — that many instances of both were due to
mechanical translation of an erratic and confusing French
source — is strengthened, I believe, by the fact that the
two constructions are far more rare in careful translations
from Latin than in the translations I have seen from French.
In Latin the usage was stable, so that the translators knew
what to expect[5].

In the whole of the Elizabeth of Spalbeck and in some
twelve pages of the Imitation of Christ [6] I have found no
instance of synthetic verb or of pleonastic pronoun. There is
one synthetic verb in twelve pages of Mary of Oignies [7]:

---

4. See L. Kellner, Historical Outlines, par. 271, 272; 287,
288, 289.
5. All of Kellner's examples of the synthetic verb after
1400 (par. 271-2), are from translations of French source
(Caxton, Blanchardyn, Berners, Huon - texts not available)
except one each from Fisher and from Ascham, in neither of
which is the subject ambiguous. Kellner's fifteenth century
examples of the pleonastic pronoun in complex sentences (Par.
288; see also par. 112-120) are all from translations, one of
which, however, the Gesta Romanorum, has a Latin source.
(Latin text for this portion not available).
6. Pp. 2-8; 50-52; 147-50.
7. Pp. 135-142; 147; 161; 165, 178-9.

(P. 550, B.)   (P. 135, ll. 24-5)

Adeo enim ab infantia   In so mykel, sooþly,
cum ea crevit miseratio   froo a childe litil,
et pietas, et quasi   grewe wiþ hir mercy and
naturali affectione   pite, & as wiþ a natural
religionem diligebat.   pite loued religyone.

I have seen only one instance of pleonastic pronoun in fifteen pages of the 1450 Revelations of St. Birgitta (Garrett
MS.) [8]:

(Lib. i, cap. xli, Vol. I,   (P. 9, l. 37-p.10, l.2)
  p. 89)

Sicut enim miles, qui   For as a kynght that
in bello sperat auxilium   in a battell he hopeth to
Domini sui, tamdiu   hafe help of hys lorde,
pugnat . . .   fyghtyth as longe as . . .

There is only one such construction in ten pages of the
Revelations of 1470 (Garrett MS.) [9]:

(Lib. II, cap. xxiii,   (P. 100, ll.23-27)
  Vol. I, p. 202)

Sicut enim cor de membro   for as þe hert ioyeth
corporis infirmo non   not of a membre of the
gaudet, antiquam iterum   body þat is seeke to-fore
receperit sanitatem, &   it resceyue helthe ayene,
recepta sanitate   and whan it is hole, the
plus laetatur.   herte is more glad;
Sic ego quantum cumque   so I, synne a man neuer
homo peccat, si ex toto   so moche, yf he turne
                                ayene to me with alle his
corde, & vera emenda-   herte and with veray amend-
tione ad me reuersus   ment, anoon I am redy to
feurit, statim parata   resceyue hym.[10]
sum recipere reuertentem.

And there is only one in thirty-five pages of the Polychronicon [11]:

_____

   8. Pp. 1-11; 88-93.
   9. Pp. 99-109.
   10. A similar analysis of the first person of the verb after an intervening clause occurs on Fol. 76, a of the Rev. of
Birg. in the Lambeth MS. quoted above, Chap. I, p. 18.
   11. III, 392-437; VII, 208-35.

(III, 396)   (III, 397)

. . . draco inde exiliit   . . . a serpente did crepe
                                    furthe of hit, other a
qui reptans undique   dragon, whiche crepenge
dum testam unde exiret   abowte and willenge to
reintrare satageret,   entre in to that egge
                                    from whom hit come, and
statim obiit   my3hte not, hit diede
                                    anoon.

Even in the freely translated _Life of St. Catharine of Siena_,
I have observed only one pleonastic pronoun and no use of the
synthetic verb [12].

(II, vi, p. 908 C.)   (II, vi, p. 267, 11.32-44)

Sicut enim Maria Magdal-   For as Marye magdelene
ena trigenta tribus   lyued xxxiij yere
annos stetit en rupe   in a Roche wythout
absque corporio cibo,   bodely mete, and all
sed in contemplatio   that tyme was I-occupyed
assiduo . . .   in contemplacyon,
sic haec virgo sacra   ryght so this holy mayde
ab illo tempore   fro that tyme that she
quo haec acciderunt,   was endowed wyth these
usque ad tricessimum   newe graces unto the age
tertium annum aetatis,   of xxxiij yere after ward,
in quo ex hac luce   whiche yere she passyd
migravit   out of thys worlde,
tam ferventer contem-   she was so occupyed in
platione vacabat   dyuyne contemplacyon
altissime quod . . .   that she hadde . . .
Et sicut illa   And yet as Mary magdelene
rapiebatur in aera . . .   was take vp in to the ayre . .
sic ista   ryght so this holy mayde
pro majori parte   for the more partye all
temporibus . . . rapiebatur   hir yeres she was rauysshed
a corporeis sensibus.   fro hyr bodely wyttes . . .[13

        The prevailing usage in translations, apparently, was
to avoid both ellipsis and redundancy of the subject pronoun.
The translators, especially those who worked from Latin, must
have developed an understanding of the needs of English syntax
when the predicate is taken from an inflected language, and it

    12. Twelve pages (6,000 words) 36-41; 265-68; 354-5.
    13. A pleonastic pronoun of similar provenance is in the ex-
ample below (p. 143) from Capgrave.

is possible that the very act of translation sharpened that understanding and led to more care in their writing of English prose. At the same time it appears that their alertness to this construction now and then operated too strongly, so that whenever the translator failed to consider the whole of his English sentence, he was likely to translate the synthetic verb by rule of thumb, whether or not the resultant English was consistent.

That a mechanical reaction of this sort could and sometimes did occur seems plain from the cases described above where some corruption or mis-reading of a source will best explain the incorrectness of the English. Here the main trouble was mere inattention brought on by the routine of translating; the translator was not so much disregarding his English as concentrating too narrowly on the foreign language before him.

Plain instances, however, are rare. It was the translator's departure from his source and not his adherence to it which most often brought trouble to the English structure. The great majority of the inconsistent constructions in the translations occur in passages where there has been some alteration, large or small. In a great many of these the real fault may have been the Englishman's habit of composing by short units. Yet the tendency to fall into a mechanical reaction undoubtedly existed, and it may have had more part than can be determined in the cases which are now to be taken up.

A translator, for instance, sometimes altered the first of two coordinate constructions but upon coming later to the second, left it in the form in which he found it. Both translators of Geoffrey de la Tour Landry have done this in the same passage:

(Livre, Cap. XXXIV, pp. 74-5)	(Book, 1450, XXXIV, p. 48. ll. 17-18)
. . . il lui sembla qu'elle veoit l'ymaige de Nostre Dame qui tenoyt une cotte et une chemise et lui disoit . . .	. . . she thought that she saw the ymage of oure ladi holdinge in her honde a cote and a smocke, and saide to her . . .

(Caxton, Book, Chap. XXXIII, p. 75)

. . . her semed that she sawe thymage of oure lady holdyng a cote and a sherte, and sayd to her . . .

Here there has unfortunately been only one alteration in each translation. Both Englishmen have provided a frequent-

ly used equivalent ('qui tenoit :: holdinge') for the first
relative modifier of Nostre Dame :: our ladi. But at the
second of the relative clauses, they both have suddenly returned to the exact construction of the source; and when
the French had, without ambiguity, omitted to re-state the
subject of disoit, the translators have mechanically omitted
to provide one themselves, forgetting that their preceding
alteration had left the logic of the English constructions
very different from that of the French. Their lack of a
sense of form may account for their composition here, but
it is equally possible that when they came to the second coordinate construction they mechanically accepted what they
saw, thinking at the moment, only of the meaning of the
French[14].

It is hard to see how this could happen in the first
sentence of a prologue, but it is almost more difficult to
believe that Gilbert of the Haye could have committed the
following confusion if he had taken any thought to his
English at all:

(Bonet, Arbre, Prol., p. 1)	(Buke, p. 2, ll. 26-32)
La sainte couronne de France, en laquelle au-jourd'huy par l'ordon-naunce de Dieu regne Charles le VIe en cellui nom tres bien amé par tout le monde redoubte, soit donné los et gloire sur toutes seignories terriennes.	To the holy croun of Fraunce in the quhilk this day regnys Charles the Sext the quilk is lufit and redoubtit our all the warld be the ordy-naunce of God. Regn,, Till him be gevin hon-oure lof and glore abune all erdly lord-schippes maist hye prince I am callit
Tres hault . . . prince, je qui suis . . . appelé Honore Bonet . . . souvent . . . ay eu . . . etc.	. . Bonnett . . . The quhilk I have had . . . etc.[15]

When Gilbert used the French regne in the first relative
clause he omitted the preceding prepositional phrase,

---

14. Without a comparison with the source, the last
English verb in the passage would seem to be synthetic.
But it obviously was not so thought of by the translators,
to whom it was simply the equivalent of disoit.

15. I have followed the punctuation of the MS., using a
comma for every slanting bar.

'par l'ordonnance de Dieu.' But when he came to use that
prepositional phrase in a later position, he mechanically
moved right on again into the _regne_, and persisted in trying
to make sense out of it.

It must be remembered, however, that alterations by
a translator represent his own composition. The same analysis used in describing early original prose can be applied
to the following example of anacoluthon in a passage of
altered translation:

(_Livre de La T. L._, Prol., p. 3)	(_Book_, 1450, 2, 36-3, 3)
Et pour ce que je vis celuy temps dont je	And therfor bi-cause y sawe atte that tyme the gouernaunce of hem the
doubte que encore soit courant,	whiche y douted that tyme yet regnithe, And ther be suche felawes now or
je me pensay que je feroye un livret . . .	worse, And therfor y pur-posed to make a litell boke . . .

Except to make 'ce que' more precise ('the gouernaunce of
hem'), the translator has followed the original structure
as far as 'yet regnithe.' Then, perhaps forgetting how he
had begun, perhaps only intending a parenthesis, he inserted
the completed clause 'and ther be suche felowes now or worse.'
But when he came to pick up his French at 'je me pensay,' he
was so under the immediate influence of his own addition
that he made the main clause of his source coordinate with
the main clause which he had just inserted, rounding out the
sense with a new and redundant 'therfor,' yet not making the
further departure of striking out the misleading 'bi-cause.'
A passage from the _St. Catharine_ shows the same inability of
a translator to think of structure in terms of the whole
sequence:

(I, i, p. 869, A)	(I, p. 37)
Addiditque dicta Lapa _dum_ semel quidam ejus concivis, contra omne debitum justitiae malitiose opprimat eum pe_tendo_ maximam summam quam nulla ratione deb-ebat; _et_ amicorum poten-tia calummniisque simpl-	And in special lapa, his wif, reherseth that _whan_ on a tyme one of his ney-bours dysyred hym _and_ wrongfully _asked_ hym a grete somme of monye whiche he owed not by none reson, _and_ soo moche _he vexed_ hym, that symple man, wyth the

icem virum adeo <u>supplatando</u> <u>vexaret</u>, quod deduxerat eum quasi ad perditionem omnium bonorum suorum; numquam tamen potuit sustinere . . . <u>etc</u>.	might of other frendes and <u>supplanted</u> hym wyth grete wronges, that he brought hym to the losse of alle his godes, <u>and</u> in alle this tyme this good man myght neuere suffre . . . <u>etc</u>.

The English sentence has been begun like the Latin with a
temporal clause. The translator has then made the slight
alteration of a gerundive to a coordinate temporal clause.
But at the second Latin temporal clause, perhaps having
already forgotten how he had begun his English sentence,
perhaps mechanically analysing the Latin synthetic verb,
he has written <u>he vexed</u>, a principal clause, still keeping,
however, the Latin coordinating conjunction; consequently,
when he arrived at the original principal clause, he considered it coordinate with the English principal clause
which he had just written, and so inserted another coordinating conjunction. He did not look back sufficiently to
realise that the new paratactic structure which he had
composed required still another change in the omission of
the <u>whan</u> which he had taken from his source at the beginning of the sentence.

Sometimes an insertion by the translator, without
any further alterations, will badly disrupt the sentence
because the new part is not constructed to accord with the
translated parts:

(<u>Livre</u> <u>de</u> <u>la</u> <u>Chasse</u>, VI, p. 45)	(<u>Master</u> <u>of</u> <u>Game</u>, II, p. 13)
Lièvres n'ont point de sayson de leur amour;	The hares han no sesoun of her loue, <u>for as I said it is cleped rydyng tyme</u>, for in euery month
quar il ne sera ja moys en l'en qu'il n'y en ait de chaudes.	of the yere ne shal not be þat some ne be with kyndeles. [for French cheaulx?]
(<u>Vita</u> <u>S</u>. <u>Catharine</u> <u>Senensi</u>, II, xvii, p. 941, C.)	(<u>Life</u> <u>of</u> <u>St</u>. <u>Catharine of Siena</u>, II, xii, p. 355, 27-8)
sed propter desederium quod habebat, ad con-suetum recurrit orationis refugium: et prosternens	But for hyr grete desyre that she had to that blyssed sacramente, <u>and</u> <u>myghte</u> <u>not</u> <u>receyue</u>

se apud quoddam sessor-
ium, in extrema quasi
parte ecclesiae positum,
coepit acanso corde orare
Sponsum . . .

it, she prayed oure lorde
deuoutely in the ferrest
place of the chirche.[16]

Or what amounts to an awkward insertion is really only an
awkward equivalent for an original appositive construction:

(Livre de la Chasse,
VI, p. 45)

(Master of Game, II, p. 13)

Et aussi quant elles vi-
ardent deux herbes,
l'une que l'on appelle
le serpol et l'autre
poulioul, elles sont
fortes et tost allantes.

And also whan þei
pasturen of too herbes,
þat oon is clepyd
Soepol and þat oþer
Pulegian, þei be stronge
and fast rennyng.

Edward has used his usual translation for l'une . . .
l'autre and also for on appelle; and in the English construction which results he has found no place for the subordinating que. There is a somewhat similar case in The
Pilgrimage of Man:

(11. 10,827-32)

(III, liv, p. 164)

Se elle qui est aumos-
     niere
De moy et dispensiere
Vouloit tant faire vers
     mon pere
Qui est son fil, elle
     sa mere
Que il a toi me redonnast
Encore n'iroies pas a
     gast.

If thilke that is aw-
     meneer

wolde do so michel to
ward my father
which is hire sone
She is his mooder
that he wolde give me
ayen to thee yit thou
shuldest not go to wast.

Perhaps the most frequent difficulty is that which
comes when the altered part coordinates inconsistently with
the rest of the sentence. The change may be considerable:

16. A similar insertion in a less altered passage appears
in the example of pleonastic pronoun from the Polychronicon,
above, pp. 134-5.

(<u>Vita</u> <u>S</u>. <u>Catharinae</u> <u>Sen-</u>
<u>ensi</u>, p. 869, D.)

non est coneptio subse-
cuta;
ut videlicet
in illa filia
inducias pariendi
haberet,

et ad finem partus
appropinquaret,

quae finem omnis perfect-
ionis deberet attingere
simul et adipisci, quasi
fuerat terminata.

(<u>Life</u> of <u>St</u>. <u>Catharine</u> <u>of</u>
Siena, p. 38, 11.44-8)

and in alle that tyme she
conceyued not, as it semed
that oure lorde for that
doughter hadde graunted
her a tyme of reste of
traueylyng of the byrthe of
chyldren, <u>and</u> <u>in</u> <u>a</u> <u>token</u>
<u>that</u> she myght come to the
ende of conceyuyng and
byrthe in that doughter
whiche sholde after ateyne
and gete the ende of alle
perfection.

(Higden, <u>Polychronicon</u>,
Vol. III, p. 410-12)

Phillipus tamen prius
a Dario rege magna
pecunia palpatus
fuerat

De qua etiam re
Alexander <u>litteras</u>
<u>acceperat</u> <u>ut</u> <u>nullo</u>
modo potionem Philippi
de manu ejus <u>sumeret</u>.

('Chronicle,' MS. Harley
2261, Vol. III, p. 411-13)

Neuerthelesse the seide
Phillippe receyuede letters
sent from kynge Darius
promisenge to hym a grete
summe of goode that he
scholde poyson kynge Alexander; of whiche thynge
Alexander <u>hade</u> <u>knowlege</u>,
<u>and</u> <u>that</u> <u>he</u> <u>scholde</u> not <u>take</u>
in any wise drynkes or med-
icynes of Philippe his
phisicion.

Or the change may be in only one sentence-member, and either
before the coordinating conjunction or after:

(<u>Livre</u> <u>de</u> <u>La</u> <u>Tour-Landry</u>,
VII, p. 16)

Car tout ne chiet que par
accoutumance <u>de</u> <u>dire</u>
ses heures, <u>d'oir</u> la
messe et le service de
Dieu, <u>de</u> <u>jeuner</u>, <u>et</u> <u>de</u>
<u>faire</u> saintes oeuvres,
comme firent les saintes
femmes, selon qu'il est

(<u>Book</u> <u>of</u> <u>La</u> <u>T</u>.-<u>Lan</u>., 1450,
VII, p. 10, 11.23-27)

for hit shall not greue
you with vsage, bothe
<u>saieng</u> youre service
<u>hering</u> youre masse
<u>fasting</u>, <u>and</u> <u>to</u> <u>do</u>
other blessed dedes,
as the saintes dede,
and as her legendes

contenu ès legendes et
ès vies des sains et des
saintes de paradis.

maken mencion,
the whiche are now
in paradise.

(Vita S. Catharinae Sen-
ensi, p. 869, E.)

(Life of St. Catharine of
Siena, p. 39, ll. 3-6)

Rapiebat enim eam unusque
quisque vicinorum et
consanguineorum et ad
domum propriam ducebant,
ut audirent
prudentula verba ejus
infantilis laetitiae
consortio pruerentur

Eche man aboute of her
neybours and of her kyn-
rede lad her home and
glad they were who myght
haue her to here her wyse
speche and that they myght
haue felawshyp and the
gladnesse of that yonge
mayde.

(Livre de la Chasse,
I, p. 17-18)

(Master of Game, III, p. 18)

Et ce leur vient de leur
mere et de bonne
engendure et de bonne
norreture et de bonne
naissance en bonnes con-
stellacions et signes
du ciel.

. . . and commeþ to hem of
the good kynde of hure
good fadere and of hure
moder and of good
nurture, and to be born
in good constellacions
and in good sygnes of
heuen.

(Ibid., Prol., p. 4)

(Ibid., Prol., p. 5)

. . . et n'aura que fere
de penser fors de la be-
songne qu'il a et est oc-
occupe.
Quar il n'est point ocieux;
ansois a assez a fere de
ymaginer de se lever matin.

and shall not haue a do
ne think but on þe nedys
that he is ordegned
for to
and henys not ydel for
he hath ynow ado to
ymagine to aryse erly.

(Revelationes S. Birgittae,
II, xxiii; I, 203)

(Revelations of St. Birgitta,
translation of 1470, p. 102,
ll.11-12)

Unde enim procedit nubes
nisi de humore &
vaporibus procedentibus
de terra, quae, cum cal-
ore ascendentes in cael-
um, densatur in super-
ioribus.

Whereof cometh cloudes or
skyes but of humours and
moistures goyng oute of
the erthe, and arne lift
up in-to þe firmement,
and there waxe thicke.

(Rolle, *Incendium* *Amoris*,
Prol., p. 145)

(Misyn, *Fire* *of* *Love*,
I, p. 2, ll. 6-8)

Admirabar magis quam
enuncio quando siquidem
sentiui cor meum pri-
mitus incale*scere*, et
uere non imaginarie
quasi sensibile igne
es*tuare*.

Mor haue I meruayled
þan I schewe, fforsothe,
whan I felt fyrst my
here wax warme, *and* treu-
ly not ymagynyngly_bot
as_it were with sensible
fyre by*rned*.

Without the Latin, this *byrned* might pass for a synthetic
verb, with subject either *I* or *hert*; but Misyn was probably
misled by the equivalent which he had interjected for *quasi*
-- '*as it were*.' There is a somewhat similar instance in
Capgrave, where faulty coordination is created by the insertion of an improper object pronoun:

(Vita S. Gilberti, p. xix*)

(Life of St. Gilbert, p. 141,
II. 20-4)

. . . quod spontaneam ili-
gens paupertatem,
omnia temporalia, sibi
a Deo praestita,

. . .þat wilfully he
chase honest pouerte and
all his temporal goodes
þat God had sent him he
freely relisid to þe
necessessite and sustenta-

fratrum et sororum
quos sub regulari
disciplina prudenter in-
stituit et sollicite
custodivit, necessitatibus
deputavit.

cion of þoo breþerin and
sisteres whom he sette
vndyr reguler discipline
and kept *hem* ful bysily.

The relative *quos* :: *whom* is sufficient for both members, but
Capgrave, as it were losing count, provided a personal pronoun object for the second verb.
    Sometimes the inconsistency is less a matter of formal
construction than of sense or simply of ease:

(*Livre* de La *T.-L.*, V,
p. 10)

(Caxton, *Book* of La *T.-L.*,
V, p. 22)

qui plus en [d'oraisons]
dist devottement, et
plus vault et en l'en
plus de merittes.

and *when_more is_said
deuoutely*, than is it
more worthe, and more
deseruyth *he* meryte.

Caxton has changed the French active voice with <u>qui</u> to a
passive with <u>plus</u> :: <u>more</u>; then when he draws back toward
the French construction, he has no antecedent for his <u>he</u>.
Again, from the following sentence by the translator of
the 1450 <u>Polychronicon</u>, we must take it that 'the treasure
moneschethe to releve costes':

> (Vol. III, p. 425)
>
> Wherefore y sende to the a bridelle, a balle, and
> a purs with siluer and golde in hit: the balle mov-
> ethe the to play conueniente to thyne age; the bri-
> delle moneschethe the to attende to discipline, and
> the treasure in the purs to releve thy costes in
> this journey.

But the whole was ineptly re-arranged from:

> (Vol. III, p. 424)
>
> ad quod assequendum, mitto tibi scuticam, pilam,
> et loculum cum aureis. Habena scutica monet te
> disciplina indigere. Pila ad ludum aetatis <u>congruit</u>.
> Aurei ad revelandum sumptus in itinere.

Edward of York wrote:

> (Master of Game, III, p. 17)
>
> Many men iugeth dure of mony coloure of heere and
> specially of iii coloures some be called broun and
> some donn and some ʒelowe heere and also here
> heuedes ben of divers maners.

He has only slightly altered from:

> (Livre de la Chasse, I, p. 17)
>
> Des cerfs juge l'en le poil en moult de manières;
> especiallement en trois que on dit l'un brun
> l'autre fauve et l'autre blont. Et assui leurs
> testes sont de diverse fourmes.

But Gaston 'Phoebus' has subordinated the member which
states his 'moult de manières,' so that the 'Et aussi . . .
sont de diverse fourmes' coordinates in structure as well
as in significance with 'juge l'en . . . en moult de manières.' From these various examples there appears, in brief,

a correlation between a translator's adherence to his original and the correctness of his prose sentences; and also
between the incorrectness of his sentences and his departure
from his source. We cannot of course reverse the correlation between incorrectness and departure; that is, although
adherence usually brought correctness, departures did not by
any means always bring incorrectness. Most of the multi-
tudinous alterations, slight or radical, in each of the group
of eight translations not normally close, have left the sentence structure perfectly logical. However, two of these
highly altered translations, the La Tour-Landry and the St.
Catharine, have a greater proportion of illogically constructed sentences than does any of the close translations
I have observed. A third, Gilbert of the Haye's Book of the
Law of Arms, contains scarcely a correct sentence not closely translated; but Gilbert's work, in its unique position as
the earliest known piece of Scottish literary prose, cannot
well be considered in an estimation of the average habits of
composition in English prose. At the same time, it must be
noted that three of the altered translations which remain
correct are of a simple sentence structure, characterized
either by plain parataxis or by an absence of long hypotactic periods. The translators of the Conquest of Ireland
and of The Alphabet of Tales both wrote correctly, but they
both composed in a close succession of subject, verb, object, with the few modifying members at the beginning or
end of the sentence, so that they gave themselves, if we may
put it this way, little opportunity to become illogical.
Again, in thirteen pages of the Ponthus and Sidone[17] there
are only eleven sentences which are over twenty-five words
in length and hypotactic in structure; the longest of the
eleven is of only fifty words, and five of them really are
split into two parts by a coordinating conjunction. Only
two of the altered translations, Love's Mirrour and Capgrave's St. Gilbert are both correct and hypotactic. And
it is further noticeable that in each of the examples of incorrectness cited above, there has been some mismanagement
of a complex or hypotactic sentence in the original.

Since the grammatical details of the altered sentences are the translators' own responsibility, a comparison
with fifteenth century practice in original composition is
inevitable. The mis-managed sentences quoted above are of
the same nature and often have the same explanation as those
found in prose which is wholly original. They indicate that
the translators, like the other English prose writers of the
period, were not well accustomed to thinking of the individual constructions in terms of the whole sequence.

17. Chap. VIII-XI, pp. 18-32.

In a period, then, when the grammatical logic of the prose sentence was often violated, it is remarkable that the translated compositions of the sort described as close should have normally maintained a very high percent of correct or logically consistent sentences.

This correctness is found not only late in the century but early. It must be credited even to the over-literal translations, Misyn's and The Pilgrimage of Man, of the 1430's, but it is more noteworthy in the work of translators who have well Anglicised their expression. In fifteen pages of the Three Kings of Cologne, dating soon after 1400, an early example of narrative translated in complex structure, there is only one instance of anacoluthon and none of asymmetrical coordination[18]. In the whole of the Life of St. Elizabeth of Spalbeck, of c. 1430, there are only four such coordinations, and I have seen only one in the Life of St. Mary of Oignies, of the same date[19]; neither contains any example of anacoluthon. The Imitation of Christ, c. 1450, shows no instance of illogical construction whatever. In the 1450 Revelations of St. Birgitta of the Garrett MS., there is only one, the anacoluthon noted above (p.128), and in the translation of 1470, in the same MS., no anacoluthon and only one illogical coordination. Among the translations from French, Earl Rivers' Cordiale is without any inconsistent constructions in its first ten pages. Fifteen pages of the Melusine[20] show considerable use of the synthetic verb but only one instance of anacoluthon[21]. Caxton's translations go for page after page with the same correct, hypotactic structure of his sources. In twenty-two pages of his La Tour Landry[22]there are but five illogical constructions. It is chiefly the quantity of Caxton's translated prose that is important. From time to time he grows careless. There are four faulty constructions in the sixteen pages of the Curial; one of these is due to a sheer omission, either by the copyist of the French manuscript or by the printer of Caxton's[23],but two of them are due to a misunderstanding of the French que[24]. One of those in his La Tour Landry is a similar mis-translation[25].

---

18. Version in the Royal MS. pp. 3-7; 33-41; 49-69.
19. About 6000 words, pp. 135-142; 147; 161, 165, 178-9.
20. Pp. 1-10; 100-105.
21. P. 3, ll. 8-16.
22. Pp. 13-28; 74-6; 152-3; 176-7.
23. P. 3, ll. 8-12; see the note by the editor, Paul Meyer.
24. P. 7, 1.2; p. 12, 1.11.
25. Chap. ii, first sentence, p. 18; French, p. 8. Pour ce becomes because that without completion. The translators of The Master of Game and of the Polychronicon sometimes fall into such blunders.

But there is no need to cite every rare exception. The fact remains that in Caxton's, as in the many other close translations, practically every individual construction which made up each sentence was correctly imitated -- consciously or unconsciously -- from a correct original. Relatively little of the correctness could have been unconscious with the translators, mere blind transference; most of it must have resulted from conscious effort. This is apparent from the care taken to Anglicize the expression. My own term 'stencil translation' obviously applies only in the sense that there seldom was any alteration of the relationship between one construction and another; that each separate unit was fitted into the structural pattern in the same way that it had been in the source. But by their usual practice of finding a native equivalent for every construction translated, with the many small readjustments thus required, the great majority show considerable objectivity toward their sources and understanding of English composition [26].

Within the pattern of the original they composed by broad structural units. It was uniquely when they ceased to imitate that they wrote incorrectly and revealed the inadequacy of their own habits. The presence of the correct foreign model and the act of translation, therefore, appear to have been a discipline to the many English writers who still lacked the tradition and the habit of thinking clearly in terms of complex prose structure. In the native prose, formal congruence of all constructions within a sentence was not yet an established usage. The circulation of a large and growing number of translations which were highly accurate in this respect must have refined the practice of other writers and contributed to the gradual change in usage which began in the latter half of the century.

---

26. This is apparent from every passage of close translation I have cited. Specific instances have been pointed out in Chapter V, above, pp. 113 ; and in Chapter VI, pp. 128.

Chapter Seven

THE EFFECTS OF CLOSE TRANSLATION:

II -- PLAN IN THE WHOLE SEQUENCE

For the study of consistent construction, only short sequences have been examined. In the structural composition of long sequences -- the period and what we may call the paragraph -- the effects of close translationare more easily perceived and perhaps more significant. Yet here it is not possible to make the close correlation between a translator's treatment of his source and the nature of his prose. One cannot say that unity or proportion disappeared uniquely when a translator turned to original writing of his own. For a few of the sources were themselves composed crudely, by short units, the structure being inadequate to the meaning. Two of these I have mentioned before[1]. Perhaps a better example is Les Dictes des Philosophes. Though often hypotactic in short sequences, this book is simply a list of sayings, composed as it were from filing cards. Both Stephen Scrope, about 1450, and Earl Rivers twenty years later translated it closely, structure and all. Rivers' own original prose shows more ability at combining the parts into a structural whole[2].

But such composition, as I have explained, was rare in the books chosen for translation. Most of the sources were composed habitually with more maturity than could be achieved by English writers, and consequently in almost all comparisons available there is a very considerable difference between the same man's work as translator and as original writer. Three such comparisons have been presented at some length in connection with the effects of close translation upon a writer's prose style[3]. All of them show the

---

1. The Merlin and L'Image du Monde.
2. Neither the French text nor Rivers' is available. I have used only Scrope's translation and the description of his procedure and of Rivers' given by the editor, Miss Margaret E. Schofield. See Appendix A, below. Rivers' original prologue is in Prol. and Epil.of Caxton, ed. Crotch, pp. 111-112.
3. Chapter I, above, pp. 20-31.

same difference: in the original prose the broadest unit of form commonly observed by the writer was the single sentence-member; while in the same man's translation the unit was extended, associating the form with the sequence of thought.

This difference may also be seen between the two long passages quoted in another connection from the La Tour Landry[4]. The first of these, which is fairly close translation, is grouped and varied in structure according to the events of the story and their causes, results, etc. The second, largely original, is half in lengthy sub-dependence and half in parataxis; for instance:

> oure lorde . . . faught . . . for pitee that he hadde
> . . . whanne he deliuered us from . . . dampnacion
> . . . where as [he] faught . . . whanne he suffrede
> . . . and bought . . . and receiued deth . . . and
> fraunchised us . . . and restored . . . [5]

The original prologue of Earl Rivers to his Dictes contrasts in the same way with the opening of his translated Cordiale [6]. The structure of the first eight lines of the prologue has no plan whatever:

> Where it is so that every human Creature . . . is
> boren . . . to be subgette . . . vnto the stormes
> of fortune And so in diuerse . . . wyses man is
> perplexid with worldly aduersitees Of the whiche I
> . . . haue largely & in many different maners haue
> had my parte And of hem releued by thynfynyte grace . . .
> whiche grace hath compelled me . . . [7]

---

4. Above, pp. 106-110.
5. Caxton's close translation of the same general material (Chap. CVI, p. 153) provides an interesting contrast to this:

> . . . as the swete Ihesu Cryst dyd, which faught for the pyte of vs and of al the humayn lygnage. For grete pyte he hadde to see them goo and falle in the tenebres of helle; wherefore he suffred and susteyned alone the bataylle moche hard and cruell on the tre of the holy Crosse; and was his sherte broken and perced in fyue places, that is to wete the fyue dolorous woundes whiche he receyued of his debonayr and free will, in his dere body, for the pyte that he had of us.

6. Quoted above, pp. 116-119.
7. Ed. by Crotch, op. cit., p. 111.

In fact Nicholas Love in his Mirrour and Capgrave in his two
Saints' Lives -- if these really contain much original composition[8]-- are the only writers I have seen whose original
prose is not characteristically different in structural maturity from their translated work[9].
    A more important comparison is between the structure
of early original writing taken at large and that of the
typical translation. Here, within similar types or genres of
composition, the same differences continue to exist.
    Early structural style of original narrative, both
secular and religious, has been analyzed in the discussion of
the changes in it which took place in the latter half of the
century[10]. Typically, it was found, the structure was extremely uniform and simple. There is no indication that the
writers had any working concept of the relation between form
and thought, or any sense of form as a need in itself. The
unit of composition was the single statement, and there was a
minimum use of syntax to combine the statements. The tendency
toward combination appears not to have begun until well into
the third quarter of the century.
    But among the translations there is an abundance of
early narrative prose in complex structure. Two examples of
c. 1430 have already been quoted, The Life of St. Elizabeth
of Spalbeck[11] and the Letter Touching St. Catherine of
Siena[12]; both of which show not only a variety of constructions but also accuracy in the logical relationships. Mid-
century translations of the same sort which have been quoted
are the Disciplina Clericalis, the La Tour Landry, and the Life
of St. Catherine of Siena[13], the latter two, however, being

---

    8. See Appendix A, below, 'Bonaventura' and 'Saints' Lives.'
    9. The bulk of Capgrave's certain original writing is in
his Chronicle, ed. by F. C. Hingeston, London, 1858. Though
this is not of the extremely plain structure observed in the
earliest English chronicles, it never shows hypotaxis through
long sequences. The least uniform structure, about like that
described in the early parts of the Ponthus (above, p.145),
is in his later entries, e.g., the Lollard rising, p. 309, or
the campaign before Agincourt, p. 311.
    10. Chapter II, above, pp. 42-57.
    11. Chapter IV, above, pp. 76-78 ; and Chapter V, pp.91-92.
    12. Chapter V, above, pp.114-116.
    13. Chapter V, above, pp. 95, 106, and 110.
The tale from the Disciplina Cl. quoted with the same tale in
an altered, paratactic translation, is a good illustration of
the contrast in narrative effect between varied and uniform
structure.

occasionally altered and not always accurate in the combination of constructions; Caxton's _Aymon_, of 1489 [14], is a further illustration, though less important because of its late date.

One of the very early fifteenth century translations, _The Three Kings of Cologne_, which maintained considerable popularity and was printed by Wynkyn de Worde in 1496 and 1499 [15], is an excellent example of the effects of close translation upon narrative structure:

Whan þes .ij. kynges Melchior and Balthasar were come and abiden in þes plaas aforeseyde in þe clowde and in derkenesse, þan þis clowde bigan to ascende and to wax clere; but þe sterre apperid not. So whan þes .ij. kyngis siȝen þat þei were nyȝe þe Citee þouȝ noon of hem ȝit knew oþir, þei toke her wey toward þe Citee, with all her oost and men. And whan þei com to þis hiȝe-weye bisyde þe Mounte of Caluarye, þer as þes .iij. weyes mette to-gidir, þan com Iaspar, kyng of Thaars and of þe yle of Egriswell, with all hys oost. And so þes .iij. glorious kynges eueryche wiþ his oost, and wiþ her cariage and beestis metten to-gidir in þis hiȝe-weye bisyde þe hille of Caluarye. And not-wiþstondynge þat noon of hem neuer to-fore had seye oþir ne noon of hem neuer knewe oþer persone ne of oþer comynge, ȝit at her metyng euerych of hem anoon-riȝt wiþ greet ioye and greet reuerence kissed oþir and made moche ioye euerych to oþir. And þouȝ þei were of diuers language, ȝit euerych of hem as to her vnderstondynge spak all o maner of speche. And whan þei þus had mette to-gedir and euerych of hem had tolde to oþir his wille and hys entent, and all her wille and her cause was acordyng in one, than þei were moche more gladdere and more feruent in her weye. And so þei riden forþe, and sodeynlich þei com in to þe Cite of Ierusalem atte þe vprisyng of þe sunne. And whan þei knew þat Ierusalem was þe kyngis cyte þe which her predecessoures and þe Caldees of olde tyme had biseged and destroyed, þei were riȝt gladde, supposyng to haue founde þe kyng of Iewes bore in þat Cyte.[16]

14. Chapter I, above, pp. 13-15.
15. See Chapter III, above, p. 62.
16. P. 55, l. 31 - p. 57, l. 30. For this and for the following close translations, it does not seem necessary to quote the source, the typical procedure of close translation having been widely illustrated in my previous chapters. A text of the Latin _Historia_, with variants which the English translator

The translator has followed English narrative convention in
the frequent use of _and_ to begin a sentence. But the structure is not paratactic. The real connectives are subordinating: 'whan,' 'þouȝ,' 'notwithstonding þat,' 'supposyng.'
In only three places are successive statements coordinated
by means of _and_, one of these being a series of three subordinate clauses. The greatest importance of hypotaxis in
narrative is for expository purposes. Note the variety in
order and construction in the two such sequences above: 'So
whan þes .ij.kyngis siȝen þat þei were nyȝe þe Citee, _þouȝ_
noon of hem ȝit knew oþir, þei toke her wey toward þe Citee,
with all her oost and men . . . . And _whan_ þei knew _þat_
Ierusalem was þe kyngis cite _þe whiche_ her predecessoures
. . . had beseged . . . þei were riȝt gladde, suppo_synge to_
have _found_ þe kyng . . . _bore_.'
       The English _Polychronicon_ of _c_. 1450, a close trans-
lation, is often compared with the earlier one by Trevisa,
which is greatly altered toward uniformity of structure, the
Latin subordinating constructions being frequently 'resolved'
into coordination. Trevisa's may be preferred for its occasional naturalness; and the tendency of the version of 1450
to follow the Latin closely in the use of participial or
gerundive phrases may sometimes seem unsuited to English.
But certainly it is the close translation, and not Trevisa's,
which bears a resemblance to most of the original English
chronicles after 1470 [17]. The following notice of a her-
etic is not unlike Fabyan's account of Richard III. Note the
amount of comment and other expository material, and the variety of constructions used.

        Nicholaus the secunde succedid Benedict the pope,
        eiecte or expulsede allemoste ij. yere. In the
        tyme of whom the churches of Fraunce were trowblede
        moche by Berengarius archidiacon Turonense, whiche
        seide the blissede sacramente in the awter not to
        be the very body of Criste, but a similitude of hit.

used, is in Horstmann's edition of the English; for the above
passage, see Cap. XV, p. 231-232.
   17. The second editor of Trevisa and the 1450, J. R. Lumby,
prefers Trevisa (Int. to Vol. III, pp. lix-lxi, lxix); and so
did Caxton, if he knew the later one at all. But see the opin-
ion of Trevisa by R. Huchon, _Histoire de la Langue Anglaise_,
II, Paris, 1930, 324-25; and the stylistic arguments for the
1450 by Berte L. Kinkade, _The English Translations of Higden's Polychronicon_, Diss., University of Illinois, 1935, pp.
12-13. For the original English chronicles of _c_. 1450 see
Chapter II, above, pp. 42-46, 54.

Wherefore this pope callede a cownesayle of cxiij
bischoppes at Vercell in Ytaly, in whiche cownesaile
Berengarius did retract his erroure, as hit is schew-
ede in the decrees de consecrationibus, distinctione
secunda, 'Ego Berengarius.'   But this heresy spryng-
ynge after his dethe, Hiltebrandus the pope kepede
a cownsayle ageyne his folowers, where Lanfrancus
prior of Beccun, and specially Wymundus bischop
Aversan in Apulia, a man of noble eloquence, repugn-
ede ageyne his erroures.   But this Berengarius correcte his lyfe so in his olde age that mony men sup-
posede hym to be a seynte, expownynge the apocalips
after that, attendynge to mekenesse and almes, esch-
ewynge the siȝhte of women, and was contente with
poore clothynge and exhibicion, whom Hildebertus
bischop Cenomannensis commendethe in his versus, say-
enge: [four lines of Latin verse follow]. A man may
perceyve hére howe that laudable bischop makethe ex-
cesse in lawde of the seide Berengarius, but the use
of poetes and of rethoricions is to wryte soe. But
hit is to be advertisede that thauȝhe this Berengarius correcte his lyfe, he correcte not alle peple
whom he hade infecte with his heresy in diverse cun-
tres, for thauȝhe his synne was doen away the synne
of other men schalle greve hym. Whiche thynge ven-
erable Fulbert bischop Carotense, laborynge in grete
infirmite in his extreme daies, perceyved, whiche,
seenge Berengarius comme to visitte hym amonge oþer,
seide: 'Expelle hym, for y see a develle folowynge
hym þat dothe corrupte the aiere.' Also the seide
Berengarius dienge in the day of the Epiphany, and
havynge in remembraunce how mony wicked peple he
hade causede thro his erroure in his yowthe, seide:
'As y suppose, Criste schalle appere to me in þis day
of his apparicion, other for my penaunce to glory,
other to peyne for oþer men that y have averte from
Criste.'[18]

Narrative prose that is preponderantly exhortatory and
rhetorical -- of the sort illustrated from the St. Catherine
of Siena or of the sort so often used by Bishop Fisher -- can
be found in many translations of the first half of the cen-

18. English, Cap. XXVII, VII, 207, 209, 211. Latin, ibid.,
pp. 206, 208 , 210.

tury[19]. The Life of St. Jerome, of about 1440, another
book selected for printing toward 1500, is interesting because of its composite character. Except for the first chapter it is not from the Legenda Aurea, as the incipit states,
but from two letters supposedly exchanged between St. Augustine and Cyril. The following short chapter has less use of
the first and second persons than most and yet is typical of
the structural nature of the whole:

But ffor-thy that trouthe shuld be declarid by mo wit-
nesse than be oon, I confferme more playnly the trouthe
of this thing. A worthy man, callid Severe, excellent
in wysdome and cunnyng, with thre other men, being the
5   same day and oure of the passing of seint Jerom in the
Cite of Turon, see a vysyone like vnto myn; of whiche
the same Severe witnessith vnto me, for that the highe
Joye of Jerome shuld not be hidde to the worlde, leest
thay that haue delyte to folowe the steppis of his holy-
10   nesse, yf thay knewe not that he hathe so grete a re-
ward, thay myght wex wery and cesse from the way of
holynesse. Godde wold that they shuld see and knowe
how many and worthy rewardis of holynesse he hathe yeff
vnto him, that they shuld the more sikerly drawe after
15   steppis of his vertu -- ffor the hope of rewarde les-
sith the strengthe of laboure. The day of seint Jerome
passing, at complyne-tyme, the said Severe was in his
owne house, and thre other goed men with him, of whiche
too were monkis of seint Martynes monastorye, entending
20   to holy redingis. Sodenly thai herd in heuen, in erthe
and in the ayre innumerable voycis of moest swete songis,
vnherd, vnspekable, and the sound of organys, symphanys
and of instrumentis of all musyke: with the whiche, as
than semyd, heuene and erthe and all thing sownyd on
25   euery syde; so that with swetnesse of that melody theyre
soulis were in poynt to go out of her bodies. And thus
astonyd, thay lokid up in to heuen: and see all the
ayre and all that is about the firmament shyne with
light brighter thane the sonne, out of whome come the
30   swetnesse of all swete odoure. And than thay prayid
god that they myght witt why all this was. Than ther
come a voyse out of heuen and sayd: 'Lat no merueyle

---

19. For the St. Catherine see above, Chapter I, p. 26 .
For Fisher, the example quoted by J. A. Gee, Works of Lupset,
p. 192, is typical; or see the story of Ahab, Mayor's ed. of
Fisher, pp. 132-35, or of the last pennance of Henry VII,
pp. 269-81.

mene yowe, nor think hit not mervelous, thoughe ye
see and here sucche thingis, ffor this day king of
35 kingis and lord of lordis, Crist Jhesu, comythe ffeestifully ayeynyst the soule of gloriouse Jerome in Beth-
elem going out of this wicked world, to lede him to
the kingdome of hevene; so more excellently and highe
toffore other, as he shynyd tofore other in this world
40 by merytis of more highe and holy lyving. This day
the orderis of all angelis, Joying and singing with
sucche voycis as ye here, comyng with thayre lord;
this day all compaynis of patriarkis and prophetis,
this day all holy martyris, this day all confessoris,
45 and this day the gloriouse and moest·highe virgyne
Mary, moder of god, with all her holy virgenys aboute
her, and the soulis of all that bene in blisse, com-
yth Joyfully and ffeestifully ayaynyst thayre contre-
mane, there citezeyne and eyre of heuen with theme'.
50 These thingis said, the voyse was still. But the light,
odoure, and song abode an oure affter, and so seasid.
By this thingis, ffadir, is his shewid that he is of
the hyest Cetecezns of heuenly Jherusalem; and no-man
dout but that, as his will is more nere to goddis will,
55 so he may gitt there what he will, rather than other.[20]

The chapter contains not only straight narrative but doctrinal
exposition, epigram, and visionary description. In contrast
with the misarray of constructions observed in contemporary
original prose of similar type, here the structure clearly
indicates the grouping of ideas into periods. Appropriate
variation in length appears three times: short for transition
(ll. 30-31) and for finality (ll. 50-51), long for panoramic
and climactic effect in the message from the voice (ll. 40-49).
There is no lengthy sub-dependence, and the one extended series — of only four members — is carefully planned (ll. 40-49).
A wide variety of constructions and arrangements has been
handled and always with considerable ease, the whole, in fact,
having a noticeable forward rhythm. Suspended constructions,
for instance, occur six times yet only twice with more than
one clause or phrase inserted after them, only once — in the
climactic series — with more than a few words.[21] There is
some alliteration and polyptoton or translacing[22], but with
only two instances of parison[23], one of isocolon[24], and

20. Pp. 337, l. 17 - p. 338, l. 18. Latin, ed. Migne, Patr.
Lat., XXXIII, Augustini Opera, II, col. 1124.
21. Ll. 4-6; 10-11; 20-21; 22-23; 40-49; 54-55.
22. E.g., ll. 9-15 and 30-33.
23. Ll. 38-39 and 54-55.
24. Ll. 15-16.

one of anaphora[25], the use of structural figures cannot be
called excessive.

The figures are conspicuous, though seldom too much
so, in many of the translations[26]. Though they became of
importance in sixteenth century prose, they are chiefly interesting here not as rhetorical ornament but because they
impart an effect of control over the form, appearing to be
the result of careful manipulation or artifice. This is
especially true of those which require arrangement of the
small structural units. Anaphora, isocolon, or homeoteleuton are impossible in a haphazard length of sub-dependent
cosnstructions; and they cease to be figures if the constructions are forever uniform. Thus in the following passage --
from the Life of St. Mary of Oignies, translated about 1430
-- whatever may have been the appeal of the ornament, the
presence of a plan must have been evident to any reader.
Anaphora and isocolon, used in a variety of ways, indicate
the three main divisions of the first period and, later, the
antithesis between the opening of the whole sequence and the
summation of it.

> And for it profetiþ litil to eschew yuel þurgh þe
> spirite of drede, to do good by þe spirite of pite,
> to haue discrecyone in alle þinges by þe spirite
> of connynge, but if we wiþstande yuell by strengthe,
> 5 kepe oure good dedys by pacyens, endure to the ende
> by sadnesse, & abyde þe mede of euerlastynge lyfe
> by perseuerans and suffraums: þerfore þe fadir vn-
> cuuered his tresours and onoured his doghter wiþ a
> grete precyous stone, þat is þe spirite of strengþe,
> 10 & warisshed hire agayne alle contraryes, atte she
> shulde not be broken wiþ assaylynge of aduersite
> nor made proude wiþ glauerynge of prosperite, atte
> she shulde suffre scornes wiþ pees & tranquillyte,
> atte she shulde doo to no man yuel for yuel. She
> 15 answeryd not to vntrewe accusers, she prayed for
> her pursuers; abidynge in hir purpos by sadnesse of
> mynde, berynge alle thynges esely by sikernesse of
> resone, takynge on hande wilfully harde þinges by
> strengþe of herte, not dredynge harmes euen atte
> 20 hande by sykernesse, hauynge certeyne hope by triste

---

25. Ll. 40-49.
26. Examples in the Curial and in two different Revelations of St. Birgitta have been pointed out above, Chapter I,
pp. 10-11 and 16-17. See also the two translations from
Rolle quoted on pp. 96-98, and the passage from the Life of
St. Catherine of Siena, p. 113.

to brynge hir gode purpos to a good ende, and by my-
kelnesse of myghte gyuynge a ful fynyshynge of hir
holy & pure purpos[27].

The long suspended constructions, 'for it profetiþ litill
. . . but if . . . þerfore . . . ' (ll. 1-7), recall the use
of this device in the early original prose. Here, as in the
quotations from Rolle, Hilton, Love, Lydgate, and others[28],
several short sentence-members have been inserted between the
connectives. But here they do not seem random; they number
only three in the first series and four in the second; no one
of them is in subdependence; no one of them seems an after-
thought. By the elaborate repetition, each short phrase is
plainly marked as one of a series and yet two types of verbal
construction distinguish the two different series. The repetition of by, re-appearing in a new series at the end of the
paragraph, marks the basic thought of the whole, the contrast
in motives for doing good; so that when the end is reached the
writer appears to have chosen the very first constructions
with a view to the very last ones.
        The effect of artifice requires a wide variety in the
expression. The St. Mary shows this in the many epigrammatic
passages to which the Latin author was given. These may be
terse and direct, relying for effect upon the interplay of
meaning:

        lat þe discrete reder take hede þat priuilege of a
        few makiþ not a commun lawe[29].

Or they may be elaborately figured:

        For yuel is nye to þe gode, and oþere-while, while
        we esshewe o vyce, wee slyde in to þe contrary: as,
        whan a man fleeþ superfluyte, sumtyme fallith into
        chynchery, or whanne he eschewiþabyte of seculere
        cloþynge, haþ ioye in foule araye[30].

Several pages earlier the same idea had been put differently;
the typical balance and sound-play were used, but this time
terseness was achieved through ellipsis:

        Sooþly she eschewyd fayre araye & foule booþ ilike:
        for þat one sounes delytes and lustes, & þat oþer
        ypocrisy and preisynge of þe pepil[31].

---

27. English, p. 165, ll. 18-36; Latin, p. 563, E.
28. Chapter II, above.
29. English, p. 136, 116-7; Latin, p. 550, C.
30. English, p. 161, ll. 30-34; Latin, p. 562, A.
31. English, p. 147, ll. 11-14; Latin, p. 555, D.

        This wide use of the possibilities of the language
is characteristic of the mid-century Imitation of Christ.
If the effect of the style in this book is of simplicity,
that is almost altogether because the sentences are short;
suspended constructions, while frequent, seldom lasting for
more than one sentence-member. For variety in construction
and arrangement is constant, and figures of sound or of
structure occur in almost every line. Within the last page
of Book III, for instance, we find a short sequence in plain
structure, relying, like the example from St. Mary, on antithesis of meaning:

        All oÞir askiÞ & sekiÞ her ovne comodites; Þou per-
        tendist allone myn helpe & my profityng, & turnist
        all Þinges to me into good[32].

A few lines later, though the clauses are equally short, the
structure is anything but plain, isocolon and a kind of
chiasmus or reversal of order occurring within a sequence of
three:

        In Þe Þerfore, my lorde god, I put all myn hope & all
        my refuge. In Þe Þerfore I sette all my tribulacion
        & myn aunguisshe, for I finde all vnferme & vnstable
        what euere I beholde oute of Þe[33].

In the prayer which ends the book the chief ornaments are of
sound. The sentences are longer and there is much subordination. But the structure displays mainly a very appropriate
firmness; and this firmness seems artless until we realize
that the three last sentences are equalized in length and in
number of main divisions, and that the variety of constructions appears to have been carefully arranged:

        To Þe are myn eyen dyrecte, my god, fader of mercies.
        Blesse & sanctifie my soule with an heuenly blessing,
        Þat it mowe be Þin holy habitacion & Þe sete of Þin
        euerlastinge glory; & Þat no Þynge be founded in Þe
        temple of Þi dignite Þat mowe offende Þe eyen of Þi
        godenes & Þe multitude of Þi miseracions, & here Þe
        praier of Þy poure seruaunt, beyng in exile al a fer,
        in Þe region of Þe shadowe of deÞe. Defende and kepe
        Þe sould of Þy litel seraunt amonge so many perels of
        Þis corruptible lyf, and, Þy grace going wiÞ, dyrecte

---

32. English, p. 149, ll. 12-14; Latin, III, lix, 20-22.
33. English, p. 149, ll. 20-23; Latin, III, lix, 28-31.

hym by þe wey of pes to þe cuntrey of euerlasting
clerenes[34].

The first of the three long sentences is built on one principal and two relative constructions, the others on two
principal and one participial each, the order and bearing of
the participial in the third being slightly varied from that
in the second and giving the further effect of a suspended
construction.
                At times, though not often, the Imitation of Christ
shows a high complexity of structure, but it is always skilfully measured. The following passage illustrates another
variety of construction in the inversion and ellipsis at the
end; but note especially that while there are two suspended
constructions in the first sentence, neither is held for
longer than one phrase, though the second is further varied
by a brief inversion:

> Lorde, for þou were paciente in thi lyve, þere inne
> fulfyllynge þe commaundement of thi fader, hit is
> worþi þat I, most wrecched synnar, after þi wille
> susteyne my selfe paciently, and þat as longe as
> þou wolte þat I bere þe burdon of þis corruptible
> lyve. ffor if þis lyve be onerouse and hevy, yette
> bi thi grace hit is fulle meritory, and, bi þine
> ensaumple & þe steppes of thi dedes, to the feble
> and þe seke the more tolerable and the more clere[35].

                Rhetorical arrangement of the structure is especially
interesting in ordinary exposition. A doctrinal passage on
canonization in the Life of St. Catherine of Siena, for instance, is introduced and concluded with suspended constructions, the paragraph thus being marked off as a full unit:

> This is the cause why our moder holy chyrche, whan
> she wold canonize ony saynte, fyrste she enquyreth
> of the vertue of pacyence, thenne of the shewing of
> myracles. And that is for two skylles: One is, for
> many euyll lyuers haue do wonder thynges and shall
> do, þat semeth myracles all-though they be none, as
> Simon magus dyd and Anticryst shall do in hys tyme.
> Another is, by-cause som ther hath ben that haue done
> and shewed myracles by vertue of our lord Ihesu the
> whiche haue be dampned afterward, as Judas and all

---

34. English, p. 150, ll. 1-13; Latin, III, lix, 45-55.
35. English, p. 87, l. 29 - p. 88, l. 4; Latin, III, xviii,
15 - 23.

tho þat our lord speketh of in the gospell where he
sayth that som shall stande on þe lyfte syde on the
day of the generall dome and saye to hym in excus-
yng of themself, 'Lord, haue we not in thy name
shewed and do wonderfull myracles?' to whom our lord
shall answere agayne and say, 'Go ye from me, werkers
of wickydnes.' By these two skylles ye may vnderstond
þat holy chyrche in erthe may not only be certyfyed
by myracles whether þat persone be holy or not by
whom they be shewed, all-be-it þat they shewe pre-
sumpcyon of holynesse, and namely tho myracles that
ben shewed after the deth of a persone. For though
they were no sayntes at whos graues myracles ben
shewed, yet were possyble þat our mercyable lord
sholde haue them excused and yelde them after theyre
meke byleue the which beleuen that they be sayntes,
not for them that ben there beryed, but for the glo-
rye and the ioye of hys owne name, lest they the
whiche beleue in hym be defrawded from theyre de-
syre. Wher-fore oure moder holy chyrche in erthe,
that is gouerned by the holy ghost, desyryng for to
be certifyed of the merites of holy sayntes as moche
as it is possyble in this lyf, enquyreth specyally
of theyr vertuous lyuyng and of tho thynges þat they
wrought whyles they lyued in erthe[36].

The bulk of the structure here is in the normal or 'loose'
order, the subordinate members following the principal. But
unless it be in the third sentence, which is somewhat expanded from the Latin, the subordinate members all have a clear
place in the whole thought-relationship; there is an easy
command over phraseology. (E.g., 'not for . . . but for
. . . lest . . . ' at the end of the next to last sentence.)
No doubt much of this command was due to the influence of
the source and not to the translator himself[37]. But the
effect upon the reader, of course, is the same as if the
writing were original.
    In general terms, it is this effect of planned or
controlled structure which is most significant as a touch-
stone. The structural figures are only one source of the
effect; naturally they heighten it, but it can be created in
other important ways. In narrative especially one source of
it -- observed in The Three Kings of Cologne and other

---

36. English, Part III, cap. vi, p. 383, l. 40 - p. 384, l.
13; Latin, Pars III cap. vi, p. 959, E-F.
37. See the comparison between this translator's original
and translated writing, Chapter I, above, p. 24-28.

closely translated narratives or in the original narratives written late in the century -- is simply the use of
varied instead of uniform structure. In any complex structure, at the same time, inconsistency of construction must,
of course, be practically absent for the effect of control
to remain, and there must be no lengthy sub-dependence or
other insertions which destroy the accord between the whole
thought-sequence and the form.

Comparing by these standards, there is a very typical difference between the original English prose of before
1470 or 1480 and the translations of the same period. Not
all but almost all translations normally give the effect of
plan and control in the structure; while with still fewer
exceptions the original writing normally lacks it. The contrast is most striking when we have the opportunity to compare the same writers' work in both classes.

The difference, of course, is not hard to explain.
The early writers had not yet formed the habit of composing
by units broader than the separate sentence-member[38].
But in close translation, whether or not they understood
the principles by which the source was composed, their careful adherence to it resulted in an English prose of similar
structure. Thus while the original prose seems naïve, un-
practised, the translations have the structural character-
istics of the matured literature which lay behind them. But
this, while interesting in itself, is not so significant as
the fact that many of the translations long antedate the
original prose of the early sixteenth century and yet re-
selble it in precisely these qualities of structural breadth
and accuracy.

At the same time, this very sign of maturity in composition, the ability to plan and control structure by broad
units, is one of the principal differences between early sixteenth century writers and those of a hundred years before.
Mr. R. W. Chambers, while leaving out of consideration this
difference in structure, has shown many general resemblances
in spirit and tone[39]. On the other hand, Mr. G. P. Krapp[40]
and Mr. G. A. Gee[41], discussing the revival of the classics
as a cause of the difference, have pointed out that the prose
of the early humanists was not closely imitated from classical models. 'The skillful phrasing and sentence-structure of
the classics revealed the underlying principles of prose composition, and it was these principles, rather than the par-

38.   Chapter II, above, pp. 35, ff.
39.   The Continuity of English Prose, pp. ci, ff.
40.   The Rise of Eng. Lit. Prose, pp. 273-76.
41.   Life and Works of Lupset, pp. 191-92.

ticular way the ancients applied them, which determined in most instances English style'[42] .

Being thus general, however, the differences need not be explained wholly as the result of classical influence. Aside from mannerisms of style, sixteenth century practice in composition could have been affected in the same respects by concurrent or earlier influence from good medieval Latin and to a large extent from late medieval French. The literature of English prose had for a hundred years included translated writing which was composed on principles of unity and proportion taken directly from Latin or French prose.

To judge from the prose in the chronicles, the change in original prose was not sudden. By the third quarter of the fifteenth century there was already a strong tendency among obscure and average writers to adopt the structural characteristics which later became conspicuous in the hands of more able men. There is, of course, no reason to consider these chroniclers themselves of any influence; and we may still date the established change at approximately 1500. But they are a significant indication that a gradual evolution toward maturity in prose form had been at work for a long time. Even without this indication it would seem reasonable to assume that the appearance in the sixteenth century of what resemble Latin standards of composition, was to some degree simply a result of such an evolution and of lessons taken from the past.

It is not so much from the work of any one English writer that we should expect such influence to come, but from the constant accumulation and increasing circulation of prose writings in which the possibilities of structural form appeared more and more evident. It is not likely, then, that among the influences from the English past the isolated figures of Pecock or of Fortescue were of much importance. In fact, as Mr. Chambers has pointed out[43], the English writings of these men appear not to have remained long in circulation; Pecock's books were suppressed after his trial in 1457, and although there are extant ten manuscripts of Fortescue's Governance[44], this and his few other English works were left unprinted till 1714.

Nor should any one translator be regarded as especially significant. But it seems altogether likely that the effects of the translated prose would have been felt because of its very quantity. It is not as though there had been only a few books of this prose, which must be shown so revolution-

---

42. Gee, op. cit., p. 191.
43. Op. cit., pp. cxxxvi - cxxxviii.
44. Intro. to the edition by C. Plummer, Oxford, 1883, pp. 87-93.

ary that their qualities would be readily perceived in
their own day, or which must be traced in the libraries or
in the work of those who we think may have used them. The
situation was rather that the widespread activities of the
translators continued for a century to be responsible for a
very considerable proportion of all the prose circulated
among English readers. While a great many -- nearly half --
of them were religious, the books made by the translators
ranged over the whole field of medieval interests. We may
easily believe, then, that everybody who read during the
fifteenth century, and especially during the latter half,
read more or less widely in translations.

At the same time, the number of writers who put
themselves under the discipline of a foreign original was
large. Though there apparently was no literary standard to
compel them, the prevailing practice among these men was to
adhere to the original as closely as their English would
naturally permit. Only a few relied upon themselves to im-
provise the constructions with which to express the meanings
of the source. The others,as a very fast rule, simply
found an English equivalent for the type of construction
which they saw before them. At least eighty percent of the
translated books were composed in this way.

There are, then, two processes through which the
frequent practice of close translation could have been imparting maturity to English habits of prose structure:
first, through the act of translation itself, and second,
in the circulation of the translated prose. The evidence
which I have gathered from collation shows that the fifteenth
century writers produced more mature prose when translating
than they did when independent, in respect to the correctness
of logical consistency of its constructions and to the broader
qualities of its lucidity and unity. Unless it be that of
Caxton[45], I have not found any case where it can be shown
that a writer actually learned from his experience at translation to compose for himself the kind of structure he put
together out of his source. Yet with extant writing for
comparison so scarce[46], I think we may safely appeal to
probability and assume that among so many men building their
English sentences so often upon sure models, there must have
appeared at least an increased recognition of both the mechanical and the logical processes of structure, if not in many
cases a capable control over them.

45. Chapter I, above, p. 28-9.
46. Edward of York, possibly Nicholas Love, both of before
1410, and Caxton are the only translators who have left more
than a page or two of their own work.

That the circulation of translations had a similar effect upon readers is of course still more a matter only of probability. Yet in the formation of taste, the probability of influence is even higher. People must have found the translated prose occasionally difficult because of a blind error by the translator, occasionally a bit outlandish, too, because of a foreign word or idiom, and not infrequently somewhat stiff. But we can be sure that this prose was read and read widely, and that, indeed, the bulk of many people's reading must have consisted of translated books. It seems reasonable also to assume, therefore, that many Englishmen, consciously or unconsciously, acquired from them, first, a sense of the firmness of the structure in this prose as compared with the looseness of that in the original prose; and second, a perception of the advantages in facility and clarity which were brought by control over the form. Nor is it too much to suppose that in many instances his reading affected the individual's practice of composition, either in studied imitation or from new habits of casting his thoughts.

The influence upon the structural style of the translations themselves is completely tangible. Beyond that, in the absence of contemporary reference, there is no chance to trace it precisely. But the analysis of original writing and of the whole history and procedure of translation shows that what the one at first lacked -- technical adequacy -- the other was in every way in a position to supply.

APPENDIX

Appendix A

A LIST OF FIFTEENTH CENTURY ENGLISH PROSE

TRANSLATIONS, WITH THE SOURCES.

The following bibliography of translations is intended as a reference list for the examples discussed and as an indication of the quantity of translation during the century. Therefore it is largely made up of texts which are accessible in modern editions; yet it also lists many pieces which are to be found only in manuscript or early print but which are known to have had a foreign original. The latter usually are connected with some well-known translator, as the Vitas Patrum of Caxton; or else they represent separate translations of a work of which a translation is published, as the earlier prose Golden Legend. The one text belonging to the fourteenth century -- Trevisa's Polichronicon -- and the several from the early sixteenth -- as certain of Robert Copland's -- appear for their interest in connection with translations or translating activities of the fifteenth.

The sources of the translations are even more often inaccessible than the translations themselves. I have noted all sources by reference to the place most accessible -- modern re-print, old print, or manuscript. In cases where I am not certain of the exact source, I have briefly discussed the evidence under the listing of the text in question.

Although the chief interest is in the translations and the translators, I have listed all pieces under the name of the original author or title. There are two principal reasons for this: it follows the practice of formal bibliographers, and so makes outside reference easier; and it groups together all different translations of one original work.

Under a separate chronological list, however, I have used the English name or title to head a brief cross-reference, so that all the work of any one English translator comes together within the period to which he belonged.

AESOPUS - Caxton, Wm., The book of the subtyl historyes and fables of Esope. Printed by Caxton, 1484. Modern reprints:

ed. Jos. Jacobs, London, 1889, 2 Vols.; San Francisco,
The Grabhorn Press, 1930.

Source - French: [Julien Macho] , Les subtiles fables
d'Esope. Lyon, Mathieu Husz, 1486, etc. See G. C. Keidel,
Manual of Aesopic fable lit. . . . for the period ending
1500, Baltimore, 1896.

ALEXANDER - Anon., . . . the lyf of gret Alexander. Ca. 1430.
Ed. by J. S. Westlake, EETS o s CXLIII, 1913.

Source - Latin: A lost prose version based on the so-called
J 3 version, which in turn is two stages removed from Leo's
Historia de Preliis. See G. L. Hamilton, 'A New Redaction
of the "Historia de Preliis",' Speculum, II (1927), 113-131;
F. P. Magoun, Jr., The Gests of King Alexander, Cambridge,
1929, pp. 55-56.

ALPHABETUM NARRATIONUM - Anon., [An Alphabet of Tales]. c. 1420.
Ed. by Mary M. Banks, EETS o s CXXVI, CXXVII, 1904-05.

Source - Latin: Alphabetum Narrationem quae ad mores et pie-
tatem faciunt. Many Mss.; e.g., Oxf. Balliol 219, Brit. Mus.
Harley 268, Arundel 378. No modern edition.

APOLLONIUS - Copland, Robert, Kynge Appolyn of Thyre. Printed
by W. de Worde, 1510, Re-printed in facsimile by E. W.
Ashbee, London, 1870. (21 copies only -- not seen.)

Source - French: A late form of the prose romance. Neither
of the two texts printed by C. B. Lewis, in Rom. Forsch.,
XXXIV, (1913), 1 - 127, is said by the editor to represent a
source for Copland. See further Elinor Klebs, Erzählung
App. . . . und spätere bearbeitungen, Berlin, 1899, pp. 414-
15.

ARISTOTLE, pseud. - Anon., The Governance of Lordschippes.   c.
1400. Ed. by Robert Steele, Three Prose Versions of the
Secreta Secretorum. EETS e s lxxiv, 1898, pp. 41-118.

Source - Latin: Secreta Secretorum. 'Eastern' Arabic form,
translation of Philip, c. 1240, revised c. 1259. Edited
(from a XIIIth cent. MS. of Roger Bacon's edition, Bodl.
Tanner 116) by R. Steele, Opera Hactenus Inedita Rogeri
Baconi, Fasc. V, Oxford, 1920.

ARISTOTLE, pseud., - Yonge, Jas., The Gouernaunce of Prynces
or Pryvete of Pryveteis. c. 1420. Ed. by R. Steele, EETS
e s lxxiv, 1898, pp. 119-248.

Source — French: Joffroi de Waterford, Secré de secrés.
MS. Bib. Nat. f.f. 1822, c. 1290 (Steele, Opera . . .
Baconi, p. xxxii). Not in print. There are short extracts
in Hist. Litt. de la France, XXI, 1897, 217-225, and by Ch.
Gidel, Association pour l'encouragement des études grecques
en France, Annuaire, Paris, 1874, pp. 305-10; the article
by Gidel reprinted in Nouvelles Études sur la Littérature
Grecque Moderne, 1878, pp. 351, ff.

ARISTOTLE, pseud. — Anon., [Secreta Secretorum] , In Ms. Bodl.
Ashmole 396, f.1. 'XVth Century.' No modern edition; R.
Steele, EETS e s lxxiv, p. 249, gives the list of chapters,
which are different, in wording as well as selection, from
the edited translations.

Source — Latin? W. H. Black, Cat. of MSS. . . Bodl. . .
Ashmole, Oxford, 1845, says of the text in the Ashmole Ms.
that it was 'Translated from the Latin of Master Phillip.'
There is, however, nothing in the few lines quoted from the
Ms. by Black which could not be as well from the French.
(Cp. the English translation in MS. Brit. Mus. Royal 18 A.
vii, as below.)

ARISTOTLE, pseud. — Anon., . . . the gouernaunce of kings and
princes. 'sec. XV.' In MS. Univ. Coll. Oxf. 85, 2. No
modern edition. Title of prologue: 'The prologue of a doc-
tour recommending Aristotle.' Begins: 'God Almyghty pre-
serve oure kynge and the prosperite of his true subgites.'
Ends: 'And thou holde the on the better parte and moost
profitable.'

Source — Latin? I am judging only from the few phrases
above, which are closer verbally to the edited English translation from Latin than to that from French, as in MS. Brit.
Mus. Royal 18 A. vii. But there were many different French
translations. (Steele, Opera . . . Baconi, p. xxxi-ii.)

ARISTOTLE, Pseud. — Shirley, John, . . . the gouernaunce of
Prynces, seyd the Secrete of Secretes. c. 1440. In MS.
Brit. Mus. Addit. 5467. (C. Bernard, Cat. Lib. MSS. Ang.
et Hib., Oxford, 1697.) No modern edition.

Source — Latin? French? Shirley made other translations
from both languages.

ARISTOTLE, pseud. — Gilbert of the Haye, The Buke of the Governaunce of Princis. 1456. Ed. by J. H. Stevenson (Scot.
Text Soc. 62), 1914.

Source — French: Haye says (pp. 74-75) ' . . . and first
the proloug as it is contenyt in the fraunch buke . . .
And syne was this ilke buke translatid out of Latyne in
the langage of Romaine nocht halely but alsmekle as thame
thocht nedefull and spedefull to the governaunce of princis.' The many French MSS. and printed versions are
listed by Steele, Opera . . . Baconi, pp. xxxi-iii. No
modern edition.

ARISTOTLE, pseud. - Anon., The Secrete of Secretes. c. 1460.
In MS. Brit. Mus. Royal, 18. A. vii. Ed. by R. Steele,
EETS e s lxxiv, 1898, p. 1 - 39.

Source — French: Secret de secres (MS. Cambg. Univ. Libr.
F f. I.33) See Steele, Opera . . . Baconi, p. xxxii. No
modern edition.

ARISTOTLE, pseud. - Copland, Robert, Secrete of Secretes of
Arystotle. Printed by Robert and William Copland, 1528.
'The Secret of Aristotyle with the Governale of Princes
and every maner of estate, with rules for helth of body
and soul, very gode to teche children to rede English,
newly translated out of French . . .' (Warton, ed. R.
Price, 1840, II, 231) No modern edition.

Source — French: I do not know what version Copland may
have used.

ARS MORIENDI - Anon., . . . tretis . . . of the crafte of
dyinge. Early XVth cent. Ed. by C. Horstmann, Yorkshire
Writers, II, 406-420.

Source — Latin: See the source for the following translation.

ARS MORIENDI - The Craft of Deyng. Early XVth cent. Ed. by
J. R. Lumby, EETS o s XLIII, 1870. An abridged translation,
or from an abridged original. The material corresponds to
the first two and one-third chapters of the earlier text
edited by Hortsmann.

Source — Latin: Ars Moriendi, a treatise, often attributed
to Gerson, which seems to have been much altered in the
XVth cent. In general, its printed texts have two forms,
one usually titled Ars Moriendi, the other De Arte bene
moriendi or Speculum Artis bene moriendi; the second,
though often abridged, being the longer. I do not know
what may have been the exact source for either of the above

translations. The xylographic editio princeps, [Cologne,
1450], ed. in facsimile, by W. H. Rylands, London, 1891,
represents the shorter form; but the shorter translation
above is only roughly like it and contains material not
in it but in the longer English text above. I have found
no modern edition of the longer De Arte.

ARS MORIENDI – Caxton, Wm., . . . a lityll treatise . . .
    spekynge of the arte & crafte to know well to die. Printed
    by Caxton,[1490]. In fac-simile, 'sold by the assignees
    of E. Lumby, deceased,' London, 1875.

    Source – French: a translation of a Latin De Arte bene . .
    etc. Of the liure intitule lart de bien mourir, printed
    by A. Verard, Paris, 1492, 1493, etc., F. M. M. Comper,
    Book of the Craft of Dying, London, 1917, p. 45, says 'it
    is quite another book.' Comper was unable to find an ex-
    act source. Possibly it was un petit traité de l'art de
    bien mourir, by Jean Mielot, MS. Bib. Nat. fr. 12,441.
    No modern edition of any French version.

ARS MORIENDI – Caxton, Wm., . . . a lytyll treatise called
    ars moriendi . . Printed by Caxton, [1491]. Ed. by W.
    B[lades], London, 1869; by E. W. B. Nicholson, in fac-
    simile, London, 1891.

    Source – Latin? 'No other copy, manuscript or printed,
    in Latin or in any other language, appears to be known.'
    (Blades, Caxton, 2nd ed., 1882, p. 359.) 'This particular
    tract appears to be a further abridgement of Caxton's al-
    ready abridged version.' (F. M. M. Comper, op. cit.,
    p. 102.)

ARS MORIENDI – Anon., . . . the art of good lyuyng & good
    deying. Printed by A. Verard, Paris, [1503]. No modern
    edition. This, like his Shepherd's Kalendar, was a
    wretched attempt by Verard to gain an English market.

    Source: French: Lart de bien vivre; lart de bien mourir.
    Printed by Verard, Paris, 1492, 1493, etc. No modern edi-
    tion.

ARS MORIENDI – Chertsey, Andrew, The craft to live well and
    to die well. Printed by W. de Worde, 1505/06 (21 Jan.)
    No modern edition. For the ascription to Chertsey by R.
    Copland, see D N B, article 'Chertsey.'

    Source – French: the Verard of 1492. (Comper, op. cit.,
    p. 49.)

ARTHUR - Bourchier, John, Lord Berners, Arthur of Lytell
Brytayne. Printed by Copland for Redbourne, 1555(?); but
translated before 1533. Ed., occasionally modernized, by
E. V. Utterson, 1814.

Source - French: Artus de la Petite Bretagne. Printed at
Lyon, 1496, Paris, 1502, etc. (Brunet, Manuel, I, 519,
ff.) No modern edition.

AYMON - Caxton, Wm., The four sons of Aymon. Printed by
Caxton, [1489]. Ed. by Octavia Richardson, EETS e s xliv,
xlv, 1885.

Source - French: Les Quatre Filz Aymon. A prose redaction (by Huon de Villeneuve?) from the verse. Printed at
Lyons 1480 , 1493, 1495, No modern edition. But see
Histoire des Quatre Filz Aymon . . . Transcription d'apres
l'édition de 1480, par Jean d'Albignac, Paris, 1908; text
fairly close, but modernized without warning.

BENEDICTUS - Anon., the holy rule of saynte Benet. Printed
by Caxton [Book of Divers Ghostly Matters, no. 3], 1491.
Ed. by E. Kock, EETS o s CXX, 1902. Dom A. M. Albarada,
Bibl. de la Regla Benedictina, Monester de Montserrat,
1933, p. 143, says Caxton's text is the same as Pynson's,
[1516], which has long been ascribed to Bishop Foxe. It
must be noted, however, that Caxton's Rule is included in
a volume with two other religious pieces which are very
old (Orologium Sapientiae, c. 1420; Twelve Profits of Tribulation, early XVth cent.)

Source - Latin: Regulum S. Benedicti. Many MSS. and early
prints (see A. M. Albarada, as above, and H. Logeman in
EETS o s XC, p. xxvi-xxix). Caxton's translation differs
considerably, though chiefly by reduction, from the standard
text as now frequently edited, (Collation EETS o s CXX, p.
xv-xvi.)

BERNARD, SAINT - Anon., Medytacons of Saynt Bernarde . . .
'translated fro Latin in to Englissh by a deuoute Student
of the unyuersitie of Cambrydge.' Printed by W. de Worde,
1496. No modern edition.

Source - Latin: Meditationes piessimae de cognitione hum-
anae conditionis. Ed. by J. P. Migne, Patr. Lat., CLXXIV
(Bernardi Opera, III), Paris, 1879, col. 485-508.

BIRGITTA, SAINT - Anon., [The Revelations of Saint Birgitta].
c. 1450. MS. belonging to Mr. Robert Garrett, Baltimore,

Md., fol. 1, r. - 63, r.   Ed. by W. P. Cumming, EETS o s CLXXVIII, 1929. This, the fullest known selection of the Revelations, by a single translator, was later added to by a second.

Source - Latin: The same source was used for all of the English Revelations. See the last entry under 'Birgitta,' below.

BIRGITTA, SAINT - Anon., [Revelations]. c. 1470. In the Garrett MS., as above, fol. 64, r. - 77, v., incomplete. Ed. by W. P. Cumming, op. cit. These additional Revelations were the work of a second translator.

BIRGITTA, SAINT - Anon., [Revelations]. Short selections (Cumming, op. cit., p. xix). Separate translations. In MS. Brit. Mus. Arundel 197, 'last half of fifteenth century,' and MS. Lambeth 432, 'Fifteenth century' (Cumming, op. cit., p. xix, and C. Horstmann, Anglia, III (1880), 320). Both unedited, except fol. 36, r. - 37, r. of Lambeth, which are part of the St. Jerome printed by Horstmann, op. cit. (See below under 'Saints' Lives'.)

BIRGITTA, SAINT - Anon., The Revelation of Sainct Bridgitte. Selections. (Concordance in Cumming, op. cit., p. xvii.) MS. Brit. Mus. Cotton, Claudius B. I. 'Fifteenth century.' No modern edition. A separate translation (Cumming, pp. xix-xxi).

BIRGITTA, SAINT - Anon., [Revelations]. Bks. I - VII. MS. Brit. Mus. Cotton, Julius, F. II. 'Fifteenth century.' No modern edition. W. P. Cumming, op. cit., pp. xvi - xxi, describes this as a separate translation. He prints 28 lines (Bk. I, Chap. VIII) pp. 123-4.

BIRGITTA, SAINT - Anon., [Revelations] Bk. IV and the beginning of Bk. V. MS. Brit. Mus. Harley 4800. 'Fifteenth century.' No modern edition.

BIRGITTA, SAINT - Anon., Revelations Selections (Cumming, p. xviii). MS. Bodl. Rawlinson C. 41. 'End of the fifteenth century.' No modern edition. This translation 'differs in method . . . and in style from all the others.' (Cumming, p. xx.)

Source, for all translations - Latin: Revelationes, written in Swedish and translated into Latin 1345 - 1373. The collection totals over 650 Revelations. Many MSS. (some are listed by Cumming, p. xx, n. 2). I have used a satisfactory text ed. by Consaluus Durantus, Rome, 1628, 2 Vols.

BLANCHARDINE - Caxton, Wm., Blanchardyn and Eglantyne.
Printed by Caxton 1489. Ed. by Leon Kellner, EETS e s
lviii, 1890.

Source - French: Blancadin et l'orgueilleuse d'amor, a
XVth prose redaction of the roman in verse. MS. Bib. Nat.
f. fr. 24,371 is close to the one used by Caxton (Kellner,
op. cit., p. cxxii). No modern edition.

BONAVENTURA, St., pseudo - Love, Nicholas, The Mirrour of the
blessed lyf of Jesu Christ. Before 1410. Many MSS.
Printed by Caxton, 1487, etc. Ed., from MSS., by L. F.
Powell, Oxford and London, 1908. (The edition of 1908 for
the Roxburghe Club is exactly the same.)

Source - Latin? French? The Meditationes Vitae Christi
were attributed to Cardinal Bonaventura. Not included in
the Florence 10 vol. ed. of Bonaventura, 1882-1902; I have
used the ed. of Venice, 1756, Vol. 12, p. 380, ff., and
the text printed by Zegner at Augsburg, 14[68], which is
essentially the same. Early in the XVth century, Jean de
Gallopes (see Guillaume de Deguileville, Pilg. Soul) made
a translation of it into French, Le Livre dore des Meditacions de la vie Nostre Seigneur Jesu-crist. MSS. Brit.
Mus. Royal 20. B. IV, Bib. Nat. anc. f. 7274, 7274-2. etc.
(P. Paris, Les MSS., VII, 247 - 9). No modern edition.
Love claims to have gone to the Latin, and at the beginning he explains how to distinguish what is translated
from what is added. However, the whole work is so considerably different from the Latin, even where he is supposedly following it (e.g. Chap. III, de altercacione),
that suspicion of an intermediate source is inevitable.
Blades (Caxton, 2nd ed., 1885, p. 318) stated, and has
been often followed since, that the source was Gallopes'
translation. Dedicated to Henry V, however, this French
version seems too late for Love, unless one argues of it
as W. L. Hare (Apollo, XIV (1931), 211) did of Gallopes'
Pèl. de l'ame, that the dedication had been added later.
As in the case of the Pelerinage, however, no one, unless
it be Blades, has compared Love with the French.

BONET, HONORÉ - Gilbert of the Haye, The Buke of the Law of
Armys or Buke of Bataillis. 1456. Ed. by J. H. Stevenson
(Scot. Text Soc., 44), 1901.

Source - French: Arbre des Battailles. C. 1385. Ed. by
E. Nys, Brussels, 1883. 'How far Haye's work is that of
recension, how far mere translation is a matter of doubt
. . . All the early MS. copies of Bonet's book differ
from each other.' (Stevenson, p. lviii.)

BRANT, SEBASTIAN - Watson, Henry, The shyppe of fools. [In prose.] Printed by Wynkyn de Worde, 1509. No modern edition. Fr. Zarncke, Sebastian Brant's Narrenschiff, Liepzig, 1854, prints (pp. 242 - 245) the prologue, chaps. 1, 4, 62, and the epilogue.

Source - French: La grant nef des folz du monde, translated into prose from Jacob Locher's Latin verse by Jean Drouyn. Printed by Balsarin at Lyons, 1498. No modern edition. Zarncke (op cit., p. 226 - 230) prints from the prologue, the epilogue, and chaps. 1, 4, 62.

BRANT, SEBASTIAN - Barclay, Alexander, . . . the Shyp of folys. Printed by R. Pynson, 1509. Ed. by T. H. Jamieson, Edinburgh, 1874, Vol. 1, The Prologue, pp. 5 - 10, and the argument, pp. 17 - 18, are in prose.

Source - Latin: Jacob Locher's Stultifera Navis, printed at Basel by J. Bergman, 1497, etc. No modern edition. Fr. Zarncke, op. cit., pp. 210 - 217, prints part of the Prologue and Argument. The last third of Barclay's argument is from the French of Drouyn, as above.

BUONACCORSSO DE PISTOJA - Tiptoft, John, Earle of Worcester, . . . the Declamation of Noblesse. C. 1465. Printed by Caxton, 1481 (with the two translations from Cicero; this piece is not listed separately in the Short Title Cat. or in Duff. See Blades, 2nd ed. p. 230.) Ed. by R. J. Mitchell in her John Tiptoft, London, 1938.

Source - French: Jean Mielot, La controversie de noblesse. C. 1449. From the Italian? Many Mss.: e.g. of the Bib. Royale de belgique, containing also the ordre de chevalerie (Lull). (A. T. P. Byles, RES, VI (1930), 305 - 08). Printed by C. Mansion, Bruges [1475] and by A. Verard, Paris, 1497 (with the Gouvernement des Princes). No modern edition.

CANUTUS (KANUTUS) - Anon., A . . . boke . . . aȝenst the Pestilence. Printed by [Wm. de Machlinia] before 1500. No modern edition.

Source - Latin: Regimen contra pestilentiam. There are five XV cent. prints without place or date; another, Lyons, 1498; another, Copenhagen, 1508; etc. No modern edition.

CAORSINUS, GUILIELMUS - Kay, John, . . . the siege . . . of Rhodes. Printed by Lettou and Machlinia? about 1482? No modern edition.

Source — Latin: _Rhodie obsidionis descriptio_. Printed at Rome by E. Silber, [1478]; again, without name or place, 1481; as No. 1 in _Opera_ by J. Reger de Kemnat, Ulm, 1496. No modern edition.

CATHARINE OF SIENA — see under Saints' Lives, below.

CATO, DIONYSIUS — Caxton, Wm., . . . _this book which is sayd or called Cathon_. Printed by Caxton, 1483. No modern edition. The matter translated by Caxton is commentary or gloss to the _Disticha_ as translated by B. Burgh, and printed in the same edition.

Source — French: one of the many prose glosses of the XVth century. M. Förster (_Archiv_, CXLV (1923), 209) says, 'wie ich sie z. B. in einem späteren Lyoner Druck von 1521 fand.' i.e. _Les mots et sentences dorees du maistre_ . . . _Caton_ . . . _avecques bons enseignemens_ . . . _a ung chacun_, O. Arnoullet, Lyons, 1521.

CESSOLIS, JACOBUS DE — Caxton, Wm., _The game and playe of the chesse_, 1474. Printed by Caxton [1476]. Ed. by Wm. E. A. Axon, London, 1883; there were also three limited editions of a re-print, with remarks signed by Vincent Figgins, London, 1855, 1860, and 1862 (80 copies only).

Source — French: _le jeu des Echez moralisé_; a work existing in two mid-fourteenth century translations from the Latin _Moralisatio super ludo Scachorum_, one by Jean Ferron, the other by Jean de Vignay. Both are found in many MSS., but only the Vignay was printed — by A. Verard, in a volume with _L'ordre de chevalerie_ (Lull) etc., at Paris, 1504. (Again, M. le Noir, Paris, 1505). There is no modern edition of either French translation. Caxton is stated (Blades, 2nd ed. 1882, p. 174; etc.) to have used mostly the Vignay, but also parts of the Ferron. There are some MSS., like Bib. Nat. 7389, which contain a compilation of both, 'en prenant puis l'une puis l'autre, ainsy que bon a semble au compilateur.' For full bibliography of the Latin, French, and English versions, see Antonius van de Linde, _Geschichte und Literatur des Schachspiels_, Berlin, 1874, Vol. I., Beilagen, pp. 34 – 125.

CHARLES — Caxton, Wm., _thystorye and lyf of_ . . . _Charles the grete_. Printed by Caxton, 1485. Ed. by S. J. H. Herrtage, EETS e s xxxvii, 1881.

Source — French: _Fier a Bras_. A prose redaction from the verse. Printed at Geneva, 1478, at Lyons by Le Roy, 1487,

etc. Frequently reprinted, under the title of La Con-
queste du grant roy Charlemaigne . . . etc. , in the XVI
century, sometimes in the XVII, and in the XVIII at Troyes
'chez la Ve Oudot' (Brunet Manuel, II, i, 229). Each re-
print, including the Troyes, said to depend only on its immediate predecessor. No modern edition.

CHARTIER, ALAIN - Caxton, Wm.,   . . . the Curial. Printed by
Caxton, [1484]. Ed. by F. J. Furnivall and P. Meyer, EETS
e s, liv, 1888.

Source - French: Ed. by Ferd. Heuckenkamp, Le Curial par
Alain Chartier. Texte francais du XVe siecle avec l'orig-
inal Latin publiés d'apres les manuscripts. Halle, 1899.
See p. xxxv - vi for Caxton's relation to the MS. stemma.

CHRISTINA, SAINT - See under Saints' Lives, below.

CICERO - Tiptoft, John, Earl of Worcester,   . . . Tullius de
Amicicia. C. 1465. Printed by Caxton, 1481. No modern
edition.

Source - Latin: Cicero's Laelius de Amicitia. See H. B.
Lathrop, 'The translations of John Tiptoft', M. L. N.,
LXI (1926), 496 - 501.

CICERO - Worcester-Botoner, Wm.? . . . Tulle of olde age.
C. 1470. Printed by Caxton, 1481. Ed. by H. Susebach,
Halle, 1933 (St. z. Engl. Phil., LXXV). Long attributed
to John Tiptoft, this has been given to William of Worcester by H. B. Lathrop, M. L. N. LXI (1926) 496 - 501,
and by Susebach, p. xv - xviii.

Source - French: Laurent de Premierfait, Le livre de
Tulle de Viellesse. C. 1405. MSS. Brit. Mus. Addit. 17,433,
Harley 4917,etc. (Susebach, xiii, n. 1). Susebach believes
on a basis of common errors that the English translator
actually used the Addit. MS. I have found no early print
and no modern edition.

CREED AND PRAYERS (Betson) - Betson, Thos., . . . a ryght
profytable treatyse compendiously drawn out of many &
dyvers writings of holy men. Printed by W. de Worde, 1500.
Modern reprint in the Cambridge XVth cent. Facsimiles,
1905.

Source - Latin: the catechism, prayers mostly occasional,
excerpts from St. Bernard, etc.

CORDIALE - Woodville, Anthony, Earl Rivers, Memorare nouis-
sima. 1478. Printed by Caxton 1479. No modern edition.

Source - French: Jean Mielot, Les Quatre Dernières Choses.
1453. A translation of a Latin Cordiale, Quatuor Novissima, which exists in various forms, as do the several different French translations. Mielot's was printed by Caxton
at Bruges, 1476. From rapid collation I believe this to be
the exact text used by Rivers.

DICTS - Scrope, Stephen, . . . the Doctryne & the Wysedome of
The Wyse Auncyent Philosophers . . . 1450. Ed. by Margaret
E. Schofield, Phila., 1936.

Source - French: See the source for the following translation.

DICTS - Woodville, Anthony, Earl Rivers, The dictes or say-
ingis of the philosophres. C. 1476. Printed by Caxton,
1477. Fac-simile, by Wm. Blades, London, 1877.

Source, for both translations of the Dicts - French: Guil-
laume de Tignonville, les Dicts Moraulx des philosophes.
C. 1420. Printed by C. Mansion at Bruges [n.d.]: by A
Verard, Paris, 1486, etc. No modern edition.

DIODORUS SICULUS - Skelton, John, Diodori siculi histor-
iarum Priscarum a Poggio ref. In English. First five books.
Before 1490 (cited by Caxton, Prologue to Eneydos, 1490).
MS. Cambridge, Corpus Christi College, 357. No modern edi-
tion. An excerpt (int. to Bk. V) given by H. B. Lathrop,
The Classics in Translation, Madison, 1933, pp. 26-7.

Source - Latin: 'Diodori Siculi Historiarum Priscarum a
Poggio in Latinum traduci . . . ' [1449] Printed at Bologna,
1472, at Venice 1476, 1497. No modern edition.

ELIZABETH OF HUNGARY, SAINT - Anon., . . . the reuelacions of
Saynt Elysabeth, the Kynges doughter of hungarye. Printed
by W. de Worde, [1493], with the Life of Catharine of
Siena. Ed. by C. Horstmann, Archiv, LXXVI (1886), 392-400.

Source - Latin?: I do not know the source of this translation.

ELIZABETH OF SPALBECK - see under Saints' Lives, below.

EYNSHAM (Revelation) - Anon., . . . a meruelous reuelacion
. . . by sent Nycholas to a monke of Euyshamme. Printed
by Wm. de Macklinia, London, 1485. Ed. by E. Arber,
English Reprints, no. 10, London, 1869.

Source – Latin: . . . de quadam visione terribili de
suppliciis . . . facta Edmundo monacho de Eynesham. C.
1189. Found in Roger of Wendover's Flores Historiarum,
ed. by H. O. Coxe, London, 1841, III, 97 ff., and by H. G.
Hewlett, Rolls Series no. 84, I, 246 ff. Thence it passed
into Mathew Paris' Chronica Majorica, ed. H. R. Luard,
Rolls Series no. 57, V, 423 ff. However, both these texts
are abbreviated, or the work much expanded in other versions; for the English contains many times more material,
mostly pointedly the numerous individual histories.

FROISSART, JEAN – Bourchier, John, Lord Berners, Chronicles.
Printed by Pynson 1523 and 1525. Ed. by W. P. Ker, Tudor
Translations no. xxvii, London, 1901.

Source – French: Chroniques. Ed. by Kervyn de Lettenhove,
Oeuvres de Froissart, Paris, 1867 – 77. Chroniques de J.Fr.,
pub. pour la Soc. de l'hist. de la France, Paris, 1869-1931.

GASTON III, PHOEBUS – 'Plantagenet,' Edward (Edward of Norwich),
second Duke of York, The Master of Game. C. 1406. Ed. by
W. A. and F. Baillie-Grohman, London, 1904. (The edition
of 1909 contains a modernised text only).

Source – French: Livre de la chasse. C. 1360. Ed. by
Jos. Lavallée, Paris, 1854; 2nd ed. 1897.

GESTA ROMANORUM – Anon., [Gesta Romanorum] C. 1430. MS. Brit.
Mus. Harley 7333. Ed. by Fr. Madden, for the Roxburghe
Club, 1838; by S. J. H. Herrtage, EETS e s xxxiii, 1879.

Source – Latin: Approximately the same source was used
for all three translations of the Gesta Romanorum. See
under the third entry below.

GESTA ROMANORUM – Anon., [Gesta Romanorum] C. 1430. MSS. Brit.
Mus. Addit. 9066, Camb. Univ. Lib. Kk 1.6. Ed. by S. J. K.
Herrtage, op. cit. These two MSS. represent an independ-
ent translation.

GESTA ROMANORUM – Anon., [Gesta Romanorum] Printed by W. de
Worde. C. 1510. No modern edition (except for five stories
not in the MSS., Madden, p. 486 – 503, Herrtage, 429-444).
For the nature of this text see Madden, p. xvii, Herrtage,
p. xxii and the variants in Herrtage's notes (esp. p. 451).

Source, for all three translations – Latin: the so-called
Anglo-Latin type, considerably different from the contin-

ental type. There are at least 30 MSS. of the A.-Lat.
(list in Herrtage, p. xxvii) also considerably different
from one another. There are editions of the continental
type (H. Oesterley, Berlin, 1872; W. Dick, Erlangen,
1890); but none of the A.-Lat., except one story, from
MS. Brit. Mus. Harl. 2270, by A. Wallensköld, Acta Soc.
Scientiarum Finnicae, xxxiv, no. 1, 1907, 111-116. (This
is quite close to the English translation of Harl. 7333
(Madden, p. 251 - 60, Herrtage, p. 311 - 19.) The position of the Ang. - Lat. MS. Harley 5369 as exact source
for the W. de Worde translation, stated as above by Madden
and repeated by Oesterley (p.242), appears doubtful. R.
Kapp (Heilige und Heiligenlegenden in England, Halle,
1934, p. 105) notes that this MS. does not contain either
the Alexius or the Placidas stories of the print; and
Wallensköld (as above, p. 26, n. 1) found that the name
Menelay (for Merelaus) in the W. de Worde is written
Gerelaus in Harley 5369.

GILBERT, SAINT - See under Saints' Lives, below.

GIRALDUS CAMBRENSIS - Anon., [The English Conquest of Ire-
    land] c. 1420. Ed. by F. J. Furnivall, EETS o s CVII
    1896.

    Source - Latin: the Expugnatio Hibernica, c. 1188. There
    are at least three recensions in various MSS., of which an
    abridged one in MS. Harley 177 is noted by Furnivall (as
    above, p. ix - xii) as closest source for the English.
    Modern edition (of MSS. of the second recension) by Jas. F.
    Dimrock, Rolls Series no. 21, V., London, 1867.

GODEFROY DE BOLOGNE - See Heraclius.

GOVERNAL - Caxton, Wm., . . . this tretyse that is cleped the
    Gouernayle of helthe . . . Printed by Caxton, 1489. Ed.
    by W. Blades, London, 1858.

    Source - French?: No source for this treatise, originally
    written in Latin, has turned up.

GUEVARA, ANTONIO DE - Bourchier, John, Lord Berners, The
    Golden boke of Marcus Aurelius. C. 1533. Printed by T.
    Berthelet, 1635. Ed. by J. M. Galvez, Berlin, 1916
    (Palaestra no. 109).

    Source - French: Rene Bertaut de la Grise, Livre doré de
    Marc Aurele. Printed by G. Du Pre at Paris, 1531, by J.
    André, 1537, and at Lyons by J. de Tornes, 1577. No
    modern edition.

GUILLAUME DE DEGUILEVILLE - Anon., The Pilgrimage of the Lyf of the Manhode. C. 1430. MS. Camb. Univ. Lib. Ff. 5. 30. Ed. by W. A. Wright, for the Roxburghe Club. 1869.

Source - French: The Pèlerinage de la Vie Humaine. First recension, c. 133C. Ed. by J. J. Stürzinger, for the Roxburghe Club, 1893.

GUILLAUME DE DEGUILEVILLE - Anon., [The Pilgrimage of Man]. Besides the one edited as above, there are at least six other XV cent. MSS. in English prose: Bodl. Laud 740, of which two late copies are known; Glasgow, Hunteriam Mus. Q. 2. 25; Camb. St. John's Coll. G. 21; London, Sion College Library. (K. B. Locock in EETS, e s lxxvii, 1899, p. lxiv; J. B. Wharey, A Study of the Sources of Bunyan's Allegories, Baltimore, 1904, p. 14). None of these except the St. John's MS. has been collated. Wright (as above p. x - xi) judged from specimens of the Laud and of the Hunterian MSS. that they were of the same translation as he printed. However, he says the St. John's MS. 'contains a translation of the poem which is clearly distinct from that here given, and is written in a Northern dialect.'

Source - French: First recension of the Pèl., as above? I am judging only from the variants from the St. John's Coll. MS. given by Wright (cp. cit.) in his textual notes.

GUILLAUME DE DEGUILEVILLE - Anon., . . . the pilgrymage of the soule. 1413. Six MSS. (List. Paltsists, N. Y. Pub. Lib. Bulletin,XXXII(1928), 719). Printed by Caxton, 1483 (Duff, sub Lidgate, no. 267). Ed. by Katherine I. Cust, The Second Pilgrimage of De Guileville . . . , London, 1859. (Selections from Caxton.) The ascription to Lydgate rejected by MacCracken (EETS e s cvii, p. xliii, n. 2)

Source - French: Le Pèlerinage de l'ame. Written in verse 1356. Ed. by J. J. Stürzinger, for the Roxburghe Club, 1895. Turned into prose by Jean de Gallopes, who dedicated it to the Duke of Bedford as Regent of France - i.e. after 1422 (P. Paris Les MSS. Fr., V, 131 - 3). Printed by A. Verard, Paris, 1499. No modern print. The date of 1422 seems to invalidate the assertion (Blades, Caxton, 1863, II, 129; and others since; e.g. Paltists, Bull. N. Y. Pub. Lib., XXXII (1928) 717) that Gallopes' prose was the source for the English. Wharey, (Sources of Bunyan's Allegories, 1904) pointing out the discrepancy of dates, said (p. 12) 'The English prose version printed by Caxton does not differ sufficiently from the original of Deguileville

to justify the supposition that the translator had any
other text before him than the original French verse.'
This is not exact; the English represents a revised version of the poem, not only in wording, sentence order,
etc., but in various small additions, altered transi-
tions, and in the use of Book and Chapter division; e.g.
Book II, cap i begins, if it is following the poem at
all, right in the middle of a sentence of verse. (Compare the fac-simile in N. Y. Pub. Lib. Bull. XXXII (1928),
716 -- the most accessible piece of text -- with Stürzinger ll. 2631 - 2557.) No discussion that I have seen
of Gallopes' part in this revision has undertaken actually to set his version beside the English for comparison.
When W. L. Hare argued (Apollo, XIV (1931) 205 - 13) that
'Gallopes made a new MS. dedication of his early work for
Bedford in 1430,' it may have been that his comparison of
the two forced him to believe Gallopes the English original, dates to one side.

GUILLAUME DE DEGUILEVILLE - Skelton, John, 'Of Mannes Lyfe
    the Peregrynacioun.' In the Garlande of Laurell, 1219 -
    1222 (ed. Dyce, Vol. I, p. 410), Skelton says he had
    translated, 'Out of Frensshe into Englysshe prose
                   Of Mannes Lyfe the Peregrynacioun..'
    This, if actually made, is lost. 'The Peregrinatio Humani
    Generis printed by Pynson in 1508 is not the same thing,
    being in ballad verse or stanzas or seven lines' (Ames,
    Typ. Ant., ed. Dibden, ii, 430).

    Source - French: Recension unknown.

HELYAS - Copeland, Robt., Helyas, Knight of the Swan. Printed
    by W. de Worde, [1512]. Ed. by W. J. Thoms, Early Eng.
    Prose Romances, London, 1858, III, i - 149; by R. Hoe for
    the Grolier Club, 1901.

    Source - French: la genealogie . . . du tres preux . . .
    Godfroy de Boulion . . . vssus . . . du . . . chevalier
    au Cyne. Printed at Paris by J. Petit, 1504. No modern
    edition.

HERACLIUS, EMPEROUR [Guilelmus, abp. of tyre] - Caxton, Wm.,
    . . . Eracles and also of Godefrey of Bologne. Printed
    by Caxton 1481. Ed. by Mary N. Colvin, Godefroy of
    Bologne, (EETS e s lxiv) 1893.

    Source - French: Livre (roman) d'Eracle, redaction from
    the Historia rerum in partibus transmarinis gestarum of
    William, archbishop of Tyre. Ed. by Paulin Paris, Guil-

laume de Tyr et ses continuaturs, texte français du XIIIe siècle . . . Paris, 1879 - 80, 2 Vol.

HIGDEN, RANULPHUS - Trevisa, John, Ranulphus of Chestres Bookes of Cronykes. C. 1380. Printed by Caxton, 1482. Ed. by C. Babington, Vols. I - II, 1865 - 69, by J. R. Lumby, III - VIII, 1871 - 86, Rolls Series, no. 41.

Source - Latin: See under the following entry.

HIGDEN, RANULPHUS - Anon., . . . Cronicle. C. 1450. Ed. by Babington and Lumby, as above (parallel text).

Source - Latin: Polichronicon. Ed. by Babington and Lumby, as above (parallel text).

HIGDEN, RANULPHUS - Bokenham, Osbern, Mappula Anglie. C. 1440 Ed. by C. Horstmann, Englische St., X (1887), 1 - 40.

Source - Latin: Higden's Polychronicon (as above) Book I, Chaps. 39 - 50.

HUON DE BORDEAUX - Bourchier, John, Lord Berners . . . Duke Huon of Burdeux. C. 1530. Printed [by W. de Worde, 1534?] Ed. by S. L. Lee, EETS e s xl, xli, xliii,1,1882 - 1887.

Source - French: A prose redaction of the Chanson de Geste, 1454. Printed by M. le Noir at Paris, 1513, 1516. No modern edition.

INFORMATION - Anon., Informacion for pylgrymes vnto the holy londe. Printed by W. de Worde, 1498. Ed., in fac-simile, by E. G. Duff, London, 1893.

Source - Latin: The exact source is not known. However, at about one-fourth from the end, the translator left his very crude English and continued in equally crude Latin, presumably the text he had been translating.

JEROME, SAINT, LIFE - see under Saints' Lives, below.

JEROME, SAINT - Caxton, Wm., Vitas Patrum. 'Here foloweth the right deuoute, moche louable, & recommendable lyff of the olde Auncyent holy faders hermytes, late translated out of latyn in to frenshe and dylygently corrected in the cyte of lyon ye yere of our lord M.CCCC. lxxxvi. upon that whiche hath be wryten and also translated out of Greke in to Latyn by the blessyd & holy saynt, Saynt Ierome . . & other solytarye relygyouse persones after

hym.' Translated in 1491. Printed by W. de Worde, 1495.
No modern edition. An edition of Caxton's Vitas Patrum
was undertaken and announced in 1894 by the Kelmscott
Press, but was not proceeded with. (See S. Moore, 'Cen-
sus,' MLN, XXV (1911), 167). A specimen page, being p.
75, is listed in the Kelmscott Press Annexe, London,
Frank Hollings, 1933, no. 47.

Source – French: From the Latin. There were various
French translations. P. Meyer in Hist. Litt. de la France,
T. 33, pp. 254 ff., gives liberal extracts from four different XIII and early XIV century versions. The text used
by Caxton was apparently one printed by N. Philip and J.
Dupré at Lyons, 1486. 'Ensuite la tres devote, tres louable et recommandable vie des anciens saintz peres her-
mites, nouellement translatée de latin en françois, et
diligentement corrigee. Sur ce que en ont escript et aussi
translate de grec en latin monseigneur saint Jerome et
autres, solitaires religieux après luy.' (Brunet, Manuel
III, i, 163). No modern edition.

JOANNES DE HILDESCHEIM – Anon., . . .bree holy and worship-
full kyngis of Coleyn. C. 1400. Printed by W. de Worde,
[1496], [1499], etc. Ed. by C. Horstmann, (EETS o s
LXXXV) 1886.

Source – Latin: Historia Trium Regum, c. 1370. Many MSS.,
with considerable variations. Horstmann, as above, pp.
206 – 312, prints a text with variants from an MS. related
to the source MS. of the translation.

JOHN OF ARRAS – Anon., Melusine. C. 1500. MS. Brit. Mus.
Harl. 4418. Printed in 1510 by W. de Worde (known from
fragment only). Ed. by A. K. Donald (EETS e s lxviii)
1895.

Source – French: L'histoire de la belle Melusine. 1382.
Printed by A. Steinschaber, Geneva, 1478. Ed. by Ch.
Brunet, Paris, 1854 (Bibl. Elz.); also, in fac-simile, by
W. J. Meyer, Neuchâtel, 1924 (not seen).

KINGS' SONS – Anon., [The Three Kings' Sons]. MS. Harley
326, C. 1500. Ed. by F. J. Furnivall, (EETS e s lxvii)
1895.

Source – French: ung liure traitant des filz daucuns
roys de France dangleterre et descoce, MS. Bib. Nat. 6766;
printed at Lyon by J. le Vingle, 1501, C. Nourry, 1503,
etc. No modern edition. In the Bib. Nat. MS. David
Aubert claims part authorship.

LA TOUR LANDRY, GOEFFREY DE - Anon., The Book of the Knight
of La Tour Landry. C. 1450. Ed. by T. Wright, (EETS o s
XXX) 1868 [1906].

Source - French: le livre du chevalier de la Tour pour
l'enseignement de ses filles. 1371. Ed. by A. de C. de
Montaiglon, 1854 (Bibl. Elz).

LA TOUR LANDRY, GEOFFREY DE - Caxton, Wm., . . . the book
whiche the kynghte of the toure made. Printed by Caxton
[1484]. Ed. by G. B. Rawlings, New York, 1903. Selections only, but not modernised. (See also Th. Wright's ed.
of the anon. translation of 1450; the last fourth of the
text, p. 167 ff., is Caxton's translation).

Source - French: As above. Caxton may have known the earlier English translation (e.g. the opening sentences of
each agree in a peculiar fault of structure); but his is
essentially independent.

LA TOUR LANDRY, PONTHUS DE - Anon., [King Ponthus and the
Fair Sidoine]. C. 1450. Ed. by F. J. Mather, Jr., PMLA,
XII (1897), i - lxvii; 1 - 150.

Source - French: See under the following entry.

LA TOUR LANDRY, PONTHUS DE - Anon., The Noble Historye of
Kynge Ponthus. Printed by [W. de Worde, 1501 - fragment]
and again by de Worde, 1511. No modern edition. Fr. Brie,
however, published a fragment of the two printed leaves of
this translation, under the title of 'Surdit,' in Archiv
. . . neueren Spr., CXVII (1907), 325 - 28, undoubtedly
from the de Worde edition of 1501. (It agrees with the
French against printers' errors in the de Worde of 1511;
Cf. Brie, p. 328 and Mather, p. 75, notes 5 and 7. Thus
the entry titled 'Surdit' in the Short Title Cat., 23435 a,
really represents the second known fragment of the 1501 or
else a third edition re-set from this.) Brie did not know
what he had and put the leaves in the wrong order. His
leaf 2 corresponds to Mather, p. 74, 1.24 - p. 76, 1.19;
and leaf 1 to Mather, p. 79, 1.14 - p. 80, 1.13. The
printed version is a revision of the earlier translation
based on the French source. (Mather, as above, p. xxxiii
ff.) Thus through the first third (Mather, 1 - 61), where
the earlier is most free, the two are most apart; in the
second third they become closer, and in the last third,
where Digby translates literally, the two English texts
are almost identical.

Source, for 1 and 2 - French: . . . liure du Roy Pontus.
C. 1420. MS. Brit. Mus. Royal 15, E. VI, etc. (Mather,
p. xviii, ff.) No modern edition. C. Dalbanne, Livres
à gravure . . . à Lyon au XVe siècle, no. 4, 1926, gives
a fac-simile of the first and last pages of the Gme. le
Roy, Lyons, 1484.

LAURENTIUS GALLUS - Anon., The Boc of Vices and Vertues.
C. 1400. MS. Brit. Mus. Addit. 17,013. No modern edition.

Source - French: Approximately the same source was used
for all three translations from Laurentius. See under
the third entry, below.

LAURENTIUS GALLUS - Anon., The Mirrour of the worlde that
some calleth vice and vertu. C. 1440. MS. Bodl. 283.
No modern edition.

LAURENTIUS GALLUS - Caxton, Wm., . . . thys presente book
entytled & named Ryal. Printed by Caxton, [1486]. No
modern edition.

Source - French: La somme des vices et vertus. (Le
miroir du monde; Li libres roiaux; etc.) 1279. MSS. Brit.
Mus. Cotton, Cleopatra, A v.; Royal 19, c. II; etc.
Printed by A. Verard at Paris, [1495]. No modern edition.
Specimen from Cotton MS., fol. 177, v. by R. Morriss,
EETS XXIII, 1866, int. p. [vi].

LE FEVRE, RAOUL - Caxton, Wm., . . . the recuyell of the
historyes of Troye. Printed by Caxton, Bruges [1475].
Ed. by H. O. Sommer, London, 1894. 2 Vols.

Source - French: . . . le recueil des histoires de Troyes.
Written 1464. Printed [by C. Mansion, at Bruges, 1477].
No modern edition.

LE FÈVRE, RAOUL - Caxton, Wm., . . . thhistories of Jason.
Printed by Caxton [1478]. Ed. by John Munro, EETS e s
cxi, 1913.

Source - French: Les fais et prouesses du noble et vail-
lant cheualier Jason (Roman de Jason et Medee - etc.)
Printed by Mansion, 1474? etc. No modern edition.

LEGRAND, LACQUES - Shirley, John, The Boke cleaped 'les
bones meurs.' 1440. MS. Brit. Mus. Addit. 5467. No
modern edition.

Source - French: See under the following entry.

LEGRAND, JACQUES - Caxton, Wm., The book of good maners.
Printed by Caxton, 1487. No modern edition.

    Source - French: Liure des bonnes moeurs, c. 1400.
'An edition in French was printed at Chablis in 1478 [by
P. le Rouge], and it was no doubt from it that Caxton made
his translation.' E. G. Duff, Caxton, Chicago, 1905, p.
10. No modern edition.

LULL, RAMON - Gilbert of the Haye, The Buke of the Ordre of
    Kynchthede. C. 1456. Ed. by J. H. Stevenson, (Scot. Text
Soc. no. 62) 1914.

    Source - French: See under the following entry.

LULL, RAMON (BOOK) - Caxton, Wm., . . . the book of the
    Ordre of Chyualry. Printed by Caxton, [1484]. Ed. by
A. T. P. Byles, EETS o s CLXVIII, 1926.

    Source - French: liure de lordre de Cheualerie, c, 1400,
a translation of the libre de cavayleria by Ramon Lull.
List and classification of MSS. and early prints in Byles'
ed. of Caxton (as above), p. xvi - xix; another MS., Bib.
Roy. de Belgique 10493 - 97, noted by Byles in R. E. S.,
VI (1930), 305 - 08. No modern edition.

MARY - Anon.,[Miracles of Mary] C. 1420? MS. Lambeth 432.
Ed. by C. Horstmann, Anglia III (1880) 320 - 325.

    Source - See under the following entry.

MARY - Anon., The myracles of oure blyssyd Lady. Printed by
W. de Worde, 1496. No modern edition. This is (to judge
from the beginning, in Duff, Fifteenth Cent. Engl. Books,
no. 297) a separate translation of a different collection
from the one in the Lambeth MS.

    Source - Latin? French? No source known for either
English collection.

MARY OF OIGNIES, SAINT - see under Saints' Lives, below.

MERLIN - Anon.,[Merlin]. C. 1450. Ed. by H. B. Wheatley,
    EETS o s X, 1865, XXI, 1866, XXXVI, 1869, CXII, 1899.

    Source - French: Roman de Merlin. Many MSS., from late
XIII cent. Ed. by G. Paris and J. Ulrich (from the Huth

MS. - corresponds to p. 1 - 107 of the English) Paris,
1886 (SATF); and by H. O. Sommer (from MS. Brit. Mus. Addit. 10,292) London, 1894. Neither of these editions of
course is critical. Mead, EETS o s X, p. CLXXIV-XXVI,
finds the closest MSS. to be Bib. Nat. fr. 105 and 9123.

OLIVER OF CASTILLE - Watson, Henry,   . . . ye hystorye of
Olyuer of Castylle. Printed by W. de Worde, 1518. Ed.
by R. E. Graves, for the Roxburghe Club. 1898.

Source - French: Phillipe Camus, de Olivier de castille
et de Artus Dalgarbe. Ed. by Paul Bergmans and Armand
Heins, Gand, 1896. (Not seen.)

OVIDIUS - Caxton, Wm., Ovyde hys Booke of Methamorphose. 1480.
MS. in the Pepysian Library It contains only books X -
XV. Ed. by G. H. Hibbert, for the Roxburghe Club, 1819;
and by S. Gaselie and H. F. B. Brett-Smith, Oxford, 1924.

Source - French: Ouide . . . moralisé par maistre thomas
Waleys . . . translate & compile par Colard Mansion.
Printed by Mansion, Bruges, 1484. It is an augmented trans-
lation of the Latin Metamorphosis Ovidiana Moraliter made
c. 1280 not by Thomas Waleys (Valois or Wallensis) but by
Peter Berchorius (Bersuire, Berçoir). No modern edition.

PARIS, LE CHEVALIER - Caxton, Wm.,   . . . Paris . . . and . . .
Vyenne. Printed by Caxton, 1485. Ed. by W. C. Hazlitt,
for the Roxburghe Library, 1868.

Source - French: Paris et Vienne. As printed by Gherard
Leeu, Antwerp, 1487, D. Meslier, Paris, 1500 , J. Trepperel, Paris, [1525], etc., and as used by Caxton, a short-
ened and somewhat rewritten form of the romance as it circulated in MS. See pp. 351, ff. of the edition of the
older form, by Robert Kaltenbacker, Romanische Forschungen,
XV (1904), 321 - 688 a. No modern reprint of the redacted
form; the limited ed. by Alfred de Terre-basse, Paris, 1838,
uses the MS. form.

PETRUS ALPHONSIS - Anon., [Disciplina clericalis]. C. 1460.
Ed. by W. H. Hulme, Western Reserve Univ. Studies in
English, no. 5, Cleveland, 1919.

Source - Latin: Disciplina Clericalis, XIIth cent. The
many MSS. are studied, and passages peculiar to MS. Cam.
Univ. Lib. Ii. VI. 11 and the English translation paralleled by A. Hilka and W. Söderhjelm with their edition
of the Latin, Acta Soc. Scientiarum Fennicae, Tom. XXXVIII,

no. 4, Helsingfors, 1911. The same text is in Hilka's
Sammlung mittellateinischer Texte, no. 1, Heidelberg, 1911.

PETRUS BLESENSIS - Anon.,   . . . the xij proffites of tribu-
lacyon. Early XV cent.? Printed by Caxton, 1481, by W.
de Worde 1499.. No modern edition. To judge by the beginnings (see G. Duff, Fifteenth Cent. English Books, nos.
55 and 400), part of this tract is in MS. Brit. Mus. Harley
1706; but it there occupies only fol. 54 v. - 55 r., whereas in the prints it goes to 30 and to 26 leaves. C. Horstmann, who published an early version of the Twelve Profits
from MS. Brit. Mus. Royal 17.B. xvii, (Yorkshire Writers,
II, 45 - 60), said, 'A different treatise on tribulation is
that in MS. Harley 1706 and other MSS.' However, the ending of the version in the Royal MS. (Yk. Wr., II, 60) is
'Thorou mony tribulacions byhoues vs entre in to þo kyngdome
of heuen.' The ending of the print is only slightly different (Duff, no. 400): 'It behouyth vs by many trybulacyons
to entre in to the kyngdome of heuen'; and I take it the
prints represent only a different translation of the same
treatise. I must note, however, that on fol. 55b of the
Harleian MS. begins another (?) Twelve Profits.

Source - Latin: Duodecim utilitates tribulationis, only
doubtfully attributed to Peter of Blois   Ed. by J. A.
Giles, Opera, London, 1848, III, 307 - 33.

PISAN, CHRISTINE DE - Caxton, Wm., The . . . Fayttes of Armes
and of Chyvalrye. Printed by Caxton, 1489. Ed. by A. T. P.
Byles, EETS o s CLXXXIX, 1932.

Source - French: 'Les Faits d'Armes et de Chevalerie'.
Many MSS. and two early prints, studied by Byles (as above,
pp. xiv - xxviii). No modern edition Prologue printed
by Byles in his edition of Caxton, as above, pp. 5 - 8.

PISAN, CHRISTINE DE - Babyngton, Anthony, [The Epistle of
Othea to Hector] about 1475. In Brit. Mus. MS. Harley 838.
No modern edition. See H. N.. MacCracken, M. L. N., XXIV
(1909), 122 - 3.

Source - French: See under the following entry.

PISAN, CHRISTINE DE - Scrope, Stephen, The Epistle of Othea
to Hector or the boke of Knyghthode. 1444 - 1450.   Ed.
by G. Warner, for the Roxburghe Club, no. 141.

Source - French: L'épistre d'Othea Deesse de Prudence à
Hector. 1401. Many MSS. (for those in England, see

P. G. C. Campbell in Rev. de Litt. Comparée, V (1925),
663 - 4). No modern edition. C. 1450, Jean Mielot issued an edition of L'Epistre which was 'accopagnée d'ex-
plications que Mielot a allongées' (P. Perdrizet, Rev.
d'hist. Litt. de la France, XIV (1907), 472 - 82). No
modern edition. (Miniatures of MS. only by J. van de
Gheyn, Brussels, 1913)

PISAN, CHRISTINE DE - Anslay, B., . . . the cyte of Ladyes.
Printed by H. Pepwell, 1521. No modern edition.

Source - French: Le livre de la cité des Dames. 1405.
Many MSS. (two (?) in England; see Campbell, as above).
No modern edition.

PISAN, CHRISTINE DE - Anon., . . . the body of Polocye. C.
1470. In MS. Cam. Un. Coll. Lib. Kk I.5. No modern edition.

Source - French: See under the following entry.

PISAN, CHRISTINE DE - Anon., . . . the body of polycye.
Printed by J. Skot. 1521. No modern edition. Campbell
(as above, p. 668) says, 'Par une comparison assez som-
maire de ce livre avec la traduction en manuscript . . .
nous sommes portés à croire que les deux versions ne sont
pas de la même main.'

Source for the Body of Policy - French: le livre du corps
de policie. C. 1405. Many MSS. (See Campbell, as above,
p. 663). No modern edition.

PLUTARCH - Wyatt, Sir Thomas, . . . Quyete of Mynde. C.
1527. Printed by R. Pynson, [1531?]. Ed., in photo-fac-
simile, by C. R. Baskerville, Cambridge, Mass., 1931.

Source - Latin: 'Liber de Tranquilitate et Securitate
Animi Gulielmo Budaeo . . . interprete,' p. 5 - 40 of Tom.
II of Plutarchi Moralium . . . Paris, 1566.

PONTHUS - See La Tour Landry, Ponthus de.

REGISTER OF GODSTOW - Anon., [The English Register of Godstow
Nunnery]. C. 1450. Ed. by A. Clark, EETS o s CXXIX, CXXX,
CLXII, 1911.

Source - Latin: the same Register as found in a MS. of
the Public Records Office Exchequer, King's Remembrancer,
Miscellaneous Books, no. 20. No modern edition.

REGISTER OF OSENY - Anon., The English Register of Oseney
Abbey 1460.   Ed. by A. Clark, EETS CXXXIII; CLXIV, 1913.

Source - Latin: the same Register as found in MSS. Oxford
Christ Church 343 and Brit. Mus. Cotton Vitellius E 15.
No modern edition.

REYNARD THE FOX - Caxton, Wm., . . . the historye of reynart
the foxe. Printed by Caxton, 1481. Ed. by W. J. Thoms,
Percy Soc., Vol. XII, London, 1844; by Edw. Arber, London,
1878; by Wm. Morris, Kelmscott Press, 1892.

Source - Dutch; an anonymous redaction of the Reynard mate-
rial, printed by Gherard Leeu, Ter-Gouw, 1479. Ed. by H.
Logeman and J. W. Muller, 'vergleken met William Caxtons
Englesche vertaling,' Zwolle, 1892 (not seen).

ROBERT THE DEVIL - Anon., . . . the lyfe of . . . Robert the
Deuyl. Printed by W. de Worde, [1502]. Ed.by W. J. Thoms,
Early Eng. Prose Romances, London, 1858, I, 1 - 56.

Source - French: La vie du terrible Robert le Diable, a
prose redaction from a version in verse. Printed by P.
Mareschall, Lyon, 1496; by N. de la Barre, Paris, 1497;
by J. Herouf, Paris, 1520; etc. No modern edition.

ROLLE, RICHARD - Misyn, Richard, þe fyer of lufe. 1435. Ed.
by R. Harvey, EETS o s CVI, 1896.

Source - Latin: Incendium Amoris. Ed. by Margaret Deanesley, Manchester and London, 1915 (Manchester Univ. Mono-
graphs, xcvii).

ROLLE,RICHARD - Misyn, Richard, mendynge of lyfe. 1434. Ed.
by R. Harvey, EETS o s CVI, 1896.

Source - Latin: See under the following translation.

ROLLE, RICHARD - Anon., . . . of the Amendement of Mannes
Lif.C.1460. Ed. by W. H. Hulme, Western Reserve Studies,
Vol. I, no. 4, Cleveland, 1919.

Source, for both the above translations - Latin: De Eman-
datione Vitae. Many MSS. No modern edition. A text
which serves general purposes is in the Magna Bibliotheca
Veterum Patrum, ed. by Margarinus de la Bigne, Paris,
1654, XXV, 609, B. ff. (ed. also Cologne, 1618, Lyons and
Geneva 1677).

ROME – Anon., [The seven wise masters of Rome]. Printed by
R. Pynson, 1493, by W. de Worde [1520], etc. Ed., from
the 1520, by G. L. Gomme, for the Villon Society, London,
1885.

Source – Latin: Historia Septem Sapientum. Many MSS. and
early prints. No critical edition. Georg Buchner in Er-
langer Beitrage zur Engl. Phil., V, 1889, prints the text
of one MS. (Insbruck, Cod. Lat. 310) with some corrections
from four others. For detailed comparison, this is not
adequate, as the French translation of Geneva, 1492, shows
(Ed. by G. Paris, SATF, Paris, 1876). In fact, it seems
quite possible that the English translator had the French
text before him as well. Both the English and the French
translations are so close to the Latin that any one of the
three texts could be emended from the other two.

ROYE, GUY DE – Caxton, Wm., . . . the doctrinal of sapvence.
Printed by Caxton, 1489. No modern edition.

Source – French: a translation of a Latin Manipulus Cura-
torum, wrongly attributed to Guy de Roye, Archbishop of
Sens (d. 1409); it was known in French under various
titles, (Blades, Caxton, 2nd ed. 1882, p. 326) and printed
by [S. du Jardin at Geneva 1475], [G. le Roy, Lyons, 1490],
R. Mace, Rouen [1502]. No modern edition.

SAINTS' LIVES: Augustine – Capgrave, John, . . . þe lif of
Seynt Augustyn. C. 1450. Ed. by J. J. Munro, EETS o s
CXL, 1910.

Source – Latin?: It is not certain that this life is properly a translation at all. No source has been found, and
Munro, (as above, p. vi) was 'inclined to conclude that he
(Capgrave) is himself the original composer.' However,
Capgrave says that he intends 'to translate hir truely oute
of Latyn' (p. 1. 1. 17); and while this may refer to his
use of Augustine's books – chiefly the Confessions, from
which he occasionally translates short passages – it must
be noted that Capgrave himself wrote a Vita S. Augustini
which is lost. His translating himself would account for
the unusual number of phrases in the first person.

SAINTS' LIVES: Catharine of Alexandria – Anon., . . . þe
lyfe of þe glorus uirgyne seynt Katryne. First quarter
of the XV century? MS. Porkington 10, fol. 92, r. – 130,
r. No modern edition. I have used a transcript kindly
lent me by Professor G. H. Gerould.

Source - Latin: I do not know what version of the Latin
Vita may be the source of this translation.

SAINTS' LIVES: Catharine of Siena - Anon , . . . a letter
touchynge þe lyfe of seint Kateryn of Senys. C. 1430.
MS. Bodl. Douce 114. Ed. by C. Horstmann Anglia, VIII
(1885), 184 - 196.

Source - Latin: Dom Stephen of Siena, Epistola de gestis
et virtutibus S. Catharinae. Ed., 'ex Rubaevallis, prope
Bruxellus,' in the Acta Sanctorum, April, III, Paris and
Rome, 1866, pp. 969 - 975.

SAINTS' LIVES: Catharine of Siena (Vineis) - Anon., . . .
the lyf of saint Katherin of Senis. C. 1450? No.MS.
Printed by W. de Worde [1493]. Ed. by C. Horstmann,
Archiv fur das St. der n. Spr., LXXVI (1886), 33 - 112;
265 - 314; 353 - 391.

Source - Latin: Raimundus de Vineis, Vita S. Catherinae
Senensi. Ed., 'ex editione coloniensi collata cum MS.,' in
the Acta Sanctorum, April, III, Paris and Rome, 1866, pp.
862 - 967.

SAINTS' LIVES: Christina mirabilis - Anon., . . . þe lyfe
of seint cristyn þe meruelous. C. 1430. MS. Bodl. Douce
114. Ed. by C. Horstmann, Anglia, VIII (1885), 119 - 134.

Source - Latin: Thoma Cantipratano, Vita S. Christinae
mirabilis. Ed., 'ex . . . MS. Canerensi in Belgio Brux-
ellas cum pluribus alliis collato,' in the Acta Sanctorum,
July, V, Paris and Rome, 1867, 550 - 581.

SAINTS' LIVES: Dorothea - Anon., [S. Dorothea] C. 1425? MS.
Lambeth 432. Ed. by C. Horstmann, Anglia, III (1880),
325 - 328. Horstmann said (p. 320) that this version is a
prose redaction of the verse Dorothea in MS. Harl. 5272
(Sam. Alt. Leg., Heilbroun, 1878, p. 191 - 197), 'mit der
sie im ganzen und einzelnen übereinstimmt, nicht selten im
wortlaut.' If this were the case, it would be interesting.
Fr. Brie (Archiv fur das st. der n. spr., CXXX (1913),
40 - 52; 269 - 385) thought he had in the prose Sege of
Thebes and Sege of Troy the only English instances of this
very common continental practice. But that Horstmann was
mistaken can be quickly shown by a mis-translation in the
prose (p. 326, 1. 20: Than ffabricius arose up from his
pilloire and sett his ydollis ther-on), where the verse
is plain enough (1. 130:

Then Fabricius lifte vp on hie
A pilere of a mawment there vpone
So shewid forthe hys ydolatrie).
(The prose translation in the Royal MS., listed below,
reads, f. 238, col. 1: Than had Fabricius raised up a
grete pelour.)   J. M. Peterson, The Dorothea Legend
. . . Middle English Versions . . . , Heidelberg, 1910,
p. 26 ff. disregards Horstmann's statement and considers
the prose as a separate translation.

Source - Latin: See under the third Life of Dorothea,
below.

SAINTS' LIVES: Dorothea - Anon., [S. Dorothea]. MS. Brit.
Mus. Royal 2. A. XVIII. C. 1425? No modern edition.
Peterson, (see above, pp. 41 - 44) has demonstrated this
to be a separate translation.

SAINTS' LIVES: Dorothea - Anon., [S. Dorothea]. MSS. Brit.
Mus. Addit. 11,565 and Addit. 35,298, and MS. Lambeth 72.
No modern edition. Peterson (as above, pp. 38 - 41) has
demonstrated the Life found in these three MSS. to be a
separate translation.

Source, for the three English Lives above - Latin: the
'younger Version', a text of which is ed. by Th. Graesse,
Leg. Aurea, pp. 910 - 12 (not properly part of the collection by J. de Voragine). Graesse's text, however, differs from all of the texts used for the English translations, which appear as well, to differ from each other.
No text of the exact type used for any of the three is
now known. (Peterson, as above, pp. 17; 28 - 35; 41; 44.)

SAINTS' LIVES: Elizabeth of Spalbeck - Anon., . . .be lyfe
of seint Elizabeth of Spalbeck. C. 1430. MS. Bodl. Douce
114. Ed. by C. Horstmann, Anglia, VIII (1885), 107 - 118.

Source - Latin: Phillip of Clairveaux, Vita Elisabeth
sanctimonialis in Erkenrode. Ed. by the Bollandists in
Cat. codicum hagiographicorum Bib. Reg. Brux., II (1889),
362 - 78.

SAINTS' LIVES: Gilbert - Capgrave, John, . . .be lif of
Seint Gilbert. 1451. Ed. by J. J. Munro, EETS o s CXL,
1910.

Source - Latin: Roger of Sempringham, Vita S. Gilberti
Confessoris. MSS. Brit. Mus. Cotton Cleopatra B. I,
and Harl. 468; Bodl., Digby 36. Ed., from the Cotton

MS. with omissions, in Wm. Dugdale's Monasticon, London, 1830, 1846, Vol. VI, Part II (bound as Vol. VII), p. v* - xix*. If Capgrave used a text like this one, he at times not only added, as he says, but omitted, condensed, and rearranged freely.

SAINTS' LIVES: Jerome - Anon., . . . the lyff of seint Jerome as hit is take of legenda aurea. C. 1440? MS. Lambeth 432. Printed by W. de Worde before 1501 (Duff. no. 236). Ed. by C. Horstmann, Anglia, III (1880), 328 - 360. Only the first chapter is from Leg. Aurea, much abbreviated after the residence in Bethlehem. Chaps. II - V (pp. 333 - 340) are the pseudo-Augustinian epistle to Cyril on Jerome, and Chaps. VI - XIX 9340 - 359) the reply of the pseudo-Cyril concerning Jerome's miracles. Chap. XIX contains two Revelations of St. Birgitta on Jerome.

Sources - Latin: The Life is in the Leg. Aur., ed. by Th. Graesse, Leipzig, 1847, 1852 (I have used the print by J. Koelhoff, Cologne, 1479). The two epistles are in the Benedictine ed. of Augustine, Paris, 1836, II, 1411, D - 1421, A; 1421, B - 1461, A (same text beneath the French translation of H. Barreau, Paris, 1873, VI, 380 - 90; 390 - 438; and in J. P. Migne, Patr. Lat., XXXIII (Augustini Opera, II), Paris, 1865, col.1120 ff.). I have not been able to find Birgitta's revelations on Jerome in the ed. by C. Duranto, Rome, 1628.

SAINTS' LIVES: Mary of Oignies - Anon., . . . þe lyfe of Seint Mary of Oeginies. C. 1430. MS. Bodl. Douce 114. Ed. by C. Horstmann, Anglia, VIII (1885), 134 - 184.

Source - Latin: Jacobus de Vitriaco, Vita S. Mariae Oigniacensi. Ed., 'ex variis Codicibus MSS.,' in the Acta Sanctorum, June, V, Paris and Rome, 1867, pp. 550 - 581.

SAINTS' LIVES: Winifred - Caxton, Wm., . . . the lyf of the holy & blessid vyrgyn saynt Wenefryde. Printed by Caxton, [1485]. Ed. by C. Horstmann, Anglia III (1880) 293 - 313.

Source - Latin? This S. Winifred is more elaborate than the lives in Mirk's Festial and in the Leg. Aurea. No source, Latin or French, has been found. See Blades, Caxton, 1885, p. 302, Horstmann, as above, p, 294, R. Kapp, Heilige und Heiligenlegenden in England, Halle, 1934, p. 37.

SALLUSTIUS - Barclay - Alexander, . . . the famous cronycle of the warre . . . agaynst Iugurth. Printed by P. Pynson, [1520]. No modern edition. Excerpts in H. B. Lathrop,

Translations from the Classics, Madison, 1933, p. 81 - 3
(Preface and passage paralleled with Jug. X, 8; XI, 1 - 2);
in E. Flügel, Neuenglisches Lesebuch, Halle, 1895, p. 307
(Chap. I :: Jug. V, 1 - 3).

SEVEN WISE MASTERS - see Rome.

SHEPHERD'S KALENDAR - Anon., The Kalendayr of shyppars.
Printed by A. Verard, Paris, 1503. A faulty Lowland Scotch
translation. Ed., in fac-simile, by H. O. Sommer, The Kalendar of Shepperds, London, 1892, III Vols, in I; Vol. II.

Source - French: The same source was used for all three
translations of the Shepherd's Kalendar. See under the
third entry, below.

SHEPHERDS' KALENDAR - Anon., The Kalendar of Shepherdes.
Printed by R. Pynson, London, 1506. A revision of the Ver-
ard, 1503, based only in part on the French. Ed. by H. O.
Sommer, as above, Vol. III.

SHEPHERDS' KALENDAR - Copland, Robt., The Kalendar of shepe-
herdes. Printed by W. de Worde, 1508. No modern edition.
Sommer, as above, Vol. I, p. 66, gives a short extract. In
1518, Julian Notary published an edition composed mainly of
Copland's translation but revised on Pynson's of 1506. This
is reprinted, somewhat modernised, by G. C. Heseltine, London, 1913.

Source for all three translations - French: Le Compost et
kalendrier des Bergiers. Printed by G. Marchant, Paris,
1493. Ed., in fac-simile, by Pierre Champion, Paris, [1926].
This is the text used by the English translators. A similar
text, by J. Bellot, Geneva, 1497, is re-printed by Bloesch,
Berne, 1920; and another, N. le Rouge, Troyes, 1529, by B.
Guégan, Paris, 1925. [Neither of these seen].

SOLOMON (DIALOGUE) - Anon., . . . the dyalogus . . . betwixt
Salomon . . . and Marcolphus. Printed by G. Leeu at Antwerp,
[1492]. Ed. by E. G. Duff, London, 1892.

Source - Latin: Conflictus verborum inter regem Salomonum
et rusticum Marcolfum. Many MSS., with different versions.
See the int. to the edition of a text very close to the
English by W. Benary, Heidelberg, 1914(Sammlung mittella-
teinescher Texte, no. 8). A Latin text was printed by
Leeu c. 1489.

STEWART CHRONICLE - Shirley, John, . . . Cronycle of the
dethe and false murdure of James Stewarde. C. 1440. Ed.

by Jos. Stevenson, in The Life and Death of King James the
First of Scotland, for the Maitland Club, 1837; by J.
Pinkerton, Ancient Scottish Poets, 1787, Vol. 1, Appendix.

Source – Latin: according to Shirley's statement; but the
text itself has not been discovered.

SUSO, HENRICUS – Anon., . . . þe seuene poyntes of trewe loue
and euerlastynge wisdame. C. 1430. MS. Bodl. Douce 114.
Printed by Caxton, [Book of Divers Ghostly Matters], 1490.
Ed. by C. Horstmann, Anglia, X (1888), 323 – 389.

Source – Latin: Horologium Sapientiae. C. 1380. Ed. by
J. Strange, Cologne, 1861. (Not seen.)

TEN COMMANDMENTS – Chertsey, Andrew, Ihesus. The floure of
the commaundements of god. Printed by W. de Worde, 1510.
See H. G. Pfander in Library, 4th Ser., XIV (1933), 299, n.

Source – French: . . . la fleur des commendemens de Dieu
. . . Printed by J. le Bourgeois, Rouen, 1496, by A.
Verard, Paris, 1499, by N. Despres, Paris, 1502, etc.

THOMAS A KEMPIS – Anon., . . . þe tretise called Musica ec-
clesiastica [The Imitation of Christ]. C. 1450. Ed. by
J. K. Ingram, EETS e s lxiii, 1893, pp. 1 – 150.

Source – Latin: See under the following translation.

THOMAS A KEMPIS – Atkinson, Wm., . . . of the Imytacion a.
folowynge the blessed lyfe of oure Sauyoure Criste. The
first three books. Printed by R. Pynson (with the fourth
book by Margaret Beaufort), 1504; by W. de Worde, [1515],
etc. Ed. by J. K. Ingram, EETS e s lxiii, 1893, pp. 151 –
258.

Source for the two translations – Latin: De Imitatione
Christi. Many MSS. and editions. I have used the 'Textum ex
autographo Thomae' . . . Carolus Hirsche . . . Berolini,
1891.

THOMAS A KEMPIS – Beaufort, Margaret, Countess of Richmond and
Derby, . . . the forthe boke of the folwynge of Iesu cryst.
Printed by R. Pynson, 1504, by W. de Worde, [1515], etc.
Ed. by J. K. Ingram, as above, pp. 259 – 283.

Source – French: . . . de la Ymitacion de Jhesucrist . . .
Printed by H. Meyer, Toulouse, 1488, by R. Lambert, Paris,
1493. No modern edition. Le Livre de l'Internelle Con-

solation, printed [by J. du Pré, Paris, 1486], by du Pré,
Paris, 1520, etc., re-printed by J. Molland and Ch. d'Her-
cault, Paris, 1856 (Bibl. Elz.) is an older, freer French
version, omitting, besides, book IV.

TREATISE — Anon., 'This tretyse is of loue . . . that our
lord Ihesu cryste had to mannys soule . . . translated out
of frenshe Into englyshe [1493] . . . by a Right well dys-
posed persone . . . '   Printed by W. de Worde, [1493.] No
modern edition.

Source — French: as the translator informs us. But the
text is unknown.

TWICI, GUILLAUME? (BOOK) — Berners, Dame Juliana, [The Book
of Hawking, Hunting, and Blasing of Arms].   Before 1450?
(See W. W. Skeat, in the Engl. Dialect Soc. Pub. no. 41,
a, 1885, p. v.) Printed at St. Albans, 1486; by W. de
Worde, 1496.   Ed., from the print at St. Albans, by Wm.
Blades, London, 1881.

Source — French: Le art de venerie, c. 1320. Privately
printed from the Phillips MS. by Sir Henry Dryden, 1843;
1845.   This 'Twici,' however, furnishes only the basis
for the 'Book of St. Albans,' which used an expanded form
of it and added whole treatises for which the French
source has not been found.

VALENTINE — Watson, Henry, The hystory of Valentyne and Orson.
Printed by [W. de Worde, 1510?], by Wm. Copland [1548],
[1565].   Ed. by Arthur Dickson, EETS o s CCIV, 1937. See
also Valentine and Orson, a study of late medieval romance,
N. Y. 1929.

Source — French: . . . hystoire des deux vaillans cheual-
iers Valentin et Orson.   Several early prints, discussed
by Dickson in his ed. of Watson, as above, pp. xvii –
xviii. No modern edition. A specimen, parallel text (2
pages) in Dickson, Study, as above, p. 280.

VINCENTIUS, BELLOVACENSIS, Caxton, Wm., . . . the myrrour
of the worlde. Printed by Caxton [1481]. Ed. by Oliver H.
Prior, EETS e s ox, 1913.

Source — French: a prose redaction from the first version
in verse, which was once thought to have been translated
from a lost Speculum vel Imago Mundi by Vincent de Beau-
vais. Probably the verse version is the original compilation, made c. 1245 by Maitre Gossouin of Metz. See pp.

27 ff. of the edition of the prose L'Image du Monde, by
Oliver H. Prior, Lausanne et Paris, 1913.

VIRGILIUS - Caxton, Wm., . . . the boke [o]f Eneydos.
Printed by Caxton, 1490. Ed. by W. T. Culley and F. J.
Furnivall, EETS e s lvii, 1890.

Source - French: liure des eneydes, a prose redaction of
the Aeneid, printed by G. le Roy at Lyon, 1483. No modern
edition.

VIRGILIUS - Anon., . . . of the lyfe of Virgilius. Printed
by J. van Doesborch at Antwerp, 1518. Numerous eds. (none
critical); see J. W. Spargo, Virgil the Necromancer, Cambridge, 1934, p. 421. I have used the text printed by
W. J. Thoms in Early English Prose Romances, 2nd ed.,
London, 1858, II, 1-62.

Source - French? Dutch? The known text in each language
contains materials lacking to the other but present in
the English; see J. W. Spargo, as above, pp. 236-242.
Les faictz merveilleux de Virgille is undated in the two
earliest prints: Paris, J. Trepperel, and Paris, G.
Nyverd; there are several limited reprints of the latter,
the most accessible being by Philomneste Junior (Gustave
Brunet), Genève, 1867 (for others see D. Comparetti,
Virgil in the Middle Ages, London, 1895, p. 23, n. 2, or
J. W. Spargo, as above, p. 420). Of Virgilius, Van zijn
. . . wonderlijcken wercken, printed by J. van Doesborgh
at Antwerp, also without date, there is no modern edition.

VORAGINE, JACOBUS DE - Anon., the lives of Seintis, that is
callid in Latynne Legenda Aurea C. 1430. Seven MSS. described by Pierce Butler, Legenda Aurea - Legende Dorée -
Golden Legend, Baltimore, 1899, pp. 50 - 75; 149- 155.
No modern edition. Butler, (op. cit., pp. 99 - 141) prints
nine legends.

Source - French and Latin?: See under the following translation.

VORAGINE, JACOBUS DE - Caxton, Wm., . . . the legende named
in latyn legenda aurea. Printed by Caxton, 1483. Ed. by
A. Aspland, specimen pages - ten whole lives - in fac-
simile, London, 1878; by F. S. Ellis, Kelmscott Press,
1892; by F. S. Ellis, London, Dent, 1900, 7 vols. (The
Morris-Ellis text has been slightly emended and modernised;
see Butler, as above, pp. 145 - 6.)

Sources for the 1430 and Caxton – French and Latin?: The
Latin Legenda Aurea, c. 1260, in many MSS , ed. by Th.
Graesse, 2nd ed., Leipzig, 1850. The French translation by
Jean de Vignay, c. 1340. For the many MSS. and the stages of
addition and re-arrangement see Butler, as above, pp. 35 –
49. No modern edition. Butler, pp. 116 and 122 – 130,
prints a St. Marine and St. Patrice; Cl. Dalbanne, Livres
à gravures imprimés à Lyon au XVe siècle, Lyon, 1924, no. I,
reproduces only sig. A2 of the Husz-Hongre, Lyon, 1483 and
the Husz, 1484. The sources of the two English translations
are not yet clear. Butler, after some strong evidence, has,
on p. 73, 'no doubt that the English MSS. [which all represent
one version] were translated from the Latin.' But on p. 147
he speaks of 'five fairly complete MSS. of an English prose
translation of the Legenda Aurea, made from the French of
Jean de Vignay, with some use of the Latin.' Caxton, Butler
finds, pp. 75 – 87 and 148, was largely dependent on Vignay;
but he took much from the older Eng. translation; at least
five legends are from Voragine; and a number of legends, including 18 of Biblical figures, he put together eclectically
from the Polychronicon, the Bible, etc., or wrote himself.

Appendix B

THE LIST IN APPENDIX A ARRANGED BY

PERIODS AND TRANSLATORS

The translations are here grouped by quarter-centuries.
Within each group the translator's name (or 'anon.') heads
the entry; it is followed by the heading used for the full
entry in Appendix A. The word 'Latin,' 'French,' or 'Dutch,'
coming last in each entry, refers to the language of the
source.

1400 - 1425

Anon. - Alphabetum Narrationem - C. 1420 - Latin.
Anon. - Aristotle, pseud. - 'The governance of Lordschippes' -
    c. 1400 - Latin.
Anon. - Ars Moriendi - 'tretis' - Early XVth cent. - Latin.
Anon. - Ars Moriendi - 'Craft' - Early XVth cent. - Latin.
Anon. - Giraldus Cambrensis - C. 1420 - Latin.
Anon. - Guillaume de Deguileville - ' . . . pilgrymage of the
    soule' - 1413. Printed by Caxton, 1483 - French.
Anon. - Joanes de Hildescheim - C. 1400. Printed by W. de
    Worde, 1496 - Latin.
Anon. - Laurentius Gallus - 'The Boc . . ' - C. 1400 - French.
Anon. - Mary - ['Miracles of Mary'] - C. 1420? - Latin?
Anon. - Petrus Blesensis - First quarter XVth cent.? Printed
    by Caxton, [1490] - Latin.
Anon. - Saints' Lives: Catharine of Alexandria - First quarter
    XVth cent.? - Latin.
Anon. - Saints' Lives: Dorothea - MS. Lambeth 432 - C. 1425? -
    Latin.
Anon. - Saints' Lives: Dorothea - MS. Brit. Mus. Royal 2. A
    XVIII - C. 1425? - Latin.
Anon. - Saints' Lives: Dorothea - MS. Brit. Mus. Addit. 11,565 -
    Early XVth cent.? - Latin.
Love, Nicholas - Bonaventura, St., pseud. - Before 1410.
    Printed by Caxton, 1486 - Latin? French?
'Plantagenet', Edward (Edward of York) - Gaston III, 'Phoebus -
    C. 1406 - French.
Yonge, James, - Aristotle, pseud. - 'Governaunce of Prynces' -
    C. 1420 - French.

1425 - 1450

Anon. - Alexander - C. 1430 - Latin.
Anon. - Aristotle, pseud. - ['Secreta Secretorum'] MS. Bodl.
    Ashmole 396 - Second quarter of the XVth cent.? - Latin?
Anon. - Aristotle, pseud. - ' . . . Governaunce of kings and
    princes' - Second quarter of XVth cent.? - Latin?
Anon. - Gesta Romanorum - MS. Brit. Mus., Harley 7333 - C.
    1430 - Latin.
Anon. - Gesta Romanorum - MS. Brit. Mus. Addit. 9066 - C. 1430 -
    Latin.
Anon. - Guillaume de Deguileville - 'Pilgrimage of the . . .
    Manhode' - C. 1430 - French.
Anon. - Guillaume de Deguileville - ['The Pilgrimage of Man'] -
    MS. Cam. St. John's Coll. G. 21. - C. 1430? - French.
Anon. - Laurentius Gallus - 'Mirrour of the world' - C. 1440 -
    French.
Anon. - Saints' Lives : Catharine of Siena - 'A letter . . . ' -
    C. 1430 - Latin.
Anon. - Saints' Lives : Christina Mirabilis - C. 1430 - Latin.
Anon. - Saints' Lives : Elizabeth of Spalbeck - C. 1430 - Latin.
Anon. - Saints' Lives : Jerome - C. 1440. Printed by W. de
    Worde before 1501 - Latin.
Anon. - Saints' Lives : Mary of Oignies - C. 1430 - Latin.
Anon. - Suso, Henricus - C. 1430. Printed by Caxton [1490] -
    Latin.
Anon. - Voragine, Jacobus de - ' . . . lives of seints' - C.
    1430 - French and Latin?
Berners, Dame Juliana? - Twici - Before 1450? Printed at St.
    Albans, 1486 - French.
Bokenham, Osbern - Higden, Ranulphus - 'Mappula Anglie' -
    C. 1440 - Latin.
Misyn, Richard - Rolle, Richard -'Þe fyer of lufe' - 1435 -
    Latin.
Misyn, Richard - Rolle - Richard - 'Mendynge of lyfe' - 1434 -
    Latin.
Scrope, Stephen - Dicts - 1450 - French.
Scrope, Stephen - Pisan, Christine de - 'Epistle of Othea to
    Hector' - 1444 - 50 - French.
Shirley, John - Aristotle, pseud. - ' . . . governaunce of
    Prynces' - C. 1440 - Latin? French?
Shirley, John - Legrand, Jacques - 'Boke cleaped "les bones
    meurs"' - 1440 - French.
Shirley, John - Stewart Chronicle - C. 1440 - Latin.

1450 - 1475

Anon. - Aristotle, pseud. - 'Secrete of Secretes' - C. 1460 -
    French.

Anon. - Birgitta, Saint - MS. of Mr. Robert Garrett - C.
    1450 - Latin.
Anon. - Birgitta, Saint - MS. Brit. Mus. Arundel 197 - Last
    half of the XVth cent. - Latin.
Anon. - Birgitta, Saint - MS. Brit. Mus. Cotton, Claudius B.
    I. 'Fifteenth century' - Latin.
Anon. - Birgitta, Saint - MS. Brit. Mus. Cotton, Julius F. II -
    'Fifteenth century' - Latin.
Anon. - Birgitta, Saint - MS. Brit. Mus. Harley 4800 -
    'Fifteenth century' - Latin.
Anon. - Birgitta, Saint - MS. Bodl. Rawlinson C. 41 - Late
    XVth cent. - Latin.
        [The above six translations from St. Birgitta
        are of undetermined date. Some of them prob-
        ably belong to the second quarter of the cen-
        tury.]
Anon. - Birgitta, Saint - Garrett MS. - C. 1470 - Latin.
Anon. - Higden, Ranulphus - ' . . . Cronicle.' - C. 1450 -
    Latin.
Anon. - La Tour Landry, Geoffrey de - 'Book of the Knight of
    . . .' - C. 1450 - French.
Anon. - La Tour Landry, Ponthus de - ['Ponthus and . . .
    Sidoine']- C. 1450 - French.
Anon. - Merlin - C. 1450 - French.
Anon. - Petrus Alphonsis - C. 1460 - Latin.
Anon. - Pisan, Christine de - ' . . . body of Polocye.' -
    C. 1470 - French.
Anon. - Register of Godstow - C. 1450 - Latin.
Anon. - Register of Oseney - 1460 - Latin.
Anon. - Rolle, Richard - ' . . . of the Amendement of Mannes
    Lif - C. 1460 - Latin.
Anon. - Saints' Lives: Catharine of Siena - C. 1450? Printed
    by W. de Worde, [1497] - Latin.
Anon. - Thomas à Kempis - ['Imitation of Christ'] - C. 1450 -
    Latin.
Babyngton, Anthony - Pisan, Christine de - ['Epistle of Othea
    to Hector'] - C. 1475 - French.
Capgrave, John - Saints' Lives: Augustine - C. 1450 - Latin.
Capgrave, John - Saints' Lives: Gilbert - 1451 - Latin.
Caxton, William - Cessolis, Jacobus de - 1474 - French.
Gilbert of the Haye - Aristotle, pseud. - 'Buke of the Govern-
    aunce of Princis' - 1456 - French.
Gilbert of the Haye - Bonet, Honoré - 1456 - French.
Gilbert of the Haye - Lull, Ramon - 'The Ordre of Knychthede.' -
    C. 1456 - French.
Tiptoft, J., Earl of Worcester - Buonaccorso de Pistoja -
    C. 1465. Printed by Caxton, 1481 - French.
Tiptoft, John, Earl or Worcester - Cicero - ' . . . Tullius de
    Amicicia' - C. 1465. Printed by Caxton, 1481 - Latin.

Worcester-Botoner? – Cicero – '   . . . Tulle of Olde Age' –
   C. 1470. Printed by Caxton, 1481 – French.

1475 – 1500

Anon. – Benedictus – 1491 – Latin.
Anon. – Bernard, Saint – 1496 – Latin.
Anon. – Canutus – C. 1480? – Latin.
Anon. – Elizabeth of Hungary, Saint – [1493] – Latin?
Anon. – Eynsham – 1485 – Latin.
Anon. – Information – '   . . . for pylgrymes unto the holy
   londe.' – 1498 – Latin.
Anon. – John of Arras – 1500 – French.
Anon. – Kings' Sons.– C. 1500 – French.
Anon. – Mary – 'Myracles of oure blyssyd Lady.' – 1496 –
   Latin? French?
Anon. – Rome – 'The Seven Wise Masters' – 1493 – Latin.
Anon. – Salomon – 'dyalogus betwixt Salomon and Marcolphus' –
   C. 1492 – Latin.
Anon. – Treatise – 'This tretyse is of loue . . . ' – [1493] –
   French.
Betson, Thomas – Creed and Prayers – 1500 – Latin.
Caxton, William – Aesopus – 1484 – French.
Caxton, William – Ars Moriendi – [1490] – French.
Caxton, William – Ars Moriendi – [1491] – Latin?
Caxton, William – Aymon – [1489] – French.
Caxton, William – Blanchardine – 1489 – French.
Caxton, William – Cato – 1483 – French
Caxton, William – Charles – 'thystorye of . . . ' – 1485 –
   French.
Caxton, William – Chartier, Alain – [1484] – French.
Caxton, William – Governal – 1489 – French?
Caxton, William – Heraclius, Emperour – 1481 – French.
Caxton, William – Jerome, Saint – 'Vitas Patrum' – 1491 –
   French.
Caxton, William – La Tour Landry, Geofrey de – [1484] – French.
Caxton, William – Laurentius Gallus – 'book . . . named Ryal' –
   C. 1486 – French.
Caxton, William – Le Fèvre, Raoul – '   . . . recuyell . . . ' –
   [1475] – French.
Caxton, William – Le Fèvre, Raoul – 'Jason' – 1476 – French.
Caxton, William – Legrand, Jacques – 'Book of good maners' –
   1487 – French.
Caxton, William – Lull, Ramon – 'the Ordre of chyualry' –
   [1484] – French.
Caxton, William – Ovidius – 1480 – French.
Caxton, William – Paris, le chevalier – 1485 – French.

Caxton, William - Pisan, Christine de - 'Fayttes of Armes' -
    1489 - French.
Caxton, William - Reynard the Fox - 1481 - Dutch.
Caxton, William - Roye, Guy de - 1489 - French.
Caxton, William - Saints' Lives: Winifred - [1485] - Latin?
Caxton, William - Vincentius, Bellovacensis - [1481]- French.
Caxton, William - Virgilius - 'Eneydos' - 1490 - French.
Caxton, William - Voragine, Jacobus de - ' . . . legende named
    in latyn legenda Aurea . . . ' - 1483 - French and Latin?
Kay, John - Caorsinus, Guilielmus - C. 1480 - Latin.
Skelton, John - Diodorus Siculus - Before 1490 - Latin.
Skelton, John - Guillaume de Deguileville - 'Of Mannes Lyfe
    the Peregrynaciouns.'? - C. 1485? - French.
Woodville, Anthony, Earl Rivers - Cordiale - 1478 - French.
Woodville, Anthony, Earl Rivers - Dicts - C. 1476 - French

                        1500 - 1530

Anon. - Ars Moriendi - ' . . . art of . . . good deying' -
    [1503] - French.
Anon. - Gesta Romanorum - C. 1510 - Latin.
Anon. - La Tour Landry, Ponthus de - 'Noble historye of kynge
    Ponthus' - 1501 - French.
Anon. - Pisan, Christine de ' . . . body of polyce' - 1521 -
    French.
Anon. - Robert the Devil - [1502] - French.
Anon. - Shepherd's Kalendar - 'Kalendayr of shyppars' - 1503 -
    French.
Anon. - Shepherd's Kalendar - 'Kalendar of Shepherdes' - 1506 -
    French.
Anon. - Virgilius - 'of the lyfe of Virgilius' - 1518 - French?
Anslay, B. - Pisan, Christine de ' . . . cyte of Ladyes' - 1521 -
    French.
Atkinson, William - Thomas à Kempis - ' . . . of the Imytacion
    . . . of . . . Criste' - 1504 - Latin.
Barclay, Alexander - Brant, Sebastian - 'The Shyp of folys' -
    1509 - Latin.
Barclay, Alexander - Sallustius - [1520] - Latin.
Beaufort, Margaret - Thomas à Kempis - ' . . . forthe boke of
    the folowynge of Iesu Cryst' - 1504 - French.
Bourchier, John, Lord Berners - Arthur - C. 1530 - French.
Bourchier, John, Lord Berners - Froissart, Jean- 1523 and 1525 -
    French.
Bourchier, John, Lord Berners - Guevara, Antonio de - 1533 -
    French.
Bourchier, John, Lord Berners - Huon de Bordeaux - C. 1530 -
    French.

Chertsey, Andrew – Ars Moriendi – 1505 – French.
Chertsey, Andrew – Ten Commandments – 1510 – French.
Copland, Robert – Appolonius – 1510 – French.
Copland, Robert – Aristotle, pseud. – 'Secrete of Secretes' –
    1528 – French.
Copland, Robert – Helyas – [1512] – French.
Copland, Robert – Shepherds' Kalendar – 1508 – French.
Watson, Henry – Brandt, Sebastian – 'Shyppe of fools' – 1509 –
    French.
Watson, Henry – Oliver of Castile – 1518 – French.
Watson, Henry – Valentine – [1510?] – French.
Wyatt, Sir Thomas – Plutarch – ' . . . Quyete of Mynde' – C.
    1527 – Latin.

BIBLIOGRAPHY

BIBLIOGRAPHY

Texts, either translations, or original writings, and books or articles relating to textual matters are not included; nor are catalogues of books or manuscrips, bibliographers' manuals, etc.

Amos, F. R., Early Theories of Translation, New York: 1920.

Aurner, Nellie S., Caxton: Mirrour of Fifteenth Century Letters. London: 1926.

Aurner, Robert Ray, Caxton and the English Sentence. University of Wisconsin, Studies in Language and Literature, XVIII (1923), 23-59.

Baldwin, Charles Sears, Medieval Rhetoric and Poetic (to 1400) Interpreted from Representative Works. New York: 1928.

Brunot, Ferdinand, Histoire de la Langue Française. Vol. I. Paris: 1898.

Byles, A. T. P., Caxton's Method and Style as a Translator, in the Introduction to The Book of the Ordre of Chyualry . . . printed by William Caxton. (EETS o s CLXVIII) London: 1926.

Byles, A. T. P., The Translator, in the Introduction to The Book of the Fayttes of Armes and of Chyualrye . . . printed by William Caxton. (EETS o s CLXXXIX) London: 1932.

Byles, A. T. P., 'William Caxton as a Man of Letters,' The Library, 4th Series, XV (1934), 1-25.

Chambers, R. W., The Continuity of English Prose from Alfred to More and his School, in the Introduction to The Life and Death of Sir Thomas Moore . . . by Nicholas Harpsfield, edited by Elsie Vaughan Hitchcock (EETS o s CLXXXVI). London: 1932. Also separately printed with the same pagination, London: 1932.

Cline, James M., 'Chaucer and Jean de Meung,' English Literary History, III (1936), 170-181.

Deanesley, Margaret, The Lollard Bible. Cambridge, 1920.

de Reul, Paul, The Language of Caxton's Reynard the Fox. Université de Gand, Receuil de Traveaux publiés par la Faculté de Philosophie et Lettres, fascicule 26. Gand and London: 1901.

Gee, J. A., The Life and Works of Thomas Lupset. New Haven: 1928.

Kellner, Leon, Introduction to Caxton's Blanchardyn and Eglantine. (EETS e s lviii) London: 1890.

Kellner, Leon, Historical Outlines of English Syntax.
    New York: 1892.
Kingsford, C. L., English Historical Literature in the Fif-
    teenth Century. Oxford: 1913.
Kinkade, Berte L., The English Translations of Higden's
    Polychronicon. Diss., University of Illinois: 1935.
Krapp, J. P., The Rise of English Literary Prose. New York:
    1915.
Larwill, P. H., La Théorie de la Traduction au Début de la
    Renaissance. München: 1934.
Lathrop, H. B., 'The First English Printers and their Patrons,'
    The Library, 4th Series, III (1922), 69-96.
Lathrop, H. B., Translations from the Classics into English
    from Caxton to Chapman. University of Wisconsin, Studies
    in Language and Literature, XXXV. Madison: 1933.
Norden, Eduard, Die Antike Kunstprosa vom vi. Jahrhundert vor
    Christ bis in die Zeit der Renaissance. Two Vols. Leipzig:
    1898.
Ohlander, Urban, Studies in Coordinate Expressions in Middle
    English. Lund: 1936.
Olmes, Antonie, Sprache und Stil der englischen Mystik des
    Mittlealters. Halle: 1933.
Owst, G. R., Preaching in Medieval England. Cambridge: 1926.
Owst, G. R., Literature and Pulpit in Medieval England.
    Cambridge: 1933.
Richardson, Octavia, Introduction to The . . . Historie of
    the Foure Sonnes of Aymon . . . by William Caxton. (EETS
    e s xiv) London: 1885.
Roberts, W. J. F., 'Ellipsis of the Subject-pronoun in Middle
    English,' London Medieval Studies, I, i (1937), 107-115.
Starke, F. J., Populare englische Chroniken des 15 Jahrhunderts:
    . . . ihre literarische form. Berlin: 1935.
von Wartburg, Wilhelm, Évolution et Structure de la Langue
    Française. Leipzig et Berlin: 1934.
Wortham, J. L., English Prose Style in Translations from the
    Classics. Unpublished dissertation on deposit in the Prince-
    ton University Library. Princeton: 1939.